☞ Mark Twain of the *Enterprise*

MARK TWAIN

~ OF THE ~

Enterprise

Newspaper Articles & Other Documents 1862-1864

EDITED BY HENRY NASH SMITH

With the Assistance of Frederick Anderson

University of California Press

Berkeley and Los Angeles: 1957

UNIVERSITY OF CALIFORNIA PRESS
Berkeley and Los Angeles, California

CAMBRIDGE UNIVERSITY PRESS
London, England

© *1957, by Mark Twain Company*
Library of Congress Catalogue Card Number: 57–6543

Printed in the United States of America
by the University of California Printing Department

Designed by Adrian Wilson

To the Memory of

DIXON WECTER

1906–1950

PREFACE

THE EDITORS of this book wish to express their gratitude to the anonymous friends of the University of California, Berkeley, who contributed the money that was needed to buy the Moffett Collection of Mark Twain materials in the autumn of 1954. Four of the scrapbooks in this collection contain the clippings from the *Territorial Enterprise* which have provided the texts of most of the articles reprinted here.

The editors wish to thank the following persons for help in various investigations that had to be carried on at a distance from Berkeley: Mrs. Clara S. Beatty, director of the Nevada State Historical Society, Reno; Mrs. Frances Biese, formerly archivist of the Missouri Historical Society, St. Louis; Mr. Robert B. Collagan, Mackay School of Mines, University of Nevada, Reno; Miss Margaret Dennison, California State Library, Sacramento; and Mr. Harvey McCaleb, of Columbia, Missouri.

Two members of the faculty of the University of Nevada have been signally generous in their aid to this project: Professor Austin E. Hutcheson, who read the manuscript and placed at the disposal of the editors his expert knowledge of early Nevada history; and Professor William C. Miller, who discovered Mark Twain's report of "The Sanitary Ball" (pp. 45–47, below) in a stray copy of the *Territorial Enterprise* in the collection of the Nevada State Historical Society. Professor Miller's transcript of the article, with explanatory comment, is to be published in a forthcoming issue of the *California Historical Society Quarterly*.

The editors are grateful to the following persons and institutions for permission to have access to or to publish materials in their possession or custody: Bancroft Library, University of California, Berkeley; California State Library, Sacramento; Mackay School of Mines, University of Nevada, Reno; the Mark Twain Research Foundation, Perry, Missouri, publishers of the bimonthly journal,

The Twainian; Nevada State Historical Society, Reno; Stanford University Library; Mr. and Mrs. Samuel C. Webster, New York City; and Yale University Library, New Haven. Previously unpublished materials from the Mark Twain Papers are used with the permission of the Mark Twain Co., Inc. For permission to publish for the first time the four letters by Mark Twain written in May, 1864 (§§ 34, 39, 40, 41), the editors owe a special debt of gratitude to Mrs. Clara Clemens Samossoud.

The typesetters and proofreaders of the *Enterprise* and other Western newspapers of the 1860's were surprisingly accurate and thorough. The few typographical errors in the articles transcribed from these papers have been silently corrected (when they were noticed), and the punctuation has been tidied up a little also. The unpublished letters by Mark Twain included in Part Three, however, have been transcribed exactly from the holograph manuscripts in the Mark Twain Papers.

HENRY NASH SMITH
FREDERICK ANDERSON

Berkeley
February, 1957

CONTENTS

PART THREE: "THE AFFAIR WAS A SILLY JOKE"

ILLUSTRATIONS

following page 50 of the text

The wood engravings in the text are from the first edition of Mark Twain's *Roughing It* (Hartford: American Publishing Company, 1872).

The decorative type headings were supplied by the present office of the *Territorial Enterprise* through the courtesy of Lucius Beebe and Charles Clegg, owners of the newspaper.

PART ONE

"THOSE WERE THE DAYS"

"Unforgettable Antiquities"

☞ In 1905, when Mark Twain was almost seventy years old, he was invited to attend a pioneers' reunion in Reno, Nevada. Even though his health was uncertain, he was strongly tempted by the invitation:

... if I were a few years younger [he wrote] I would accept it, and promptly. I would go.... I would renew my youth; and talk—and talk—and talk—and have the time of my life! I would march the unforgotten and unforgettable antiquities by, and name their names, and give them reverent Hail-and-farewell as they passed: Goodman, McCarthy, Gillis, Curry, Baldwin, Winters, Howard, Nye, Stewart; Neely Johnson, Hal Clayton, North, Root,—and my brother, upon whom be peace!

The names evoked for him the image of an ancient delight. "Those were the days!—those old ones," he exclaimed. "They were so full to the brim with the wine of life; there have been no others like them."[1]

Mark Twain's emotion about frontier Nevada was not just an old man's pleasure in dreaming of his youth. Long before, he had chosen his experiences in the Far West as the subject of the first book he planned and wrote as a book—*Roughing It*, published in 1872. Despite many distractions, he found the subject entrancing: "... I am writing with a red-hot interest," he told his publisher. "Nothing

3

grieves me now—nothing troubles me, nothing bothers me or gets my attention—I don't think of anything but the book, and I don't have an hour's unhappiness about anything and don't care two cents whether school keeps or not."[2] The chapters about Virginia City in *Roughing It* bear out this joyous declaration. The narrator identifies himself with everything he sees; yet he is committed to nothing and accepts no responsibility. He recalls life on the Comstock Lode during the boom of 1863 as a kind of pageant—a perpetual circus parade that justified its existence not by any rational function but by its vividness as a spectacle:

Virginia had grown to be the "livest" town, for its age and population, that America had ever produced. The sidewalks swarmed with people—to such an extent, indeed, that it was generally no easy matter to stem the human tide. The streets themselves were just as crowded with quartz-wagons, freight-teams, and other vehicles. The procession was endless. So great was the pack, that buggies frequently had to wait half an hour for an opportunity to cross the principal street. Joy sat on every countenance, and there was a glad, almost fierce, intensity in every eye, that told of the money-getting schemes that were seething in every brain and the high hope that held sway in every heart. Money was as plenty as dust; every individual considered himself wealthy, and a melancholy countenance was nowhere to be seen. There were military companies, fire companies, brass-bands, banks, hotels, theaters, "hurdy-gurdy houses," wide-open gambling-palaces, political pow-wows, civic processions, street-fights, murders, inquests, riots, a whisky-mill every fifteen steps, a Board of Aldermen, a Mayor, a City Surveyor, a City Engineer, a Chief of the Fire Department, with First, Second, and Third Assistants, a Chief of Police, City Marshal, and a large police force, two Boards of Mining Brokers, a dozen breweries, and half a dozen jails and station-houses in full operation, and some talk of building a church.[3]

Joe Goodman, Denis McCarthy, Steve Gillis, and the rest were the leading actors in the wonderful fable that Mark Twain conjured up against the backdrop of boom times on the Comstock. But it happens that they were also actual men. Their words and deeds on the level of fact as contrasted with fiction make up a large part of the matter of the newspaper articles by Mark Twain which are collected here, and which form a historical footnote to the chapters of *Roughing It* dealing with Virginia City and the *Enterprise*.

Sam Clemens came to Virginia to go to work for the paper in September, 1862, fifteen months after his first arrival in Nevada.

He had spent most of this time prospecting for gold and silver, enduring hard manual labor, wretched quarters, and lean fare without attaining the slightest success in either mining or speculation. By midsummer of 1862 his apparently inexhaustible optimism—together with his money—had given out, and he wrote from the Esmeralda mining district to his brother Orion in the territorial capital, Carson City, a hundred miles to the north: "My debts are far greater than I thought for . . . I owe about $45 or $50, and have got about $45 in my pocket. But how in the h——l I am going to live on something over $100 until October or November, is singular. The fact is, I must have something to do, and that *shortly*, too."[4]

For a time he had even thought of giving up and going back home to Missouri. But his pride was involved: he would not return without the fortune he had so confidently announced he would make in Nevada.[5] In this extremity his mind turned toward newspaper work, in which he had had a little amateur experience. He wondered whether he could get a job writing regular correspondence for the Sacramento *Union* or the Carson City *Silver Age.*[6] As it happened, he had already sent some humorous letters to the Virginia City *Territorial Enterprise* over the signature "Josh," and the solution to his problem came from that source. On August 7 he wrote Orion that he had accepted a position as local reporter on the *Enterprise.*[7] He was still in Esmeralda on September 9, however, and therefore cannot have reported for duty before the second week of that month.[8] The earliest certain evidence that Sam Clemens had begun writing regularly for the *Enterprise* is the reprinting, on October 15 in the San Francisco *Daily Evening Bulletin,* of his hoaxing report that a "petrified man" had been dug up near Virginia City.[9] The article must have been first published in the *Enterprise* about October 5.

The atmosphere of the *Enterprise* office seems to have been like that of a fraternity house without a housemother. The youngsters who put out the paper (most of them were in their twenties; Joe Goodman, the editor in chief, was twenty-four in 1862) inhabited a kind of bachelors' paradise. They played billiards and had passes to the theaters; they smoked cigars and drank a special "reporter's cobbler"; they received presents of "feet" in mines which they could sell for enough money to finance vacations in San Francisco.

It was a way of life that Mark Twain enjoyed immensely for a time, despite the seamy side of things suggested by a reporter's notation of "a woman under the influence of liquor . . . perambulating C Street . . . shaking a thousand dollars in gold coin at the passers-by" or a "notorious courtezan, known as 'Buffalo Joe'" lying in the street dead drunk, surrounded by a crowd of spectators, her fingers and breast "bedecked with diamonds."[10]

The picturesque aspects of the boom years on the Comstock Lode have been described many times (best of all by Mark Twain himself in *Roughing It*; more recently by Ivan Benson in *Mark Twain's Western Years* and by Effie Mona Mack in *Mark Twain in Nevada*). The present book is focused on a much narrower subject: Mark Twain's work as a reporter while he lived in Virginia City. Up to now this work has been represented by seventeen letters written for papers outside Nevada and twenty contributions to the *Enterprise* that have survived because they were reprinted in other papers.[11] But not one single article written by Clemens for the *Enterprise* while he was on the staff has previously been known in its original form, because no file of the paper before 1865 is extant.[12]

The present volume makes available some thirty additional letters and dispatches, not previously reprinted, that he wrote for the *Enterprise* between December 5, 1862, and the end of May, 1864. Clippings of these pieces had been preserved (mainly by Orion) in four scrapbooks that turned up among the possessions of Anita Moffett, Mark Twain's grandniece, at her death in 1952. They add appreciably to what is known about Mark Twain's life during his Nevada period. In order to make the record as complete as possible I have included an article reprinted from the *Enterprise* in Myron Angel's *History of Nevada* (1881) and one reprinted in Kate M. Rabb's *Wit and Humor of America*, Volume V (1907). In the third section of the book I have gathered a number of documents bearing on Mark Twain's abrupt departure from Virginia City in May, 1864. Some of these have been reprinted, in whole or in part, by Mr. Benson, Miss Mack, and Professor Austin E. Hutcheson (in a series of articles in *The Twainian*). But the three letters written by Mark Twain to Orion and Mollie Clemens just before his departure (§§ 34, 39, and 40) and the unsent draft of a note to W. K. Cutler (§ 41) have not previously been published.

Sam Clemens and Mark Twain

Mark Twain's writing for the *Enterprise* falls into four categories: (1) routine "local" items (enlivened occasionally by hoaxes to which he resorted in the dearth of genuine news, or from sheer exuberance—the best-known example being the "Empire City massacre" story, published October 28, 1863, and reprinted by both Albert B. Paine and Mr. Benson);[13] (2) an occasional unsigned editorial; (3) letters sent to the paper from Carson City (the territorial capital), San Francisco, and other places; and (4) reports of sessions of the Territorial Legislature and the Constitutional Convention of 1863 in Carson. The letters from out of town are gossipy and whimsical rather than factual; they are similar in intention to the work of twentieth-century humorous columnists, of which in fact they are among the journalistic ancestors. The local items, editorials, and political dispatches more nearly resemble the straight professional journalism of our own day. But the genres run together: as has often been pointed out, Nevada journalism of the 1860's was nonchalant and uninhibited, and a report of the most commonplace event was likely to veer into fantasy or humorous diatribe. Although the political reporting reproduced here shows a much greater quantity of serious, disciplined work than Mark Twain has traditionally been credited with at this period, most of the editorial comments which he inserted in the dispatches reporting the third Territorial Legislature are personal and comic. For that matter, the legislators themselves enlivened their deliberations with horseplay and champagne, and the function of the *Enterprise* reporter as court jester was recognized in official proceedings.

During Sam Clemens' stint as reporter for the *Enterprise* he must have written hundreds of column inches of copy. But even with the newly discovered material in the Moffett scrapbooks we still have only a small fraction of this work. Almost all the daily local items which presumably made up the bulk of his writing for the paper are lost. Mark Twain himself destroyed many clippings of his articles from the *Enterprise*. On January 20, 1866, writing from San Francisco to his mother and sister about Bret Harte's proposal that they should collaborate in publishing a book of sketches, he said:

"My labor will not occupy more than 24 hours, because I will only have to take the scissors & slash my old sketches out of the Enterprise & the [San Francisco] Californian—I burned up a small cartload of them lately—so *they* are forever ruled out of any book—but they were not worth republishing."[14]

Because examples of Mark Twain's routine reporting are scarce, I have included whatever scraps of such material I could find—mainly two batches of paragraphs, dating apparently from December, 1862, and January, 1863. The articles are of course unsigned; the evidence that they are Mark Twain's work is discussed in the headnote to section 3. The Moffett scrapbooks contain clippings of a number of other local items from the *Enterprise*, but I have not been able to convince myself that Mark Twain wrote them.

It is not clear how many scrapbooks were kept by Orion and Pamela, or by Mark Twain himself. One quite similar in contents to those in the Moffett Collection, but belonging to the period of his residence in San Francisco, was acquired by the Yale University Library with the Morse Collection, and others may turn up in the future.[15] In some instances Mark Twain seems to have submitted scrapbooks of his newspaper articles to publishers when he was discussing the possibility of bringing out a collection of articles as a book. The Yale scrapbook shows many revisions and explanatory footnotes in Mark Twain's handwriting, as if he were preparing copy for a printer, and there are a few revisions of this sort in the Moffett scrapbooks. The volume published by Charles H. Webb in 1867 under the title *The Celebrated Jumping Frog of Calaveras County, and Other Sketches* was probably compiled from scrapbooks which have since disappeared. With one or two exceptions, the pieces in the *Jumping Frog* collection belong to a period after Mark Twain's departure from Nevada.

The newspaper articles collected here cover the period during which the apprentice journalist Sam Clemens began to use the pseudonym "Mark Twain," but unfortunately the evidence is still not conclusive with respect to the exact date when "Mark Twain" was first used in print. The pseudonym is signed to a letter published on February 3, 1863 (see the headnote to § 4). It may have been used earlier, but Albert B. Paine is certainly in error in saying that all Clemens' work henceforth was signed "Mark Twain."[16] The daily dispatches to the *Enterprise* reporting the first Nevada Constitutional Convention (November 2—December 11, 1863) are, after the first two, given the heading: "Reported in Phonographic Short-Hand for the *Territorial Enterprise*, by A. J. Marsh and Sam. L. Clemens." In other words, the *Enterprise* recognized two aspects of Clemens' work: routine political reporting, a technical process without a personal flavor, ascribed to Clemens; and personal journalism, mostly humorous, ascribed to Mark Twain. Mark Twain refers to this distinction in his Autobiographical Dictation: "Every Sunday I wrote a letter to the paper [from Carson City], in which I made a resumé of the week's legislative work, and in order that it might be readable I put no end of seasoning into it. I signed these letters 'Mark Twain.' "[17] The pseudonym designated an invented personality, a mask, a *persona*—a comic sensibility which provided a characteristic perspective upon people and events. A single issue of the paper—for example, that of December 8, 1863—might contain both a legislative report signed by Marsh and Clemens and a "Letter from Mark Twain."

The distinction between the "straight" journalist Sam Clemens and the irresponsibly imaginative Mark Twain was taken for granted by a Virginia City politician, Cornelius M. Brosnan, in objecting to the published charge that he had confused "Nestor" and "Nessus" in a speech at a Union Party mass meeting on December 30, 1863. "Now, if that facetious sinner, blunderer and *sagebrush painter* 'Mark Twain,' had thus libelled me," wrote Brosnan, "I could forgive him; but to be thus misrepresented (though undesignedly) by the 'intelligent' reporter of the ENTERPRISE is, as Mrs. Partington would say, assolutely inseparable."[18]

Political Reporting

Although Mark Twain was privileged to say anything—or almost anything—he pleased, Sam Clemens was expected to practice serious journalism, and most of the time he accepted this professional responsibility. It was Sam Clemens the hard-working political reporter who wrote the greater part of the material preserved in the Moffett scrapbooks. The two pieces that have survived from his first stint as a political reporter (during the session of the second Territorial Legislature, November 11—December 20, 1862) are examples of the highly seasoned weekly letters; all Clemens' routine dispatches for this session have been lost. We are therefore unable to judge how fully, at this early stage of his apprenticeship, he had reconciled himself to the treadmill of factual reporting. But his work during the session of the Constitutional Convention beginning in November, 1863, has been preserved, and it proves that he was capable of buckling down to a stiff daily chore.

The *Enterprise* made elaborate arrangements for reporting the Convention. In the absence of provision for an official transcript of the proceedings, at least two Nevada newspapers—the *Enterprise* and the Virginia City *Union*—carried daily dispatches based on shorthand notes. The *Enterprise* shorthand reporter at the Convention, Andrew J. Marsh, was an expert borrowed from the Sacramento *Union* who later wrote a widely used textbook of shorthand.[19] The assertion that the proceedings were "Reported in Phonographic Short-Hand for the *Territorial Enterprise,* by A. J. Marsh and Sam. L. Clemens" can hardly be taken literally, because it is unlikely in the extreme that Mark Twain knew shorthand well enough to take down legislative debates. He mentions shorthand occasionally at this period, but always in jest. In his burlesque report of the session of the "Third House" of the Convention, at which he presided, he says, "The President addressed the house as follows, taking his remarks down in short-hand as he proceeded" (§ 16). Introducing a preposterous burlesque of a legislator's windy oratory, he asserts: "I took it from my own mysterious short-hand notes, which are mighty shaky, I am willing to admit . . ." (§ 14). On another occasion he remarks, ambiguously, "I have a notebook full of interesting hieroglyphics, but I am afraid that by the time I am ready to write them out, I shall have forgotten what they mean" (§ 10). All the evidence indicates he was not skilled in shorthand.[20]

It is not clear exactly how Marsh and Clemens worked together. On one occasion the Virginia City *Bulletin* asserted editorially that "no two reporters living can possibly fairly report the proceedings of such a body as a Constitutional Convention and do justice to its members." Marsh retorted that "*one* reporter living thinks he can 'possibly fairly' do the Convention up brown for the ENTERPRISE (with 'Mark Twain' for his right bower, perhaps), and 'do justice to its members'. . . ." And he concluded: "Why does the Virginia *Bulletin* talk about what two reporters can do, when it knows that the very report its scissors man stole to-day, and clipped and mangled out of all sense and shape, and then headed 'From our own reporter,' was the work of *one* man only, on a morning paper?"[21] Although here Marsh seems to claim sole authorship of the dispatch in question, his reference above to Mark Twain as his "right bower," and the joint by-line, support the conclusion that the dispatches were prepared by both men. A few days later a "Correction" referring to what "we thought we had written" is signed "Reporters."[22] Mark Twain himself described the preparation of the dispatches as a joint undertaking. Speeches on the floor of the assembly "ought to be reported verbatim," he acknowledged;

but then we work eighteen hours a day, and still have not time enough to give more than the merest skeletons of the speeches made in the Convention. . . . Even Judge Brosnan's stately eloquence, adorned with beautiful imagery and embellished with classic quotations, hath been reported by us thus tersely: "Mr. Brosnan opposed the motion" (§14, below).

Whatever may have been the methods used, Marsh and Clemens together turned out, on an average, more than four thousand words a day for the thirty-two days the Convention was in session. Through this strenuous apprenticeship Mark Twain learned the business of reporting so well that during the session of the third Territorial Legislature, which convened about a month after the Convention adjourned, he was able to function as an equal partner in a reporting team without the aid of a shorthand expert. During the legislative session, the Virginia City *Daily Union* and the *Territorial Enterprise* carried long daily reports of the proceedings which were identical except for occasional notes by Mark Twain inserted in the *Enterprise* version. Mark Twain attended the sessions of the House, and the reporter for the *Union*, Clement T. Rice, attended those of the Council. The two men presumably collaborated in preparing a daily dispatch of which copies were sent both to the *Union* and to the *Enterprise*, those sent to the *Enterprise* containing additions by Mark Twain. The reports are more condensed than the reports of the Constitutional Convention; they could have been prepared by two quick and energetic men without the aid of shorthand. Even so, Mark Twain's share of the work—covering the House and writing his part of a daily dispatch averaging about 1,800 words for the forty days of the session—entailed hard and persistent labor with usually dull materials. Rice said as much, with feeling, in one of his letters to the *Union*:

After the week's labor in tracking those wily Councilors—giving a summary of their bills, motions, resolves and orating, however imperfectly—one feels like going to bed in a warm, snug place on a Sunday, and letting the winds and the world howl on till doomsday. People may think it's easy enough to epitomize, condense and properly set forth all these sayings and doings, and keep the run of what every Legislator is saying or hinting at, and thinking over all that he is thinking about, and masticating thoughts inaudibly expressed, . . . but I tell you it's no pleasant job at all, and Sunday comes in almost as handy as a pocket in a little boy's gown.[23]

In addition to the salaries paid by their newspapers, the reporters for the Constitutional Convention were subsequently given a bonus of seven dollars a day by the Legislature.[24] Their function was thus both official and unofficial. Just before the opening of the third Territorial Legislature Mark Twain announced that he had William M. Gillespie, Legislative Secretary, "figuring with the Legislators for extra compensation for the reporters" (§ 21, below). A bonus was paid to official reporters during a part of the session, but Gillespie apparently succeeded in having this stipend revoked at some point (§ 32, below). Mark Twain was formally designated as an official reporter for the Legislature; but this action may have been half in jest. On January 15, 1864, "the Chair announced Mr. Sam. L. Clemens as entitled to a seat as Reporter for the House, *while the courtesy of that body should continue to hold out*. [There was some little strategy about that, you know.—Mark.]"[25] A few days later, the reporter comments: "But I am here only during the courtesy of the House—on my good behavior, as it were . . . Mark" (§ 25, below). Toward the end of the session, he inserts the following note: "[Right here I desire to return my thanks to Col. Allen, Chief Clerk, and Mr. Gregory, Assistant Clerk of the House, for numerous favors extended to me in getting up my reports.—Rep.]"[26]

Both in the Constitutional Convention and in the Legislature, Mark Twain was treated almost as if he were a member of the house. On February 20, 1864, the last day of the session of the third

Territorial Legislature, "The Chaplain not being present, Mr. Fisher suggested that the Virginia reporter be requested to officiate in his place. By courtesy of the House, the Virginia reporter was allowed to explain that he was not on it. [Excused.]" (§ 31, below). A pupil in a school at Carson, Master Barry Ashim, had demonstrated such a proficiency in shorthand on the occasion of a visit to the school by Mark Twain and Representative William Clagett that he was invited to practice his art in reporting the last days of the proceedings of the House.[27] During the closing hours of the session, when a spirit of frivolity prevailed, the House passed a bill "for the relief of Sam. Clemens and Barrac [sic] Ashim (official reporters on the floor of the House)." The Council rejected the measure, but William M. Stewart proposed a resolution—which was adopted by the House—that each member should deposit three dollars at the Clerk's desk for the relief of Master Ashim. Later in the evening the House tendered the "usual vote of thanks" to the Sergeant at Arms and "the House Reporter."[28] While the House was waiting to hear that the Council was ready to adjourn, Mark Twain acted as the spokesman for a group of members in presenting a big wooden comb to Clagett—a practical joke suggested by Clagett's unruly hair.[29] And the choice of Twain to deliver the Governor's message to the burlesque Third House (§ 26, below) was a clear token of his acceptance by the legislators.

The Reporter as Lobbyist

Mark Twain's status with the legislature not only made him feel free to comment editorially on the proceedings but also gave him confidence in his powers as a lobbyist. In the summer of 1863, he wrote to his mother and sister:

We shall bud out into a State before many months, which will relieve Orion of his office. If I have influence enough, I mean to get him nominated a candidate for some fat office under the State Government, so that you can come out and live with him. I am a pretty good hand at such things. I was a mighty heavy wire-puller at the last [i.e., the second Territorial] Legislature. I passed every bill I worked for, & on a bet, I killed a bill by a three-fourths vote in the House after it had passed the Council unanimously. Oh, I tell you a reporter in the Legislature can swing more votes than any member of the body. We'll have rare times the coming session, & in the State [Constitutional] convention.[30]

When a slate of officers was submitted to the voters along with the first proposed state constitution (which was rejected), the *Enterprise* endorsed Orion's candidacy for Secretary of State with the comment, "In addition to all his positive recommendations, he is a brother of that 'moral phenomenon,' Mark Twain."[31] Many years later, Mark Twain maintained that he had used his position among the legislators to provide a juicy financial plum for Orion.

I was there every day in the legislature [he said in his *Autobiography*] to distribute compliment and censure with evenly balanced justice and spread the same over half a page of the *Enterprise* every morning; consequently I was an influence. I got the legislature to pass a law requiring every corporation doing business in the territory to record its charter in full, without skipping a word, in a record to be kept by the Secretary of the Territory—my brother. All the charters were framed in exactly the same words. For this record service he was authorized to charge forty cents a folio of one hundred words for making the record; five dollars for furnishing a certificate of each record, and so on. Everybody had a toll-road franchise, but no toll-road. . . . Everybody was a mining corporation, and had to have himself recorded and pay for it. Very well, we prospered. The record service paid an average of one thousand dollars a month, in gold.[32]

The contemporary records yield some support for this statement, but Mark Twain seems to have confused two different sessions of the Legislature and two different laws. A law passed by the second Legislature in 1862, to which the account in the *Autobiography* apparently refers, required that "a certificate in writing" should be recorded by each corporation "in the office of the County Clerk . . . and a duplicate thereof in the office of the Secretary of the Territory." This law, however, does not seem to have imposed on corporations the expense mentioned by Mark Twain.[33] A revision of it passed by the third Territorial Legislature in 1864 required each corporation to "file and have recorded" a certificate "in the office of the Clerk of the county . . . and a certified copy, under the hand of the Clerk and the seal of the Court of said county, in the office of the Secretary of the Territory . . ."[34] "Carl," writing to the Virginia City *Daily Union* on February 12, 1864, protested against the revision of the law, on the score that it would involve greater expense for corporations and would inconvenience "parties examining titles" by obliging them to visit both offices.[35]

No fees are mentioned in either statute. The second Territorial Legislature, however, had directed that "the records of the Probate Court of the County of Carson, Utah Territory, and Carson County, Nevada Territory" should be deposited in the office of the Secretary of the Territory, who was to provide certified copies on demand.[36] "Carl" wrote on January 30, 1864, in the *Daily Union*, that Secretary Orion Clemens had employed four or five copyists in this work over a period of several months. The Secretary had been allowed forty cents a folio for the copying, and had paid only twenty cents; the cost to the Territory had been $10,000.[37] It is possible that Mark Twain later confused this transaction with the recording of corporation charters. In any event, he was probably exaggerating when he said that he got the Legislature to act.

Of course he liked to boast to the folks back home about his power and influence, but a real innocence shines through the bluster of his letters. While he was visiting San Francisco in the spring of 1863 he wrote: "They want me to correspond with one of the dailies here, & if they will pay me enough, I'll do it. (The pay is only a 'blind'—I'll correspond anyhow. If I don't know how to make such a thing pay me—if I don't know how to levy blackmail on the mining companies,—who *does*, I should like to know?)"[38]

A few weeks later, back in Virginia City, he continued in the same vein, for the same audience:

As for money, I manage to make a living, but if I had any business tact the office of reporter here would be worth $30,000 a year—whereas, if I get 4 or $5,000 out of it, it will be as much as I expect. I have stock in my possession, which, if I had sold when it was first given me, from time to time . . . would have brought me $10,000—but I have carelessly let it go down to nothing again.

And then the most specific of Mark Twain's boasts: "Now, I raised the price of 'North Ophir' from $13 a foot to $45 a foot, to-day, & they [ga]ve me five feet. I shall probably mislay it or throw it in my trunk and never get a dollar out of it. But I am telling you too many secrets, & I'll stop."[39] In the same letter he says that in San Francisco a man offered to give him five feet of "Overman"—worth $400 a foot—but that he carelessly failed to call at the man's office to pick up the stock. "I don't care a straw, for myself," adds Mark

Twain, "but I ought to have had more thought for you. Never mind, though, Ma—I will be more careful in future. I will take care that your expenses are paid—*sure*."

The few bits of evidence concerning Mark Twain's finances while he was working on the *Enterprise* provide no hint that he had any substantial income beyond his salary from the paper (which was $25.00 a week at the outset and later increased, according to Mark Twain's recollection in *Roughing It*, to $40.00 a week).[40] His letters to his mother and sister at this period usually enclosed quite modest sums—$10.00 or $20.00 in greenbacks. A fire which destroyed his rooming house in July, 1863, left him "nothing but the clothes I had on." That he was believed to be hard-pressed for money is indicated by his statement that immediately after the fire, "a man whom I never saw before, gave me some 'feet' as I went down town, & I sold the batch for $200 & fitted myself out again half as good as new."[41] The most telling piece of evidence about his finances is the letter he wrote to Orion just before he left Virginia City asking for $200.00 (presumably as a loan; § 40, below). When he arrived in San Francisco he obviously had no more than enough money to support him for a few days while he looked for a job. Within less than a month he took an uncongenial place on the San Francisco *Call.*[42] The description in *Roughing It* of the life of "butterfly idleness" that he led in San Francisco for a time after he left Nevada, when he "kept the due state of a man worth a hundred thousand dollars (prospectively)" on the basis of his mining stocks, can hardly be anything but fictitious.[43]

Under Which Flag?

While he was working for the *Enterprise* Mark Twain was a kind of frontier Bohemian.[44] He had quickly got his fill of prospecting, and one week of labor in a quartz mill had been more than enough for him. Like everyone else, he had speculated in mining shares, but he had only lost money at it. His role as a newspaper man allowed him to be simply an enchanted spectator of the mining boom. When he was following his routine as local reporter in Virginia City he had a good deal of leisure, although probably not so much as he boasted he had to his mother and sister: "Now, I don't really work more than two hours a day, but then I am busy all the time, gadding about, you know, & consequently I don't expect to write you very often."[45] Dan De Quille said later that Mark Twain "did not much relish the work of writing reports of mines and mining affairs . . ." He was "as a reporter . . . earnest and enthusiastic in such work as suited him—really industrious—but when it came to 'cast-iron' items, he gave them 'a lick and a promise.' He hated to have to do with figures, measurements and solid facts, such as were called for in matters pertaining to mines and machinery."[46]

Nor was Mark Twain interested in national politics, despite the fact that the momentous issues of the Civil War filled the Nevada newspapers and lay just beneath the surface of everyday life in the Territory. John W. North, who had come out from Minnesota to hold office as the first surveyor-general of Nevada, said in 1863 on the floor of the Constitutional Convention: "It has already become notoriously remarked that here was the great refuge of the Copperheads—that Virginia City was their city of refuge for the Copperheads and secessionists of the East and the West—coming over the plains from Missouri, and across the mountains from California."[47]

In the summer of 1861, not long after Mark Twain arrived in Nevada, Southern sympathizers had been openly jubilant over the first battle of Bull Run; the Virginia City volunteer fire department had beaten up a number of them.[48] Thereafter pro-Confederate sentiments were suppressed, but much evidence suggests that they had not ceased to exist. A reporter for the Sacramento *Union* wrote from Carson City in December, 1862, concerning the second Territorial Legislature:

. . . a great majority of the members of the House are passably loyal, at least so far as test oaths go, but like most politicians, they are time-servers. They are looking forward to some reaction in public sentiment, and do not wish to be "nailed" so as not to be able to jump down on either side of the fence. In my opinion they greatly mistake the temper of the loyal American people in the Territory, and will find in the end that they are making a costly mistake. God help the Union if its defense were intrusted to the hands of such half-bred patriots.[49]

A few days later, a set of patriotic resolutions endorsing the conduct of the war by the Lincoln administration and affirming strong pro-Union sentiments was tabled in the Council by a vote of 8 to 6. The reporter from Sacramento commented, "So the Secesh sympathizers again succeeded in dodging the issue."[50]

As the war continued, public opinion grew more strongly pro-Union, although a Copperhead minority was always to be reckoned with. From time to time the newspapers tell of "Secesh" office-holders being summarily removed from office, and of men arrested by the military authorities for disloyalty.[51] There was much oratory against treason in the Constitutional Convention of 1863.[52] The newspapers constantly published dispatches reporting atrocities committed by Confederate troops and editorials denouncing the "Southern hell-hounds."[53] Editorial writers, with an air of intense scandal, accused one another of concealed Copperhead sympathies.[54]

In these circumstances, the question of Mark Twain's own commitment takes on a special interest. By 1871, when he was writing *Roughing It,* he recalled that on July 4, 1863, the news of the fall of Vicksburg and the Union victory at Gettysburg had come over the telegraph wire to Virginia City but could not be published because of "the journalistic monopoly that forbade the slightest revealment of Eastern news till a day after its publication in the California papers." If the news could have been revealed, he says, the United States flag on Mount Davidson "would have been saluted and re-saluted, that memorable evening, as long as there was a charge of powder to thunder with; the city would have been illuminated, and every man that had any respect for himself would have got drunk—as was the custom of the country on all occasions of public moment." "Even at this distant day," he adds, "I cannot think of this needlessly marred supreme opportunity without regret. What a time we might have had!"[55]

It must be remembered, however, that this passage was written eight years after the event and six years after Appomattox. Mark Twain's attitude toward the War in the early 1860's must have been more complex. After all, in 1861 he had served, even though briefly, in the Marion Rangers, a military unit organized in Hannibal which had been mustered into the Confederate service.[56] His devotion to the cause of Secession had evaporated quickly, and his decision to go out to Nevada with Orion was undoubtedly due in part to his desire to disentangle himself from a cause he no longer wished to defend. Nevertheless, his ideas and sentiments had to change markedly before he could become an enthusiastic supporter of the Union cause. In the early 1860's he thought of himself as a Southerner and had some of the Southern dislike for "Yankees."[57] Grant H. Smith, who habitually states the case against Mark Twain, says that in Nevada his "cronies, outside of the Enterprise office, apear to have been several prominent 'secesh.' "[58] It is true that Billy Clagett and Jack Simmons (Speaker of the House in the second Territorial Legislature), who were Sam Clemens' close friends, voted against the patriotic resolutions in the session of 1862;[59] that Hal Clayton, first presiding officer of the Third House of the Legislature, whom Mark Twain mentioned forty years later as one of the "antiquities" he remembered with pleasure, was arrested for disloyalty;[60] and that Steve Gillis was a native of Mississippi and thus probably inclined to sympathize with the Confederacy.[61] But Mark Twain was also on very friendly terms with Joe Goodman and with Clement Rice, to mention only two examples of men who were strongly pro-Union. One should not forget, too, that Orion Clemens had campaigned for Lincoln in 1860 and as acting governor took aggressive action against Copperheads (§ 25, below).

The few explicit references to the War in Mark Twain's private letters suggest that he began to identify himself with the Union cause soon after he came to Nevada. Early in 1862, writing to Clagett, he ridicules "our Missourians" for their boastful rhetoric about the "Sacred Soil" of the state and reports their defeat after retreating into Arkansas.[62] In this letter he says of the Federal troops, "they have taken Fort Henry, and Fort Donelson, and the half of Tennessee . . ."; but by the autumn of the same year he had—all unconsciously—changed his pronouns. He told Clagett that "we have been playing the game of brag" in a context that makes "we" refer clearly to supporters of the Union.[63] Throughout his stay in Nevada he avoided public reference to the War or to the issue of loyalists versus Copperheads. When Goodman went on a vacation in the spring of 1864 and left him in charge of the editorial page, he wrote to his sister Pamela: "I stipulated . . . that I should never be expected to write editorials about politics or eastern news. I take no sort of interest in those matters."[64]

Sources of Comedy

An observer who did not wish to discuss national problems or news of battles could still find amusement in the pompous official rhetoric of local politics. Mark Twain the reporter enjoyed making fun of sagebrush statesmen who took themselves and Nevada too seriously. A committee of the Constitutional Convention, for example, recommended a design for a state seal which simply translated into visual symbols the clichés of political oratory:

In the foreground are two large mountains, at the base of which is located, on the right, a quartz mill, and on the left a tunnel penetrating the silver leads of the mountain, with a miner running out a car load of ore to deposit at the dump, at which a team has loaded and started for the mill. The valley in front exhibits a sheaf, a plow and a sickle. In the background is seen a range of mountains, and from a mountain gorge is approaching, very slowly, a train of railroad cars. A telegraph line passes along the sides of the mountain, flashing news of "richer strikes" . . . On the eastern border the rising sun typifies the brilliant dawn of Nevada. Thirty-four stars encircle the whole group, which receive a silvery lustre from this youngest star of the Union. Your Committee propose the adoption of our Territorial motto, "*Volens et Potens*," expressing the two ideas of loyalty to the Union and the wealth to sustain it.[65]

This sounds very much like the usual style of L. O. Sterns, one of the members of the committee, whose oratory Mark Twain satirized on another occasion (§ 14, below). The proposed design for the seal aroused a great deal of criticism in the convention, some of it amusing. One delegate "moved to insert 'rapidly.' He thought that as these cars would be coming down the mountains, and with the fearful impetus imparted to them by our donation of $3,000,000, this word would be more appropriate." The word "dump" was objected to as undignified but was defended as more refined than "pile." It was charmingly moved "to amend the seal by adding to it a miner in his cabin, baking slap-jacks—throwing them up the chimney and running out of doors and catching them right side up in the pan," but "the Convention did not adopt this feature."[66] On a later occasion the seal was debated again at length. One member proposed "a figure of the Goddess of Freedom, armed cap-a-pie, as Minerva when she sprang from the head of Jove, transpiercing a monster representing Secession." Samuel A. Chapin, chairman of the committee which had first tried to devise a state seal, "offered as a substitute an umbrageous design got up by 'Mark Twain,' but subsequently withdrew it."[67] The original proposal was finally adopted. Mark Twain's conception, however—"a figure of a jackass-rabbit reposing in the shade of his native sage-brush, with the motto '*Volens* enough, but not so d——d *Potens*' "—is a valid comment on the boastful tone of the official design (§ 20, below).

Although the dispatches presented here reveal one brief out-burst of crusading zeal (the attacks on prosecuting attorneys, Carson City undertakers, and the "infamous telegraph monopoly," §§ 27 and 28, below), Mark Twain invests much more energy in mock verbal duels with his fellow reporters—not only with Dan De Quille, who taught him the craft of Comstock journalism, but also with Clement T. Rice, "the Unreliable" of the Virginia City *Union,* with whom Mark Twain visited San Francisco in the early summer of 1863. Horseplay in print was a standard Nevada com-modity. Dan De Quille published elaborate innuendos about how Mark Twain stole firewood from other lodgers in their rooming house,[68] and Mark Twain could fill a column with a tale about how he presented a coffin to "the Unreliable" when that worthy was ill.[69] Or he could go on indefinitely about the atrocious manners of "the Unreliable," who gorged himself on food and drink when he managed to crash a party, and then insisted on singing a solo (§ 4, below). Journalistic slapstick of this sort was so much a con-vention that when a victim was not readily found, Mark Twain was impelled to detail for his readers his own experiences with a medi-cine violently emetic and purgative (§ 9, below). The tone of the Nevada press was not delicate about such matters, even though Mark Twain could be excruciatingly coy about not mentioning the word "diaper" (§ 10, below). The society was the reverse of de-cadent, and it is of some consequence to notice that he was thoroughly at home in it.

The use of a stooge or tackling dummy for comic effects—as in the elaborate interchanges with "the Unreliable," or the repeated gibes at "young Gillespie" of the Territorial Legislature—fore-shadows the fictitious "Mr. Brown" of later travel letters, who is a kind of Caliban, an almost subhuman creature notably lacking in inhibitions.[70] In the course of time Mark Twain would see more deeply into the literary possibilities of this vernacular figure. One possible maneuver, for example, was to merge the narrator's role with that of the comic butt, and then to contrive matters so that the reader would sympathize with this character in his freedom from all pretensions to gentility. Such experiments in comic technique led eventually to the conception of Huckleberry Finn. The jokes about young Gillespie and the clinical account of the narrator's bout with the "Wake-up Jake" physic are thus among the remote literary antecedents of Mark Twain's masterpiece.

Most of the comic situations he was able to contrive in his early newspaper writing are interesting only because they are apprentice work of a man who later became a major writer. But there are one or two moments in these pieces which give promise of the mature Mark Twain. The best is probably the description of the stage driver who keeps his passenger awake through a long night with vivid anecdotes of death and mutilation in former stagecoach accidents (§ 10, below). The burlesque of Representative Sterns's oratory (§ 14, below) is uneven, but parts of it are recognizably the work of a man who would within a few years write the Buncombe trial scene in *Roughing It* (Vol. I, chap. xxxiv).[71] And even in clumsy work like the attack on prosecuting attorneys an occasional metaphor starts from the page, such as the statement that "the foul density of their intellects would put out any intellectual candle that Mr. Lawlor [the talented schoolmaster of Carson City] could lower into them" (§ 27, below). This is the firsthand experience of a mining community transmuted into poetry; one can only regret that it is wasted on so trivial a target.

Every reader will recognize in the description of Miss Clapp's school (§ 24, below) material which ten years later would go into the "Examination Evening" scene in chapter xxi of *Tom Sawyer* ("The Boy Stood on the Burning Deck" would be recited on that occasion also, and young ladies would read compositions); and here too is a suggestion of the way the Reverend Mr. Sprague would line out hymns in Tom Sawyer's Sunday school (chap. v).

Sources of Controversy

But these are merely hints of Mark Twain's later career. The *Enterprise* reporter who wrote the pieces collected here was still a young man—he was twenty-nine when he left Virginia City, and he seems younger than that. He was remarkably cocksure, even to the extent of scolding his employers in their own columns (§§ 6, 8, below), and one can understand why the Gold Hill *Evening News* would refer to "the brass and triple cheek of Mark Twain" (§ 42, below). The newly fledged reporter enjoyed giving public instruction in journalism to the editor of the Carson City *Independent* (§ 29, below). Many of his letters to his older brother Orion during this period have the tone of the master of a household addressing a servant. In August, 1863, he wrote to his mother and sister: "I lead an easy life, . . . and I don't care a cent whether school keeps or not. Everybody knows me, and I fare like a prince wherever I go, be it on this side of the mountains or the other. And I am proud to say I am the most conceited ass in the Territory."[72] There is more than a little truth in this self-portrait. His fits of arrogance and his sharp tongue must have won him the dislike of many men in Nevada.[73] Scurrilous abuse was a convention of journalism, and we know that Mark Twain's outrageous charges against Dan De Quille and "the Unreliable" did not disturb his close friendships with these men. Yet not all the epithets directed at Mark Twain were uttered in love. To describe a man as a "great demoralizer and notorious corrupter of the Saints" was doubtless an expression of affection, but to call him a "beef-eating, blear-eyed, hollow-headed, slab-sided ignoramus," or to say that he was addicted to "infernally disgusting 'platitudes' " begins to sound like something more than good-humored banter.[74] As early as 1863 there was real hostility in some newspaper comments on the Empire City massacre hoax.[75] In January, 1864, the *Daily Union* published an especially venomous letter, signed "Meriden," criticizing Mark Twain's comments on the proceedings of the third Territorial Legislature and his speech as governor before the Third House. Comparing Mark Twain to the celebrated Emperor Norton of San Francisco, a harmless lunatic who imagined himself as occupying an imperial throne, the writer says, "Both are similarly 'great characters,' both desire to become notorious as such," but Norton has none of "that cunningness of egotism which distinguishes his contemporaneous potentate." Mark Twain's editorial asides in political dispatches are characterized as "contemptible in the literary sense" and "scandalizing to the reportorial profession and public journalism."[76]

One should not take these verbal attacks on Mark Twain too seriously. If he made some enemies in Nevada, he made a greater number of friends, close friends. Yet by the early months of 1864 he was beginning to show signs of boredom, of wanting a change of scene. The boom of 1863 was giving way to an economic depression caused by declining productivity in the mines, and the bonanza days of the 1870's were far in the future.[77] Although Mark Twain glozed over the immediate circumstances of his departure in *Roughing It,* he was stating a basic truth when he said, "I began to get tired of staying in one place so long. . . . I wanted to go somewhere. I wanted—I did not know *what* I wanted. I had the 'spring fever' and wanted a change, principally, no doubt."[78] He had learned all he was likely to learn from Nevada journalism. In the last letter he wrote Orion before he left, he said of himself and Steve Gillis, "Washoe has long since grown irksome to us, & we want to leave it anyhow" (§ 40, below). Nevertheless, his decision to push on was precipitated by a dramatic series of events during the last two weeks in May, 1864. These events have long been familiar in general outline, but a number of important details have been obscure. Although the documents presented below do not remove all the obscurities, they fill in the outline appreciably and embody all that is definitely known concerning this crisis in Mark Twain's career.

The task of finding out precisely what happened is made more difficult by the fact that Mark Twain himself later set down two detailed accounts of the episode which are in some respects contradictory and inaccurate. The version in *Roughing It,* written seven years afterward, places the emphasis on a plan whereby he was to go to New York with "two citizens" in order to help sell a silver mine just discovered in a new mining district. He remarks casually that the editorials he had written for the *Enterprise* during the absence of Joe Goodman left Joe with six duels on his hands, but he says nothing more about them.[79] In Mark Twain's *Autobiography,* however, written more than forty years later, the plan to go East to sell the mine has been forgotten. Instead, he tells an elaborate story of how he was forced to leave Nevada because he was in danger of criminal prosecution for having challenged a man to a duel.[80] This narrative is in his best vein of humorous self-depreciation. He relates how, in Goodman's absence, he attacked James L. Laird of the *Daily Union* in the editorial columns of the *Enterprise*. Laird replied in kind, and Mark Twain's friends Rollin M. Daggett and Steve Gillis insisted he must challenge Laird.

The hour (according to the account in the *Autobiography*) was set for five o'clock in the morning. At four, Mark Twain and his friends went to the field of honor for target practice, only to discover that he literally could not hit a barn door. Steve seized the pistol to demonstrate how the thing should be done and shot the head off a sparrow at thirty yards. Just at that moment Laird and his people came up. Steve told them Mark Twain had shot the bird. "The second took Mr. Laird home, a little tottery on his legs, and Laird sent back a note in his own hand declining to fight a duel with me on any terms whatever."

Neither the plan to sell the silver mine nor the tale about the abortive duel with Laird is substantiated by contemporary evidence, and Mark Twain's description of the meeting with Laird on the field of honor is clearly fictitious. Professor DeLancey Ferguson has discovered the source of it: it was derived from a tall tale published by Mark Twain in *Tom Hood's Comic Annual* (London) in 1873.[81] The similar story told by Steve Gillis, which Albert B. Paine accepted as true, was apparently based on the same published sketch.[82] Mark Twain's dispute with Laird did not develop beyond the stage of high-flown insult. The progress of this affair, and of other altercations in which Mark Twain was engaged, is recorded in the documents presented below (§§ 33–42). They tell their own story, but a chronology may help the reader to find his way through the complexities of the half-farcial, half-melancholy imbroglio:

May 16, 1864. The sack of flour which was being auctioned off again and again to raise money for the Sanitary Fund (the Civil War equivalent of the Red Cross) reached Gold Hill, a mile from Virginia City. The Gold Hill *Evening News,* usually hostile to Mark Twain, said that "'tone' was given to the procession by the presence of Gov. Twain and his staff of bibulous reporters, who came down in a free carriage, ostensibly for the purpose of taking notes, but in reality in pursuit of free whiskey."[83]

May 17 (possibly May 18). Mark Twain wrote an editorial for the *Enterprise* (which is not extant) entitled "How Is It?" intimating that money raised at the fancy-dress ball given by the ladies of Carson City on May 5 "was to be sent to aid a Miscegenation Society somewhere in the East," or at least was about to be diverted from its proper destination.

May 18. Four indignant ladies of Carson wrote a letter of protest to the *Enterprise*, which the *Enterprise* refused to publish. (It was finally published on May 25 by the *Union*.)

May 20. Mark Twain wrote to Mollie Clemens saying that he had been drinking when he wrote the offending editorial and that it had got into print by mistake; but he could not bring himself to apologize publicly.

May 21. The *Union* published two articles having to do with yet another charge of Mark Twain, to the effect that the employees of the *Union* had not paid the money they had pledged to the Sanitary Fund. This charge may have been made in the "How Is It?" editorial of May 17 or 18, or in another editorial. James L. Laird, one of the proprietors of the *Union*, and J. W. Wilmington, a printer on the paper, heaped insults on the author of the editorial; but as it was unsigned, they did not call Mark Twain by name. These pieces in the *Union* set in motion the interchange of notes published later by the *Enterprise* under the heading "Personal Correspondence." Mark Twain challenged Laird to a duel, but Laird referred him to Wilmington. Steve Gillis, as Mark Twain's second, undertook to insult Wilmington so that Wilmington would be forced to challenge him.

May 23. Mark Twain wrote to Mrs. W. K. Cutler a letter explaining that he could not make a public apology to the ladies of Carson City because he was involved in "a deadly quarrel with the publishers of the *Union*, and I could not come out and make public apologies to any one at such a time." But he thanked Mrs. Cutler for her "continued friendship for Mollie [Clemens] while others are disposed to withdraw theirs on account of a fault for which I alone am responsible."[84]

May 24. The *Enterprise* published the correspondence among Mark Twain, Laird, Gillis, and Wilmington, and Mark Twain again denounced Laird for refusing to fight him. In an unsigned editorial entitled "Miscegenation" Mark Twain tried to make his peace with the embattled ladies of Carson. The Gold Hill *Daily News* made light of the whole affair in two editorials.

May 25. The *Union* published the letter of the Carson ladies. Mark Twain, in a letter to Orion and Mollie Clemens, said he was open to challenge from three persons, and was awaiting the issue of a challenge sent to a fourth. It is not now clear who these enemies were, beyond Laird and possibly Wilmington.

May 26. Mark Twain wrote Orion that he and Steve had decided to set out for "the States" on Sunday, May 29.

May 28. Mark Twain sent a note to W. K. Cutler, of which only a preliminary draft is extant. This note probably offered Cutler "satisfaction" under the code.[85]

May 29. Mark Twain and Gillis left on the stagecoach for San Francisco.

The Code Duello

One has to recognize some justice in the comment of the Gold Hill *News*, after Mark Twain's departure, that he had "in short, 'played hell' " (§ 42, below). But he had been the victim of circumstances. The whole unfortunate train of events was apparently set in motion by the mistake of a typesetter on the *Enterprise*, who put into print an editorial Mark Twain had written but had decided not to publish. Further confusion resulted from the fact that the dueling code had an ill-defined status in Nevada, so that no clear rules guided the conduct of any of the men involved.[86] A community where the code prevailed in its pristine severity could not have countenanced the kind of half-serious personal abuse that abounded in Washoe journalism. Printed insults were so customary that Mark Twain could pass the vague limit of Nevada tolerance without quite realizing it. The account in the *Autobiography*, despite its reminiscent embroidery, is accurate in suggesting that none of the participants was sure how serious he or his opponent was.

On occasion, newspaper controversy in Virginia City did lead to the field of honor. Joe Goodman of the *Enterprise* and Tom Fitch of the *Union* had fought a duel in 1863. Their first meeting was a fiasco. The antagonists met in Six-Mile Cañon at nine o'clock on the morning of August 1 but were arrested before any shots were fired.[87] Mark Twain's contemporary report of this affair in the *Enterprise* treats it as a farce. He says that with a companion he followed Goodman and Fitch out to the dueling ground on horseback

at the rate of a mile a minute, since when, being neither iron-clad nor even half-soled, we enjoy more real comfort in standing up than sitting down. But we lost our bloody item—for Marshal Perry arrived early with a detachment of Constables, and Deputy Sheriff Blodgett came with a lot of blarsted Sheriffs, and these miserable meddling whelps arrested the whole party and marched them back to town. In interfering with our legitimate business, Mr. Perry and Mr. Blodgett probably think they are almighty smart, but we calculate to get even with them.[88]

Although the two principals were placed under $5,000 bond to keep the peace, they met again. Mark Twain describes an encounter at Ingraham's ranch in Stampede Valley on September 28, witnessed by numerous spectators, in which Goodman shot Fitch in the knee.[89]

Yet contemporary newspaper references to Mark Twain's altercation with Laird treat it very lightly. The Gold Hill *News* called the fire-and-brimstone "Personal Correspondence" published by the *Enterprise* "Falstaffian" and remarked, with an allusion to Mark Twain's celebrated Empire City massacre hoax, that "The duel will perhaps come off at the pine forest at Empire City. Horrible! Most horrible" (§ 37, below). At this distance in time one can not easily determine how close the situation was to the line between make-believe and earnest. The defiance issued to W. K. Cutler by Mark Twain on Saturday, May 28 (§ 41, below), after Mark Twain and Gillis had already made arrangements to take the stage for California the next morning, leaves the historian with a conspicuous loose end in his hands. It does not even clear things up to adopt the hypothesis that Mark Twain was, as he described himself in the *Autobiography,* a coward; for Gillis, whose pugnacity was celebrated, was involved in exactly the same set of circumstances.

Mark Twain was clearly mistaken in his later memory of another aspect of the affair. He says in the *Autobiography* that a "brand-new law" made sending or carrying a challenge a penitentiary offense, and that "Governor North" caused him and Gillis to be warned that if they did not leave the Territory at once he would make them "the first victims of the new law." He "would absolutely keep us in the prison the full two years. He wouldn't pardon us out to please anybody."[90] Steve Gillis made a similar statement to Paine,[91] and this version has been accepted by later writers. But these statements cannot be accurate. For one thing, there was never a Governor North of Nevada. (The only territorial governor was James W. Nye; "North" may be a mistake for "Nye.")[92] Furthermore, there was not a brand-new law against dueling: no statute dealing with dueling had been placed on the books by the third Territorial

Legislature, which had adjourned February 20, 1864. A statute of long standing (passed by the first Territorial Legislature in 1861) made dueling or sending a challenge a criminal offense, but the Goodman-Fitch affair demonstrates that the law was not enforced.[93] Mark Twain's letter to Orion, written in the midst of the excitement, is quite explicit on this point: "We are not afraid of the grand jury . . ." (§ 40, below). He promises to wait a month, if any of the husbands of the Carson ladies want to challenge him. The letter does acknowledge some risk of arrest that might interfere with his and Gillis' plan to leave Nevada at once, but the precedent of the Goodman-Fitch affair suggests that the two men were not likely to incur worse punishment than being placed under bond to keep the peace. It is not easy to believe that they would in any event have had to do more than visit San Francisco for a couple of weeks while things quieted down. The real danger Mark Twain faced— his letters make this clear—was the danger of being ridiculous and ridiculed.

Whatever his motive, Mark Twain left Virginia City with the cordial good wishes of the *Enterprise* staff. (Steve Gillis, possibly embroidering again, told Paine many years later that Joe Goodman accompanied them all the way to San Francisco.)[94] The *Enterprise* published at least one long dispatch written by Mark Twain from San Francisco within a month after his departure.[95] From October, 1865, until he sailed for the Hawaiian Islands in March, 1866, he contributed frequently to the paper—for a time, in fact, daily.[96] The publishers would hardly have continued to buy so much copy from Mark Twain if public opinion had been hostile to him. And in October and November, 1866, soon after his return from Honolulu, he came back to Nevada for a highly successful lecture tour.[97]

In the perspective of Mark Twain's later career one can recognize that he derived solid benefits from his exposure to the rowdy flush times along the Comstock Lode. When he got on the stagecoach to leave Virginia City for San Francisco he was not yet fully aware of the imaginative power that lay hidden within him; yet he knew he was a writer, and he had undergone the discipline of a professional journalist. He had stored up the experiences that were to provide the materials for his major books, and on a few occasions he had come close to tapping this underground reserve—

as when the schoolroom in Carson City called up in his mind the memory of his own schoolroom in Hannibal. Most important of all, he had acquired on the Comstock "that shrewd, graceless, good-humored, cynical way of looking at things as they in fact are— unbullied by authority and indifferent to tradition" which was to be the root of all his best literary work.[93]

PART TWO

"THE OFFICE OF REPORTER"

1.

Letter from Carson City
December 5, 1862

☞ While Sam Clemens was prospecting for silver in Nevada in 1861 and 1862, three of his letters to his mother and sister were published in the Keokuk (Iowa) *Gate City*. During the early months of 1862 Sam contributed an unknown number of letters to the Virginia City *Territorial Enterprise* over the signature "Josh." He recalled many years later that these volunteer contributions had consisted of enthusiastic descriptions of his mining claims and a burlesque of the oratorical style of Chief Justice George Turner of the Territorial Supreme Court. The burlesque led the editors of the *Enterprise* to offer him a job.[1] None of the "Josh" letters has come to light. The first of Clemens' writings for the *Enterprise* that is extant is the "petrified man" hoax, reprinted in the San Francisco *Daily Evening Bulletin* on October 15, 1862, and included by Ivan Benson in *Mark Twain's Western Years* (p. 175). The "Letter from Carson City" reprinted here is the second of Clemens' contributions to the *Enterprise* that has survived and the earliest that is available in its original form. It is attributed by the *Enterprise* to "Our Special Correspondent." The pseudonym "Mark Twain" was not yet in use.

Young Clemens had gone to work on the paper in September, 1862, as a replacement for Dan De Quille (William Wright), who had asked for leave of absence to visit his relatives in Iowa.[2] The new employee's first duties were those of a local reporter, or "city editor." In *Roughing It* (an extremely unreliable source of autobiographical fact) Mark Twain says that he was expected to fill two nonpareil columns every day with local items, and that when he first went to work he was forced to invent news in order to turn out enough copy. He multiplied "one wretched old hay-truck dragging in from the country" by sixteen, and imagined an Indian attack on an emigrant wagon train "that to this day has no parallel in history."[3]

When the second Territorial Legislature began its session at Carson City on November 11, 1862, Clemens was sent down to report the proceedings.[4] It is not clear how often he mailed dispatches back to Virginia City, but by bringing together two passages from his reminiscences one may infer that he sent a daily factual report and a weekly letter of a more personal and humorous cast.[5] The piece reprinted here is presumably one of the weekly letters. The humor in it is forced and amateurish, but the piece is interesting as a kind of bench mark from which the young writer's development as a humorist may be measured in later dispatches of the sort.

Granting toll-road franchises was an important form of legislation. During the 1862 session, Clemens, Rice, and Andrew J. Marsh satirized the profusion of franchises by proposing a "Reporters' Toll-Road." The *Enterprise* pointed out in an editorial that if this additional franchise should be granted, no one "could find a spot between the highest peak of Mount Davidson and the lowest depths of the Sink of the Carson on which to locate said Reporters' toll-road. No! not though they searched with microscopes."[6] Myron Angel points out that the first Territorial Legislature had granted only six toll-road franchises,[7] and accuses Mark Twain of exaggeration in his statement in *Roughing It*:

The [first] legislature sat sixty days, and passed private toll-road franchises all the time. When they adjourned it was estimated that every citizen owned about three franchises, and it was believed that unless Congress gave the territory another degree of longitude there would not be room enough to accommodate the toll-roads. The ends of them were hanging over the boundary-line everywhere like a fringe.[8]

The published statutes bear out Angel's assertion about the first Territorial Legislature, but the next legislature granted twenty-two toll-road franchises and the third passed twenty-seven.[9] This is, after all, a great many for so sparsely populated a territory.

The Colonel Williams who drew the map illustrating the letter was a member of the lower house from Virginia City; possibly, although not certainly, he was the Colonel Jonathan Williams who had been one of the owners of the *Enterprise* in 1860.[10] There were many "colonels" in Nevada. Wells Drury says that "mine superintendents were universally entitled Colonel," as were all lawyers, and leading saloonkeepers, except those who were called "Judge."[11] In 1905 Mark Twain mentioned "Jack Williams" affectionately as one of the "desperadoes, who made life a joy" during his Nevada days.[12] But there is no way of knowing whether this Williams, either, was the legislator from Virginia City.

Persons mentioned frequently in the text are identified in the Biographical Directory at the end of the book.

A Pi-Ute was an early white settler of Nevada—more precisely, one who had arrived before the mining rush of May, 1860 (§ 15, below).

EDITOR ENTERPRISE: If your readers are not aware of the fact, I take pleasure in informing them that the [Nevada] Supreme Court will meet in Carson City on the 13th of the present month; and in connection with this intelligence I present the following item, giving it in the language in which I received it for fear of mistakes— for its terms are darkly, mysteriously legal, and I have not the most distant conception of what they mean, or what they are intended to have reference to—thus: "Wm. Alford vs. Nathaniel Dewing et als.—Ordered filed, denying rehearing." There it is, and I wash my hands of the matter. I don't know Alford, and I don't know Dewing, and I don't know Et Als—and I never heard of either, or any of these gentlemen until this very day, when the Clerk of the Supreme Court brought me this written nightmare, which has been distressing me up to the present moment. If it is a charge, I do not make it; if it is an insinuation, I do not endorse it; if its expressionless exterior conceals a slur, I do not father it. I simply publish the document as I received it, and take no responsibility upon myself for the consequences. I do not wish these gentlemen any harm; I would not willingly and knowingly do them the slightest possible wrong—yet, if they ought to be filed—mind, I say if they *ought* to be filed—if it is entirely right and proper that they should be filed—if, in the opinion of the people of this commonwealth, it is deemed necessary to file them—then, I say, let them be filed and be d—— [here the manuscript was illegible.—ED.] Now you have the document and the facts in the case; and if there be a fault in the matter it is the Clerk's, and I know what that Chinaman did it for. [If you have forgotten the circumstance, I said in a letter that he had been cast for a Chinaman in the recent tableaux here.]

The Roads and Highways bill was considered in Committee of the Whole in the House yesterday. A clause in it provides for a tax of $4 on each voter, or a day's work on the roads in lieu thereof. Storey was relieved from the payment of this tax, which was entirely proper, since there is not a free road in the whole county.

These grave and reverend legislators relax a little occasionally, and indulge in chaste and refined jollity to a small extent. Col. Williams is engineering a certain toll road franchise through the House, and the other night he was laying before the Committee on Internal Improvements some facts in the case, pending which he had occasion to illustrate his theme with pencil and paper, and the result was a map, which, in view of its grandeur of conception, elegance of design and masterly execution, I feel justified in styling miraculous. Mr. Lovejoy, Chairman of the Committee, captured it, incorporated it into his report, and presented it before the House yesterday, thus:

REPORT OF THE COMMITTEE ON INTERNAL IMPROVEMENTS

Map of Col. Williams' road "from a certain point to another place," as drawn by himself, and which was conclusive evidence to your Committee:

Your committee would ask that it be referred to Col. Howard of the Storey county delegation. [Signed]   Lovejoy
    Ackley, *Sec'y.*   *Chairman*

It was so referred by the Speaker.

Col. Howard will report to-day. I have procured a copy of the forthcoming document, and transmit it herewith.

REPORT ON WILLIAMS MAP

Your committee, consisting of a solitary but very competent individual, to whom was referred Col. Williams' road from a certain point to another place, would beg most respectfully to report:

Your committee has had under consideration said map.

The word map is derived from the Spanish word "mapa," or the

Portuguese word "mappa." Says the learned lexicographer Webster, "in geography a map is a representation of the surface of the earth, or any part of it, drawn on paper or other material, exhibiting the lines of latitude and longitude, and the positions of countries, kingdoms, states, mountains, rivers, etc."

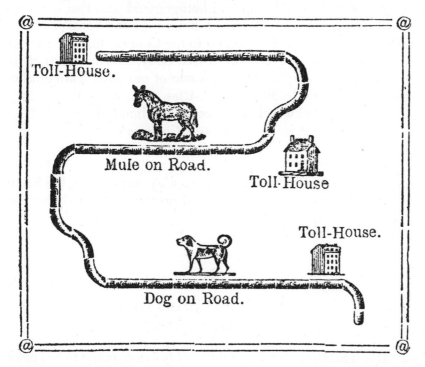

Toll-House.

Mule on Road.

Toll-House

Toll-House.

Dog on Road.

Your committee, with due respect to the projector of the road in question, would designate what is styled in the report a map, an unnatural and diabolical scrawl, devoid of form, regularity or meaning.

Your committee has in times past witnessed the wild irregularity of the footprints of birds of prey upon a moist sea shore. Your committee was struck with the strong resemblance of the map under discussion to some one of said footprints.

Your committee, during his juvenile days, has watched a frantic and indiscreet fly emerge from a pot or vase containing molasses; your committee has seen said fly alight upon a scrap of virgin paper, and leave thereon a wild medley of wretched and discordant tracks; your committee was struck with the wonderful resemblance of said fly-tracks to the map now before your committee.

Yet your committee believes that the map in question has some merit as an abstract hieroglyphic.

Your committee, therefore, recommends, the Council concurring, that the aforesaid map be photographed, and that one copy thereof, framed in sage brush, be hung over the Speaker's chair, and that another copy be donated to the Council, to be suspended over the chair of the President of that body, as a memento of the artistic skill and graphic genius of one of our most distinguished members—a guide to all future Pi-Utes.

All of which is respectfully submitted.

HOWARD, *Chairman*
and Sole Committee

A resolution passed the House yesterday, authorizing the Secretary of the Territory to purchase and preserve files of the various papers published in the Territory.

2.

Letter from Carson City
December 12, [1862]

☞ This is evidently another of the weekly letters, meant to be humorous in contrast to the factual daily dispatches about proceedings of the Legislature. It is unsigned, and does not even carry the by-line of "Our Special Correspondent" which appears at the head of the previous letter. But the authorship of the piece can hardly be in doubt. The statement that the night session of the House was "in many respects . . . much superior to a funeral" is in itself almost a signature.

The White House Hotel, Mrs. C. A. Williamson, proprietor, stood on the plaza in Carson. It was "the *aristocratic* House of the place"; no liquor was served there.[1]

The reference to mutilation of Colonel Williams' eloquence establishes the existence of earlier dispatches concerning legislative proceedings that are now lost. The Governor was James W. Nye, formerly of New York. Dutch Nick's hotel at Empire City was to figure in Mark

Twain's hoax entitled "The Latest Sensation," describing a sanguinary series of murders and a suicide in a log house "just at the edge of the great [nonexistent] pine forest which lies between Empire City and Dutch Nick's."[2]

EDITORS ENTERPRISE: Ormsby heads the world on the turnip question. The vegetable upon which I base this boast, was grown in the turnip garden of Mr. S. D. Fairchild, back here towards King's Canyon—in the suburbs—say about eight squares from the plaza. Mr. Fairchild left it at the "branch" of the ENTERPRISE office in Carson, a day or two since. The monster was accurately surveyed, with the following result: circumference, forty inches; weight, a fraction over eighteen pounds.

Col. Williams, of the House, who says I mutilate his eloquence, addressed a note to me this morning, to the effect that I had given his constituents wrong impressions concerning him, and nothing but blood would satisfy him. I sent him that turnip on a handbarrow, requesting him to extract from it a sufficient quantity of blood to restore his equilibrium—(which I regarded as a very excellent joke). Col. Williams ate it (raw) during the usual prayer by the chaplain. To sum up: eighteen pounds of raw turnip is sufficient for an ordinary lunch—Col. Williams had his feet on his desk at the time—he beamed—wherefore, I think his satisfaction was complete.

Carson also boasts the only pork-packing establishment in Nevada Territory. Mr. George T. Davis is the proprietor thereof, and he has already killed and packed two hundred and fifty fine hogs this winter. This will be cheering news to the young lady who told me the other evening that she "loved pork."

The pleasantest affair of the season, perhaps, although not the most gorgeous, was the "candy-pull" at the White House, a few nights ago. The candy had not finished cooking at nine o'clock, so they concluded to dance awhile. They always dance here when they have time. I have noticed it frequently. I think it is a way they have. They got a couple of able-bodied fiddlers and went at it. They opened with the dance called the plain quadrille, which is very simple and easy, and is performed in this wise: All you have to do is to stand up in the middle of the floor, being careful to get your lady on your right hand side, and yourself on the left hand side of your lady. Then you are all right you know. When you hear a blast of music like unto the rush of many waters, you lay your hand on your stomach and bow to the lady of your choice—then you turn around and bow to the fiddlers. The first order is, "First couple fore and aft"—or words to that effect. This is very easy. You have only to march straight across the house—keeping out of the way of the advancing couple, who very seldom know where they are going to—and when you get over, if you find your partner there, swing her; if you don't, hunt her up—for it is very handy to have a partner in these plain quadrilles. The next order is, "Ladies change." This is an exceedingly difficult figure, and requires great presence of mind; because, on account of shaking hands with the lobby members so much, and from the force of human nature also, you are morally certain to offer your right, when the chances are that your left hand is wanted. This has a tendency to mix things. At this point order and regularity cease—the dancers get excited— the musicians become insane—turmoil and confusion ensue— chaos comes again! Put your trust in Providence and stick to your partner. Several of these engaging and beautiful plain quadrilles were danced during the evening, and we might have enjoyed several more, but the rostrum broke down and spilt the musicians. I was exceedingly delighted with the waltz, and also with the polka. These differ in name, but there the difference ceases—the dances are precisely the same. You have only to spin around with frightful velocity and steer clear of the furniture. This has a charming and bewildering effect. You catch glimpses of a confused and whirling multitude of people, and above them a row of distracted fiddlers extending entirely around the room. The waltz and the polka are very exhilarating—to use a mild term—amazingly exhilarating.

Nothing occurred to mar the joyousness of the occasion. The party was very select—except myself and Col. Williams; the candy was not burned; the Governor sat down on a hot stove and got up again with great presence of mind; the dancing was roomy and hilarious, and fun went to waste. Henceforward my principles are fixed. I am a stern and unwavering advocate of "candy-pulls."

There was a slight conflagration in Mr. Helm's office yesterday morning—at least I was told so by my friend, the reporter for the Virginia Union, who is not very reliable. He also stated that no damage was done; but I don't put much confidence in what he says.

The ladies have not smiled much on this Legislature, so far. Thirty-two of our loveliest visited the halls night before last, though, which is an encouraging symptom. I cannot conscientiously say they smiled, however, for the Revenue bill was before the House. This cheerful subject is calculated to produce inward jollity, but the same is not apt to blossom into smiles on the surface. The ladies were well pleased with the night session, though—they enjoyed it exceedingly—in many respects it was much superior to a funeral. The Revenue bill was finished up last night, and in the name and at the request of the members, I invite all the ladies in town to call again, at any time, either day or night session. That Revenue bill was one of those nonsensical general public concerns that we are not used to; but the fun will be resumed right away, now that we are back on our regular toll roads again.

I went down to Empire City yesterday to see the Eagle Fire Company try their new engine (by the way, you have, so far, neglected to mention either the machine or the company in your paper). They first threw an inch and a quarter stream over Dutch Nick's hotel, and then a three-quarter inch stream over the liberty pole. This brought cheers from the multitude—(there were many ladies there from neighboring cities). The boys grew excited and ambitious. Several ladies passed by, wearing the new fashioned light-house bonnets. The Eagles, in their madness, attempted to throw a half-inch stream over those bonnets. They puffed their cheeks and strained every nerve; there was a moment of painful suspense, as the pearly column went towering toward the clouds— then a long, loud, reverberating shout, as it bent gracefully and went over, without touching a feather! But the engine broke.

If McCluskey, of the Delta Saloon, could send me a reporter's cobbler—an unusually long one—I think it would relieve my cold.

3.

Local Items, Virginia City
December, 1862—January, 1863

☞ Both the dates of these items and their authorship are conjectural but reasonably certain. The author identifies himself as "Sam" in "Our Stock Remarks" (a paragraph, incidentally, not unworthy of Mark Twain). "More Ghosts" and "New Year's Day" are labeled "Sam's Column" in pencil in the scrapbook.

As for dates: the names of legislators mentioned in "At Home" correspond to members of the Storey County delegation in the second Territorial Legislature, which adjourned December 20, 1862. "More Ghosts" and "New Year's Day" probably appeared on January 1, 1863. The report on the Sanitary Ball was published on January 10, 1863, in one of the two or three issues of the *Enterprise* for this period which have survived entire. The article was discovered and identified by Professor William C. Miller of the University of Nevada; the copy of the *Enterprise* from which it is transcribed is in the library of the Nevada Historical Society, Reno.

The Gould & Curry was one of the wealthiest mining companies on the Comstock Lode.

OUR STOCK REMARKS.—Owing to the fact that our stock reporter attended a wedding last evening, our report of transactions in that branch of robbery and speculation is not quite as complete and satisfactory as usual this morning. About eleven o'clock last night the aforesaid remarker pulled himself up stairs by the banisters, and stumbling over the stove, deposited the following notes on our table, with the remark: "S(hic)am, just 'laberate this, w(hic)ill, yer?" We said we would, but we couldn't. If any of our readers think they can, we shall be pleased to see the translation. Here are the notes: "Stocks brisk, and Ophir has taken this woman for your wedded wife. Some few transactions have occurred in rings and lace veils, and at figures tall, graceful and charming. There was some inquiry late in the day for parties who would take them for better or for worse but there were few offers. There seems to be some depression in this stock. We mentioned yesterday that our Father which art in heaven. Quotations of lost reference, and now I lay me down to sleep," &c., &c., &c.

———————

BLOWN DOWN.—At sunset yesterday, the wind commenced blowing after a fashion to which a typhoon is mere nonsense, and in a short time the face of heaven was obscured by vast clouds of dust all spangled over with lumber, and shingles, and dogs and things. There was no particular harm in that, but the breeze soon began to work damage of a serious nature. Thomas Moore's new frame house on the east side of C street, above the Court House, was blown down, and the fire-wall front of a one story brick building higher up the street was also thrown to the ground. The latter house was occupied as a store by Mr. Heldman, and owned by Mr. Felton. The storm was very severe for a while, and we shall not be surprised to hear of further destruction having been caused by it. The damage resulting to Mr. Heldman's grocery store, amounts to $2,200.

———————

AT HOME.—Judge Brumfield's nightmare—the Storey county delegation—have straggled in, one at a time, until they are all at home once more. Messrs. Mills, Mitchell, Meagher and Minneer returned several days ago, and we had the pleasure of meeting Mr. Davenport, also, yesterday. We do not know how long the latter gentleman has been here, but we offer him the unlimited freedom of the city, anyhow. Justice to a good representative is justice, you know, whether it be tardy or otherwise.

———————

THRILLING ROMANCE.—On our first page, to-day, will be found the opening chapters of a thrilling tale, entitled "An Act to amend and supplemental to an Act to provide for Assessing and Collecting County and Territorial Revenue." This admirable story was written especially for the columns of this paper by several distinguished authors. We have secured a few more productions of the same kind, at great expense, and we design publishing them in their regular order. Our readers will agree with us that it will redound considerably to their advantage to read and preserve these documents.

Sad Accident.—We learn from Messrs. Hatch & Bro., who do a heavy business in the way of supplying this market with vegetables, that the rigorous weather accompanying the late storm was so severe on the mountains as to cause a loss of life in several instances. Two sacks of sweet potatoes were frozen to death on the summit, this side of Strawberry. The verdict rendered by the coroner's jury was strictly in accordance with the facts.

More Ghosts.—Are we to be scared to death every time we venture into the street? May we be allowed to go quietly about our business, or are we to be assailed at every corner by fearful apparitions? As we were plodding home at the ghostly hour last night, thinking about the haunted house humbug, we were suddenly riveted to the pavement in a paroxysm of terror by that blue and yellow phantom who watches over the destinies of the shooting gallery, this side of the International. Seen in daylight, placidly reclining against his board in the doorway, with his blue coat, and his yellow pants, and his high boots, and his fancy hat, just lifted from his head, he is rather an engaging youth, than otherwise; but at dead of night, when he pops out his pallid face at you by candle light, and stares vacantly upon you with his uplifted hat and the eternal civility of his changeless brow, and the ghostliness of his general appearance heightened by that grave-stone inscription over his stomach, "to-day shooting for chickens here," you are apt to think of spectres starting up from behind tomb-stones, and you weaken accordingly—the cold chills creep over you—your hair stands on end—you reverse your front, and with all possible alacrity, you change your base.

New Year's Day.—Now is the accepted time to make your regular annual good resolutions. Next week you can begin paving hell with them as usual. Yesterday, everybody smoked his last cigar, took his last drink, and swore his last oath. To-day, we are a pious and exemplary community. Thirty days from now, we shall have cast our reformation to the winds and gone to cutting our ancient shortcomings considerably shorter than ever. We shall also reflect pleasantly upon how we did the same old thing last year about this time. However, go in, community. New Year's is a harmless annual institution, of no particular use to anybody save as a scapegoat for promiscuous drunks, and friendly calls, and humbug resolutions, and we wish you to enjoy it with a looseness suited to the greatness of the occasion.

THE SANITARY BALL

The Sanitary Ball at La Plata Hall on Thursday night [January 8, 1863] was a very marked success, and proved beyond the shadow of a doubt, the correctness of our theory, that ladies never fail in undertakings of this kind. If there had been about two dozen more people there, the house would have been crowded—as it was, there was room enough on the floor for the dancers, without trespassing on their neighbors' corns. Several of those long, trailing dresses, even, were under fire in the thickest of the fight for six hours, and came out as free from rips and rents as they were when they went in. Not all of them, though. We recollect a circumstance in point. We had just finished executing one of those inscrutable figures of the plain quadrille; we were feeling unusually comfortable, because we had gone through the performance as well as anybody could have done it, except that we had wandered a little toward the last; in fact we had wandered out of our own and into somebody else's set—but that was a matter of small consequence, as the new locality was as good as the old one, and we were used to that sort of thing anyhow. We were feeling comfortable, and we had assumed an attitude—we have a sort of talent for posturing— a pensive attitude, copied from the Colossus of Rhodes—when the ladies were ordered to the centre. Two of them got there, and the other two moved off gallantly, but they failed to make the connection. They suddenly broached to under full headway, and there was a sound of parting canvas. Their dresses were anchored under our boots, you know. It was unfortunate, but it could not be helped. Those two beautiful pink dresses let go amidships, and remained in a ripped and damaged condition to the end of the ball. We did not apologize, because our presence of mind happened to be absent at the very moment that we had the greatest need of it. But we beg permission to do so now.

An excellent supper was served in the large dining-room of the new What Cheer House on B street. We missed it there, somewhat.

We were not accompanied by a lady, and consequently we were not eligible to a seat at the first table. We found out all about that at the Gold Hill ball, and we had intended to be all prepared for this one. We engaged a good many young ladies last Tuesday to go with us, thinking that out of the lot we should certainly be able to secure one, at the appointed time, but they all seemed to have got a little angry about something—nobody knows what, for the ways of women are past finding out. They told us we had better go and invite a thousand girls to go to the ball. A thousand. Why, it was absurd. We had no use for a thousand girls. A thou—— but those girls were as crazy as loons. In every instance, after they had uttered that pointless suggestion, they marched magnificently out of their parlors—and if you will believe us, not one of them ever recollected to come back again. Why, it was the most unaccountable experience we ever heard of. We never enjoyed so much solitude in so many different places, in one evening before. But patience has its limits; we finally got tired of that arrangement—and at the risk of offending some of those girls, we stalked off to the Sanitary Ball alone—without a virgin, out of that whole litter. We may have done wrong—we probably did do wrong to disappoint those fellows in that kind of style—but how could we help it? We couldn't stand the temperature of those parlors more than an hour at a time: it was cold enough to freeze out the heaviest stock-holder on the Gould & Curry's books.

However, as we remarked before, everybody spoke highly of the supper, and we believe they meant what they said. We are unable to say anything in the matter from personal knowledge, except that the tables were arranged with excellent taste, and more than abundantly supplied, and everything looked very beautiful, and very inviting, also; but then we had absorbed so much cold weather in those parlors, and had had so much trouble with those girls, that we had no appetite left. We only eat a boiled ham and some pies, and went back to the ball room. There were some very handsome cakes on the tables, manufactured by Mr. Slade, and decorated with patriotic mottoes, done in fancy icing. All those who were happy that evening, agree that the supper was superb.

After supper the dancing was jolly. They kept it up till four in the morning, and the guests enjoyed themselves excessively. All the dances were performed, and the bill of fare wound up with a new style of plain quadrille called a medley, which involved the whole list. It involved us also. But we got out again—and we staid out, with great sagacity. But speaking of plain quadrilles reminds us of another new one—the Virginia reel. We found it a very easy matter to dance it, as long as we had thirty or forty lookers-on to prompt us. The dancers were formed in two long ranks, facing each other, and the battle opens with some light skirmishing between the pickets, which is gradually resolved into a general engagement along the whole line: after that, you have nothing to do but stand by and grab every lady that drifts within reach of you, and swing her. It is very entertaining, and elaborately scientific also; but we observed that with a partner who had danced it before, we were able to perform it rather better than the balance of the guests.

Altogether, the Sanitary Ball was a remarkably pleasant party, and we are glad that such was the case—for it is a very uncomfortable task to be obliged to say harsh things about entertainments of this kind. At the present writing we cannot say what the net proceeds of the ball will amount to, but they will doubtless reach quite a respectable figure—say $400.

THE MUSIC.—Millington & McCluskey's Band furnished the music for the Sanitary Ball on Thursday night, and also for the Odd Fellows' Ball the other evening in Gold Hill, and the excellence of the article was only equalled by the industry and perseverance of the performers. We consider that the man who can fiddle all through one of those Virginia reels without losing his grip, may be depended upon in any kind of emergency.

4.

Letter from Carson City
[January 31, 1863]

☞ This letter (reprinted in part in Rabb, *Wit and Humor of America*, V, 1805–1808) has a peculiar interest as the earliest extant piece signed "Mark Twain." It is, in fact, very probably, the first published piece for which the pseudonym was used. Its date is therefore of some consequence.

The slugs at the end of two advertisements physically continuous with the clipping of this dispatch in Scrapbook 4 (p. 11) place the date within the first week of February, 1863. (One, an announcement of a large number of "merchants, traders and citizens of Virginia City" that they will accept and pay out greenbacks at their value in gold at San Francisco, is dated December 16, 1862, and bears a slug "ja18 tf," which means "January 18 until further notice." The other advertisement bears a slug "ja31 1w," which means "January 31 for one week.")

The letter itself is dated "Carson, Saturday night." Since the dispatch had to come up to Virginia City by stagecoach, it could hardly have made the Sunday paper. At this time the *Enterprise* did not appear on Mondays.[1] A Tuesday is therefore the most probable day of publication, and February 3 is the only Tuesday which meets the other conditions.

Albert B. Paine asserted that "Mark Twain was first signed to a Carson letter, February 2, 1863."[2] He did not cite his authority for the statement, but it evidently rested on an undated letter to him from Joe Goodman, whom he had visited in California in 1907 when he was gathering information for his biography of Mark Twain. Goodman's letter reads as follows:

My Dear Paine:

I've just come upon an old memorandum-book containing the following note which may be of value to you as it has two exact dates:

"Clemens came on The Enterprise in 1862. He reported the Legislative session of the winter 1862–3, first signing the name 'Mark Twain' to a letter written from Carson City dated Feb. 2, 1863. The first special article to which it was signed ('The Sugar Loaf') was printed Feb. 19, 1863."   GOODMAN[3]

This is very circumstantial, and the memorandum book may have been a contemporary record. But the printed evidence seems to show that Goodman's date was wrong by one day. Could his note have meant that the letter was received in the *Enterprise* office on February 2?

One further circumstance bearing on the pseudonym "Mark Twain" should be noted. In the letter, "the Unreliable" is made to address the author very casually as "Mark, old boy." This might suggest that the pseudonym had already been in use long enough to become familiar. But the incident is evidently fiction and can hardly be made a basis for inferences concerning historical fact.

The convention mentioned was another Nevada joke: a "Grand Bull Drivers' Convention" in Washoe City, December 22, 1862, celebrating the adjournment of the Legislature. Sam Clemens reported it in a letter to the *Enterprise* which Effie Mona Mack found reprinted in the *Placer Weekly Courier* of January 17, 1863.[4]

The "gem from the horse opera" was probably a song entitled "I Had an Old Horse Whose Name Was Methusalem" that was long a favorite of Mark Twain's. When Twain returned to Virginia City to lecture on the Sandwich Islands in 1866, Joe Goodman suggested that instead of arranging for a formal introduction, he should have the curtain rise to discover him seated at a piano on the stage playing and singing this song.[5]

Eds. Enterprise: I feel very much as if I had just awakened out of a long sleep. I attribute it to the fact that I have slept the greater part of the time for the last two days and nights. On Wednesday, I sat up all night, in Virginia, in order to be up early enough to take the five o'clock stage on Thursday morning. I was on time. It was a great success. I had a cheerful trip down to Carson, in company with that incessant talker, Joseph T. Goodman. I never saw him flooded with such a flow of spirits before. He restrained his conversation, though, until we had traveled three or four miles, and were just crossing the divide between Silver City and Spring Valley, when he thrust his head out of the dark stage, and allowed a pallid light from the coach lamp to illuminate his features for a moment, after which he returned to darkness again, and sighed and said, "Damn it!" with some asperity. I asked him who he meant it for, and he said, "The weather out there." As we approached Carson, at about half past seven o'clock, he thrust his head out again, and gazed earnestly in the direction of that city—after which he took it in again, with his nose very much frosted. He propped the end of that organ upon the end of his finger, and looked down pensively upon it—which had the effect of making him appear cross-eyed—and remarked, "O, damn it!" with great bitterness. I asked him what he was up to this time, and he said, "The cold, damp fog—it is worse than the weather." This was his last. He never spoke again in my hearing. He went on over the mountains, with a lady fellow-passenger from here. That will stop his clatter, you know, for he seldom speaks in the presence of ladies.

In the evening I felt a mighty inclination to go to a party somewhere. There was to be one at Governor J. Neely Johnson's, and I went there and asked permission to stand around awhile. This was granted in the most hospitable manner, and visions of plain quadrilles soothed my weary soul. I felt particularly comfortable, for if there is one thing more grateful to my feelings than another, it is a new house—a large house, with its ceilings embellished with snowy mouldings; its floors glowing with warm-tinted carpets; with cushioned chairs and sofas to sit on, and a piano to listen to; with fires so arranged that you can see them, and know that there is no humbug about it; with walls garnished with pictures, and above all, mirrors, wherein you may gaze, and always find something to admire, you know. I have a great regard for a good house, and a girlish passion for mirrors. Horace Smith, Esq., is also very fond of mirrors. He came and looked in the glass for an hour, with me. Finally, it cracked—the night was pretty cold—and Horace Smith's reflection was split right down the centre. But where his face had been, the damage was greatest—a hundred cracks converged from his reflected nose, like spokes from the hub of a wagon wheel. It was the strangest freak the weather has done this Winter. And yet the parlor seemed very warm and comfortable, too.

About nine o'clock the Unreliable came and asked Gov. Johnson to let him stand on the porch. That creature has got more impudence than any person I ever saw in my life. Well, he stood and flattened his nose against the parlor window, and looked hungry and vicious—he always looks that way—until Col. Musser arrived with some ladies, when he actually fell in their wake and came swaggering in, looking as if he thought he had been anxiously expected. He had on my fine kid boots, and my plug hat and my white kid gloves (with slices of his prodigious hands grinning through the bursted seams), and my heavy gold repeater, which I had been offered thousands and thousands of dollars for, many and many a time. He took these articles out of my trunk, at Washoe City, about a month ago, when we went out there to report the proceedings of the Convention. The Unreliable intruded himself upon me in his cordial way and said, "How are you, Mark, old boy? when d'you come down? It's brilliant, ain't it? Appear to enjoy themselves, don't they? Lend a fellow two bits, can't you?" He always winds up his remarks that way. He appears to have an insatiable craving for two bits.

Received St Joseph July 25. 1861 of Mr Orion Clemens Three Hundred Dollars on account of his and Saml L. Clemens fare to Carson City or any other point on our Route East of Placerville in Coach leaving St Joseph July 26. 1861.

$300.00/100

*Paul Coburn Agt COC.
Per Nat Stein. & PP Exco.*

Rec'd St Jo. July 25. 1861, of Mr Orion Clemens His acceptance of this Date at 30 Days for One Hundred Dollars, favor of B.M. Hughes, Prest — in full for Balance of above fares.

$100.—

*Paul Coburn Agt COC&PP Exco
Per Nat Stein)*

1. RECEIPT FOR STAGECOACH FARE OF ORION AND SAMUEL L. CLEMENS

The receipt was made out to Orion Clemens by the agent of the Central Overland California & Pike's Peak Express Company, in payment of the fare of the two brothers from St. Joseph, Missouri, to Carson City, Nevada Territory, by overland stagecoach. *Mark Twain Papers, University of California, Berkeley.*

2. SEAL OF THE TERRITORY OF NEVADA

From a letterhead of the territorial government. The seal was based on a design submitted by Territorial Secretary Orion Clemens to the first Legislative Assembly in October, 1861. *Mark Twain Papers.*

3. GOLD HILL, NEVADA, IN THE 1860's

From an anonymous oil painting, apparently of 1864 or 1865. Virginia City lies beyond the divide at the upper right. *Bancroft Library, University of California, Berkeley.*

4. ADVERTISEMENT FOR THE *Territorial Enterprise,* 1862

In August, 1863, offices of the paper were moved from the address on A Street listed here to a new building on C Street. From *First Directory of Nevada Territory,* compiled by J. Wells Kelly.

LETTER FROM CARSON CITY.

CARSON, Saturday Night.

EDS. ENTERPRISE: I feel very much as if I had just awakened out of a long sleep. I attribute it to the fact that I have slept the greater part of the time for the last two days and nights. On Wednesday, I sat up all night, in Virginia, in order to be up early enough to take the five o'clock stage on Thursday morning. I was on time. It was a great success. I had a cheerful trip down to Carson, in company with that incessant talker, Joseph T. Goodman. I never saw him flooded with such a flow of spirits before. He restrained his conversation, though, until we had traveled three or four miles, and were just crossing the divide between Silver City and Spring Valley, when he thrust his head out of the dark stage, and allowed a pallid light from the coach lamp to illuminate his features for a moment, after which he returned to darkness again, and sighed and said, " Damn it !" with some asperity. I asked him who he meant it for, and he said, "The weather out there." As we approached Carson, at about half past seven o'clock, he turned his head out again, and gazed earnestly in the direction of that city—after which he took it in again, with his nose very much frosted. He propped the end of that organ upon the end of his finger, and looked down pensively upon it—which had the effect of making him appear cross-eyed—and remarked, " O, damn it !" with great bitterness. I asked him what he was up to this time, and he said, " The cold, damp fog—it is worse than the weather." This was his last. He never spoke again in my hearing. He went on over the mountains, with a lady fellow-passenger from here. That will stop his clatter, you know, for he seldom speaks in the presence of ladies.

In the evening I felt a mighty inclination to go to a party somewhere. There was to be one at Gover<or J. Neely Johnson's, and I went there and asked permission to stand around awhile. This was granted in the most hospitable manner, and visions of plain quadrilles soothed my weary soul. I felt particularly comfortable, for if there is one thing more grateful to my feelings than another, it is a new house—a large house, with its ceilings embellished with snowy mouldings; its floors glowing with warm-tinted carpets; with cushioned chairs and sofas to sit on, and a piano to listen to; with fires so arranged that you can see them, and know that there is no humbug about it; with walls garnished with pictures, and above all, mirrors, wherein you may gaze, and always find something to admire, you know. I have a great regard for a good house, and a girlish passion for mirrors.

At about two o'clock in the morning the pleasant party broke up and the crowd of guests distributed themselves around town to their respective homes; and after thinking the fun all over again, I went to bed at four o'clock. So, having been awake forty-eight hours, I slept forty-eight, in order to get even again, which explains the proposition I began this letter with.

Yours, dreamily, MARK TWAIN.

5. FIRST PUBLISHED ARTICLE KNOWN TO HAVE BEEN SIGNED "MARK TWAIN"

No complete copy of the issue of the *Territorial Enterprise* from which this clipping was taken is extant. The middle part of the article is omitted here; the full text is printed in § 4. *Mark Twain Papers.*

6. C Street, Virginia City—Cedar Hill in the Distance, 1865

Number 708 in a series of stereoscopic views published by Lawrence & Houseworth, San Francisco, in 1866. *Nevada State Historical Society, Reno.*

7. Advertisement for the Magnolia Saloon, Carson City, 1862

Pete Hopkins and his saloon figure prominently in Mark Twain's "Empire City massacre" hoax, published in October, 1863. (See § 12.) From *First Directory of Nevada Territory.*

8. Young America Engine Company No. 2, Virginia City

From a photograph by Robert H. Vance taken in C Street after the 1862 Fourth-of-July parade. (On volunteer firemen in Virginia City, see § 8.) *Stanford University Library.*

9. MARK TWAIN IN THE MIDDLE 1860's

From a photograph made by Bradley & Rulofson of San Francisco at some time between 1864 and 1866. This is one of the first extant pictures of Mark Twain showing him with a mustache. *Bancroft Library.*

10. WILLIAM WRIGHT ("DAN DE QUILLE")

As Mark Twain's senior colleague on the *Enterprise* Wright initiated him into the mysteries of Washoe journalism. The two men became close friends, and roomed together during much of Mark Twain's stay in Virginia City. *Mackay School of Mines, University of Nevada, Reno.*

11. Virginia City in 1864

From a lithograph published by C. C. Kuchel of San Francisco, based upon drawings by Grafton T. Brown. *Mackay School of Mines.*

12. Gould & Curry Silver Mining Company's Reduction Works

This elaborate mill in Six-Mile Canyon, a mile and a half east of Virginia City, went into operation in 1863. Both the management and the public took vast pride in it, despite the fact that it was not very efficient in processing ore. The mill was remodeled in 1864 but was closed down permanently in 1866 when high-grade ore in the mine ran out. From a lithograph in *Views of the Works of the Gould & Curry Silver Mining Company.*

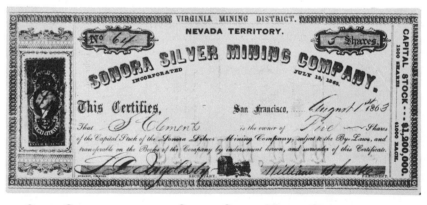

13. Stock Certificate of the Sonora Silver Mining Company

The certificate, dated August 1, 1863, and made out to "S. Clements," is an example of "wildcat" mining stock of the sort mentioned by Mark Twain in his letter to his mother and sister (§ 20). Although the stock had a book value of $5,000, it was probably given to him. *Mark Twain Papers.*

14. James W. Nye,
    Governor of Nevada
    Territory, 1861–1864

Nye was a lawyer, not a professional soldier. The pretext for the uniform was his position as commander-in-chief of the Territorial Militia. *Mackay School of Mines.*

15. Nevada State Prison, Near Carson City

The structure on the right, with a cupola, embodies much of the stonework of Abraham Curry's building at Warm Springs in which he allowed the first Territorial Legislature to hold its sessions in 1861. The ball in February, 1863, described in § 5, took place here. The additional buildings, adapted to use as a prison, belong to a later period. *California State Library, Sacramento.*

16. THEODORE WINTERS' HOUSE IN WASHOE VALLEY

The house, which was built in the autumn of 1863, is still standing, eight or nine miles north of Carson City along the highway to Reno. It is described in § 27. *Photograph by Robert B. Collagan.*

17. RESIDENCE OF THE TEACHERS OF THE SIERRA SEMINARY AT CARSON

From an original pen-and-ink drawing. Miss Hannah K. Clapp was the head mistress of the seminary, which is described in § 24. In 1863 her residence was on the southwest corner of Proctor and Nevada streets, but the picture is undated and may depict a house at some other location. *Mackay School of Mines.*

18. JANE LAMPTON CLEMENS, MARK TWAIN'S MOTHER

From a portrait painted by a traveling artist named Brady in St. Louis in 1858 or 1859. *Samuel C. Webster Collection.*

19. PAMELA CLEMENS MOFFETT, MARK TWAIN'S SISTER

From a portrait painted by Brady on the same occasion as the portrait of Jane Clemens. *Samuel C. Webster Collection.*

No. 10 — $20 enclosed Virginia, July 18.

My Dear Mother & Sister

Ma, you are slinging insinuations at me again. Such as "where did I get the money?" and "the company I kept in San Francisco." Why I sold "wildcat" mining ground that was given me, & my credit was always good at the bank for two or three thousand dollars, & is yet. I never gamble, in any shape or manner, and never drink any thing stronger than claret or lager beer, which conduct is regarded as miraculously temperate in this country. As for my company, Ma, I went into the very best society to be found in San Francisco, & to do that, you must know, of course, that I had to keep myself mighty straight. I also [cut] move in the best society of Virginia, & actually have a reputation to preserve.

As for money, I manage to make a living, but if I had any business tact the office of reporter here would be worth $30,000 a year — whereas, if I get 4 or $5,000 out of it, it will be as much as I expect. I have stock in my possession, which, if I had sold when it was first given me, from time to time, in the last [?] months.

20. LETTER FROM MARK TWAIN TO HIS MOTHER AND SISTER, 1863

Written on onionskin paper because of the high rates of postage on letters sent overland across the Plains. Jane Clemens was living with her daughter Pamela and Pamela's husband in St. Louis. The second page of the letter has been torn; a few characters are missing at the beginning of lines 6 and 7. *Mark Twain Papers.*

would have brought me $10,000 —
but I have carelessly let it go down
to nothing again. I don't think I am
any account, any how. Now, I raised
the price of "North Ophir" from $15
a foot to $45 a foot, to-day, & they
gave me five feet. That will go the
way of all the rest. I shall probably mislay it or throw it in my
trunk & never get a dollar out
of it. But I am telling you too
many secrets, & I'll stop. One
more. A gentleman in San Francisco
told me to call at his office, & he
would give me five feet of "Overman." Well, do you know I never
went after it? The stock is worth
$400 a foot, now — $2,000 thrown
away. I don't care a straw, for
myself, but I ought to have had
more thought for you. Never mind,
though, Ma — I will be more careful
in future. I will take care that
your expenses are paid — sure.
        You and Pamela only pay
$8 a week apiece for board (& lodging
too?) Well, you are not in a very expensive part of the world, certainly.
My room-mate & I pay, together, $70 a
month for our bedchamber, & $50 a month,
each, for board, besides. Put in my
washing, & it costs me $100 a month to live.
        Affectionately, Mark

21. DEVIL'S GATE, LOOKING UP GOLD CANYON, ABOUT 1864

Virginia City lies beyond this narrow passage. The tollhouse is at the left. The stagecoach is headed down the canyon toward Gold Hill, Silver City, and Dayton. *Bancroft Library*.

22. WORKMEN IN THE GOULD & CURRY MINE

The position of the ore body allowed access to the mine by long horizontal tunnels. The ore could therefore be hoisted to the cars for removal by simple hand-operated windlasses of the type shown in the drawing. From a lithograph in *Views of the Works of the Gould & Curry Silver Mining Company*.

The music struck up just then, and saved me. The next moment I was far, far at sea in a plain quadrille. We carried it through with distinguished success; that is, we got as far as "balance around," and "halt-a-man-left," when I smelled hot whisky punch, or something of that nature. I tracked the scent through several rooms, and finally discovered the large bowl from whence it emanated. I found the omnipresent Unreliable there, also. He set down an empty goblet, and remarked that he was diligently seeking the gentlemen's dressing room. I would have shown him where it was, but it occurred to him that the supper table and the punch-bowl ought not to be left unprotected; wherefore, we staid there and watched them until the punch entirely evaporated. A servant came in then to replenish the bowl, and we left the refreshments in his charge. We probably did wrong, but we were anxious to join the hazy dance. The dance was hazier than usual, after that. Sixteen couples on the floor at once, with a few dozen spectators scattered around, is calculated to have that effect in a brilliantly lighted parlor, I believe. Everything seemed to buzz, at any rate. After all the modern dances had been danced several times, the people adjourned to the supper-room. I found my wardrobe out there, as usual, with the Unreliable in it. His old distemper was upon him: he was desperately hungry. I never saw a man eat as much as he did in my life. I have the various items of his supper here in my note-book. First, he ate a plate of sandwiches; then he ate a handsomely iced poundcake; then he gobbled a dish of chicken salad; after which he ate a roast pig; after that, a quantity of blancmange; then he threw in several glasses of punch to fortify his appetite, and finished his monstrous repast with a roast turkey. Dishes of brandy-grapes, and jellies, and such things, and pyramids of fruits, melted away before him as shadows fly at the sun's approach. I am of the opinion that none of his ancestors were present when the five thousand were miraculously fed in the old Scriptural times. I base my opinion upon the twelve baskets of scraps and the little fishes that remained over after that feast. If the Unreliable himself had been there, the provisions would just about have held out, I think.

After supper, the dancing was resumed, and after a while, the guests indulged in music to a considerable extent. Mrs. J. sang a beautiful Spanish song; Miss R., Miss T., Miss P., and Miss S., sang a lovely duet; Horace Smith, Esq., sang "I'm sitting on the stile, Mary," with a sweetness and tenderness of expression which I have never heard surpassed; Col. Musser sang "From Greenland's Icy Mountains" so fervently that every heart in that assemblage was purified and made better by it; Mrs. T. and Miss C., and Mrs. T. and Mrs. G. sang "Meet me by moonlight alone" charmingly; Judge Dixson sang "O, Charming May" with great vivacity and artistic effect; Joe Winters and Hal Clayton sang the Marseilles Hymn in French, and did it well; Mr. Wasson sang "Call me pet names" with his usual excellence (Wasson has a cultivated voice, and a refined musical taste, but like Judge Brumfield, he throws so much operatic affectation into his singing that the beauty of his performance is sometimes marred by it—I could not help noticing this fault when Judge Brumfield sang "Rock me to sleep, mother"); Wm. M. Gillespie sang "Thou hast wounded the spirit that loved thee," gracefully and beautifully, and wept at the recollection of the circumstance which he was singing about. Up to this time I had carefully kept the Unreliable in the background, fearful that, under the circumstances, his insanity would take a musical turn; and my prophetic soul was right; he eluded me and planted himself at the piano; when he opened his cavernous mouth and displayed his slanting and scattered teeth, the effect upon that convivial audience was as if the gates of a graveyard, with its crumbling tombstones, had been thrown open in their midst; then he shouted something about he "would not live alway"—and if I ever heard anything absurd in my life, that was it. He must have made up that song as he went along. Why, there was no more sense in it, and no more music, than there is in his ordinary conversation. The only thing in the whole wretched performance that redeemed it for a moment, was something about "the few lucid moments that dawn on us here." That was all right; because the "lucid moments" that dawn on that Unreliable are almighty few, I can tell you. I wish one of them would strike him while I am here, and prompt him to return my valuables to me. I doubt if he ever gets lucid enough for that, though. After the Unreliable had finished squawking, I sat down to the piano and sang—however, what I sang is of no consequence to anybody. It was only a graceful little gem from the horse opera.

At about two o'clock in the morning the pleasant party broke up and the crowd of guests distributed themselves around town to their respective homes; and after thinking the fun all over again, I went to bed at four o'clock. So, having been awake forty-eight hours, I slept forty-eight, in order to get even again, which explains the proposition I began this letter with.

Yours, dreamily,
Mark Twain

5.

Letter from Carson [City]
[February 3, 1863]

☞ This letter is reprinted in part in Rabb, *Wit and Humor of America*, V, 1815–1818. The date is established by the connection between this piece, headed "Tuesday night," and the one in section 4. It is a document in the elaborate verbal feud between Mark Twain and "the Unreliable."

Edward Richardson killed Cornelius Mason in Carson City on November 24, 1862.[1]

Eds. Enterprise: I received the following atrocious document the morning I arrived here. It is from that abandoned profligate, the Unreliable, and I think it speaks for itself:

Carson City, *Thursday Morning*

To the Unreliable—Sir: Observing the driver of the Virginia stage hunting after you this morning, in order to collect his fare, I infer you are in town.

In the paper which you represent, I noticed an article which I took to be an effusion of your muddled brain, stating that I had "cabbaged" a number of valuable articles from you the night I took you out of the streets in Washoe City and permitted you to occupy my bed.

I take this opportunity to inform you that I will compensate you at the rate of $20 *per head* for every one of those *valuables* that I received from you, providing you will relieve me of their presence. This offer can either be accepted or rejected on your part: but, providing you don't see proper to accept it, you had better procure enough lumber to make a box 4 × 8, and have it made as early as possible. Judge Dixson will arrange the preliminaries, if you don't accede. An early reply is expected by

RELIABLE

Not satisfied with wounding my feelings by making the most extraordinary references and allusions in the above note, he even sent me a challenge to fight, in the same envelope with it, hoping to work upon my fears and drive me from the country by intimidation. But I was not to be frightened; I shall remain in the Territory. I guessed his object at once, and determined to accept his challenge, choose weapons and things, and scare him, instead of being scared myself. I wrote a stern reply to him, and offered him mortal combat with boot-jacks at a hundred yards. The effect was more agreeable than I could have hoped for. His hair turned black in a single night, from excess of fear; then he went into a fit of melancholy, and while it lasted he did nothing but sigh, and sob, and snuffle, and slobber, and blow his nose on his coat-tail, and say "he wished he was in the quiet tomb"; finally, he said he would commit suicide—he would say farewell to the cold, cold world, with its cares and troubles, and go and sleep with his fathers, in perdition. Then rose up this young man, and threw his demijohn out of the window, and took a glass of pure water, and drained it to the very, very dregs. And then he fell on the floor in spasms. Dr. Tjader was called in, and as soon as he found that the cuss was poisoned, he rushed down to the Magnolia Saloon and got the antidote, and poured it down him. As he was drawing his last breath, he scented the brandy and lingered yet a while upon the earth, to take a drink with the boys. But for this, he would have been no more—and possibly a good deal less—in another moment. So he survived; but he has been in a mighty precarious condition ever since. I have been up to see how he was getting along two or three times a day. He is very low; he lies there in silence, and hour after hour he appears to be absorbed in tracing out the figures in the wall paper. He is not changed in the least, though; his face looks just as natural as anything could be—there is no more expression in it than a turnip. But he is a very sick man; I was up there a while ago, and I could see that his friends had begun to entertain hopes that he would not get over it. As soon as I saw that, all my enmity vanished; I even felt like doing the poor Unreliable a kindness, and showing him, too, how my feelings towards him had changed. So I went and bought him a beautiful coffin, and carried it up and set it down on his bed, and told him to climb in when his time was up. Well, sir, you never saw a man so affected by a little act of kindness as he was by that. He let off a sort of war-whoop, and went to kicking things around like a crazy man, and he foamed at the mouth, and went out of one fit and into another faster than I could take them down in my note-book. I have got thirteen down, though, and I know he must have had two or three before I could find my pencil. I actually believe he would have had a thousand, if that old fool who nurses him hadn't thrown the coffin out of the window, and threatened to serve me in the same way if I didn't leave. I left, of course, under the circumstances, and I learn that although the patient was getting better a moment before this circumstance, he got a good deal worse immediately afterward. They say he lies in a sort of a stupor now, and if they cannot rally him, he is gone in, as it were. They may take their own course now, though, and use their own judgment. I shall not go near them again, although I think *I* could rally him with another coffin.

I did not return to Virginia yesterday, on account of the wedding. The parties were Hon. James H. Sturtevant, one of the first Pi-Utes of Nevada, and Miss Emma Curry, daughter of Hon. A. Curry, who also claims that his is a Pi-Ute family of high antiquity. Curry conducted the wedding arrangements himself, and invited none but Pi-Utes. This interfered with me a good deal. However, as I had heard it reported that a marriage was threatened, I felt it my duty to go down there and find out the facts in the case. They said I might stay, as it was me; the permission was unnecessary, though—I calculated to do that anyhow. I promised not to say anything about the wedding, and I regard that promise as sacred— my word is as good as my bond. At three o'clock in the afternoon, all the Pi-Utes went up stairs to the old Hall of Representatives in Curry's house, preceded by the bride and groom, and the bridesmaids and groomsmen (Miss Jo. Perkins and Miss Nettie Curry, and Hon. John H. Mills and Wm. M. Gillespie) and followed by myself and the fiddlers. The fiddles were tuned up, three quadrille sets were formed on the floor. Father Bennett advanced and touched off the high contracting parties with the hymeneal torch (married them, you know), and at the word of command from Curry, the fiddle-bows were set in motion, and the plain quadrilles turned loose. Thereupon, some of the most responsible dancing ensued that you ever saw in your life. The dance that Tam O'Shanter witnessed was slow in comparison to it. They kept it up for six hours, and then they carried out the exhausted musicians on a shutter, and went down to supper. I know they had a fine supper, and plenty of it, but I do not know much else. They drank so much champagne around me that I got confused, and lost the hang of things, as it were. Mills, and Musser, and Sturtevant, and Curry, got to making speeches, and I got to looking at the bride and bridesmaids—they looked uncommonly handsome—and finally I fell into a sort of trance. When I recovered from it the brave musicians were all right again, and the dance was ready to commence. They went to slinging plain quadrilles around as lively as ever, and never rested again until nearly midnight, when the dancers all broke down and the party broke up. It was all mighty pleasant, and jolly, and sociable, and I wish to thunder I was married myself. I took a large slab of the bridal cake home with me to dream on, and dreamt that I was still a single man, and likely to remain so, if I live and nothing happens—which has given me a greater confidence in dreams than I ever felt before. I cordially wish the newly-married couple all kinds of happiness and posterity, though.

Richardson's case was continued to the next term of the District Court last Thursday, and the prisoner admitted to bail in the sum of $10,000—$7,000 on the charge of murder (the killing of Con Mason), and $3,000 on the charge of highway robbery.

Three new mining companies filed their certificates of incorporation in the County Clerk's and Territorial Secretary's offices last Saturday. Their ledges are located in the new Brown & Murphy District, in Lyon county. The names, etc., of the new companies are as follows: Jennie V. Thompson G. & S. M. Company, capital stock $220,000, in 2,200 shares of $100 each; Byron G. & S. M. Company, same number of shares, etc.; Lion G. & S. Company, capital stock $230,000, in 2,300 shares of $100 each. The following gentlemen are Trustees of all three companies: C. L. Newton, J. D. Thompson, J. Ball, G. C. Haswell and Wm. Millikin. The principal offices of the companies are in Carson City.

MARK TWAIN

6.

Letter from Carson [City]
[February 6, 1863]

☞ The date of this letter is established by the reference to the Wayman-Ormsby wedding "last night." The wedding took place on February 5, 1863.[1]

A "list of certificates of incorporation recorded in the office of the Secretary, under the new Territorial law," is omitted at the end of this letter. It contains the names of twenty-four corporations, with a statement of the amount of the capital stock, the number of shares, and the location of the principal office of each. Concerning the law requiring corporations to register, and Secretary Orion Clemens' fees for this ceremony, see Part One, above.

Jack Wilde and Lytle cannot be identified, and the joke of calling Lytle "Schermerhorn's Boy" is lost. *Schermerhorn's Boy* was a favorite blackface minstrel farce in which George Christy starred in the late 1850's and early 1860's.[2]

EDS. ENTERPRISE: The community were taken by surprise last night, by the marriage of Dr. J. H. Wayman and Mrs. M. A. Ormsby. Strategy did it. John K. Trumbo lured the people to a party at his house, and corraled them, and in the meantime Acting Governor Clemens proceeded to the bride's dwelling and consolidated the happy couple under the name and style of Mr. and Mrs. Wayman, with a life charter, perpetual succession, unlimited marital privileges, principal place of business at ho—— blast those gold and silver mining incorporations! I have compiled a long list of them from the Territorial Secretary's books this morning, and their infernal technicalities keep slipping from my pen when I ought to be writing graceful poetical things. After the marriage, the high contracting parties and the witnesses there assembled, adjourned to Mr. Trumbo's house. The ways of the Unreliable are past finding out. His instincts always prompt him to go where he is not wanted, particularly if anything of an unusual nature is on foot. Therefore, he was present and saw those wedding ceremonies through the parlor windows. He climbed up behind Dr. Wayman's coach and rode up to Trumbo's—this shows that his faculties were not affected by his recent illness. When the bride and groom entered the parlor he went in with them, bowing and scraping and smiling in his imbecile way, and attempting to pass himself off for the principal groomsman. I never saw such an awkward, ungainly lout in my life. He had on a pair of Jack Wilde's pantaloons, and a swallow-tail coat belonging to Lytle ("Schermerhorn's Boy"), and they fitted him as neatly as an elephant's hide would fit a poodle dog. I would be ashamed to appear in any parlor in such a costume. It never enters his head to be ashamed of anything, though. It would have killed me with mortification to parade around there as he did, and have people stepping on my coat tail every moment. As soon as the guests found out who he was they kept out of his way as well as they could, but there were so many gentlemen and ladies present that he was never at a loss for somebody to pester with his disgusting familiarity. He worried them from the parlor to the sitting-room, and from thence to the dancing-hall, and then proceeded upstairs to see if he could find any more people to stampede. He found Fred. Turner, and stayed with him until he was informed that he could have nothing more to eat or drink in that part of the house. He went back to the dancing-hall then, but he carried away a codfish under one arm, and Mr. Curry's plug hat full of sauerkraut under the other. He posted himself right where he could be most in the way, and fell to eating as comfortably as if he were boarding with Trumbo by the week. They bothered him some, though, because every time the order came to "all promenade," the dancers would sweep past him and knock his codfish out of his hands and spill his sauerkraut. He was the most loathsome sight I ever saw; he turned everybody's stomach but his own. It makes no difference to him, either, what he eats when hungry. I believe he would have eaten a corpse last night, if he had one. Finally, Curry came and took his hat away from him and tore one of his coat tails off and threatened to thresh him with it, and that checked his appetite for a moment. Instead of sneaking out of the house, then, as anybody would have done who had any self-respect, he shoved his codfish into the pocket of his solitary coat-tail (leaving at least eight inches of it sticking out), and crowded himself into a double quadrille. He had it all to himself pretty soon; because the order "gentlemen to the right" came, and he passed from one lady to another around the room, and wilted each and every one of them with the horrible fragrance of his breath. Even Trumbo, himself, fainted. Then the Unreliable, with a placid expression of satisfaction upon his countenance, marched forth and swept the parlors like a pestilence. When the guests had been persecuted as long as they could stand it, though, they got him to drink some kerosene oil, which neutralized the sauerkraut and codfish, and restored his breath to about its usual state, or even improved it, perhaps, for it generally smells like a hospital.

The Unreliable interfered with Col. Musser when he was singing the pea-nut song; he bothered William Patterson, Esq., when that baritone was singing, "Ever of thee I'm fondly dreaming"; he interrupted Epstein when he was playing on the piano; he followed the bride and bridegroom from place to place, like an evil spirit, and he managed to keep himself and his coat-tail eternally in the way. I did hope that he would stay away from the supper-table, but I hoped against an impossibility. He was the first one there, and had choice of seats also, because he told Mr. Trumbo he was a groomsman; and not only that, but he made him believe, also, that Dr. Wayman was his uncle. Then he sailed into the ice cream and champagne, and cakes and things, at his usual starvation gait, and he would infallibly have created a famine, if Trumbo had not been particularly well fortified with provisions. There is one circumstance connected with the Unreliable's career last night which it pains me to mention, but I feel that it is my duty to do it. I shall cut the melancholy fact as short as possible, however: seventeen silver spoons, a New Testament and a gridiron were missed after supper. They were found upon the Unreliable's person when he was in the act of going out at the back door.

Singing and dancing commenced at seven o'clock in the evening, and were kept up with unabated fury until half-past one in the morning, when the jolly company put on each other's hats and bonnets and wandered home, mighty well satisfied with Trumbo's "corn shucking," as he called it.

Well, you were particularly bitter about the "extra session" yesterday morning, and with very small cause, too, it seems to me. You rush in desperately and call out all the fire engines in the universe, and lo! there is nothing but a chunk of harmless fox-fire to squirt at after all. You slash away right and left at the lawyers, just as if they were not human like other people, subject to the same accidents of fortune and circumstances, moved by the same springs of action, and honest or dishonest according to the nature which God Almighty endowed them with. Stuff! You talk like a wooden man. A man's profession has but little to do with his moral character. If we had as many preachers as lawyers, you would find it mixed as to which occupation could muster the most rascals. Then you pitch into the legislators, and say that, "with two or three exceptions, they are men who failed to complete their programmes of rascality," etc. Humbug! They never commenced any such programme. I reported their proceedings—I was behind the scenes, and I know. I talk sweepingly, perhaps—so do you, in that wild sentence. There might have been two or three first-class rascals in the Legislature—I have that number in my eye at the present moment—but the balance were fully as honest as you, and considerably more so than me. I could prove this by simply reminding you of their names. Run over the list, and see if there are not some very respectable names on it. I have acknowledged that there were several scoundrels in the Legislature, but such a number, in as large a body as the last Assembly, could carry no measure, you know, and the men I am thinking of couldn't even influence one. The Lord originally intended them to do transportation duty in a jackass train, I think. And then, how you talk about the pecuniary wants of our legislators: "Their hungry wallets yearn for a second assault on the greenbacks and franchises of the Territory." That is humbug, also. Take the House, for instance. I can name you fifteen members of that body whose pecuniary condition is very comfortable—who stand in no more pressing need of Territorial greenbacks than you do of another leg. And I can name you half a dozen others who are not suffering for food and raiment, and whom Providence will be able to take care of, I think, without bringing an extra session of the Nevada Legislature to pass. You talk like a wooden man, I tell you. Why there are not enough "Territorial Greenbacks" in the Secretary's office and the Territorial Treasury put together to start a wholesale pea-nut stand with; and why should thirty-nine legislators want to neglect their business to go to Carson and gobble up and divide such a pittance? Bosh.

Somebody made a blunder; somebody did a piece of rascality. It was not the legislators, yet only they can set the matter right—and if they want to go back to the capital and do it, it is rather a credit to them than a dishonor. I cannot see anything very criminal in this conduct of theirs. You are too brash, you know—that is what is the matter with you. You say you heard a report that the Acting Governor had decided to call an extra session. Well, what if you did? Don't you suppose that, being here, at the seat of government, I would naturally know a good deal more about it than anybody's reports? Reports lie—I do not. Why didn't you ask me for information? I always have an abundance of the article on hand. I will give you some now: the Acting Governor has *not* decided to call an extra session; he is not seriously thinking of such a thing at present; he is not expecting to think of it next week; he is not in favor of the measure, and does not wish to move in the matter unless a majority of the counties expressly desire it. Now, you have said a great many things in your article which you ought not to have said; you have done injustice to all the parties whom you have mentioned; you have hollered "wolf!" when there was nothing present but the mildest sort of a lamb; and the properest course for you to pursue will be to screw down your throttle-valve and dry up.

I have a strong inclination to continue this subject a while longer, but I promised to go down in town and get drunk with Curry and Trumbo, and Tom Bedford and Gillespie, before I leave for Virginia. My promises are sacred. I have also to receive a petition from citizens of Carson, with several thousand names on it, requesting me to extend my visit here a few years longer. It affords me great pleasure to state that several hundred sheets of this petition are covered with the autographs of intelligent and beautiful ladies.

7.

Letter from Mark Twain
San Francisco, May 16, 1863

☞ The use of "Mark Twain" in the heading, of which this is the first extant example, presumably indicates the author's growing reputation in Nevada.

The letter was written during a visit to San Francisco which Mark Twain made with Clement T. Rice, "the Unreliable," of the *Daily Union*. Mark Twain was in San Francisco several weeks, from early in May to the end of June. He returned to Virginia City on July 2.[1]

Eds. Enterprise: The Unreliable, since he has been here, has conducted himself in such a reckless and unprincipled manner that he has brought the whole Territory into disrepute and made its name a reproach, and its visiting citizens objects of suspicion. He has been a perfect nightmare to the officers of the Occidental Hotel. They give him an excellent room, but if, in prowling about the house, he finds another that suits him better, he "locates" it (that is his slang way of expressing it). Judging by his appearance what manner of man he was, the hotel clerk at first gave him a room immediately under the shingles—but it was found impossible to keep him there. He said he could not stand it, because spinning round and round, up that spiral staircase, caused his beer to ferment, and made him foam at the mouth like a soda fountain; wherefore, he descended at the dead of night and "jumped" a room on the second floor (the very language he used in boasting of the exploit). He said they served an injunction on him there, "and," says he, "if Bill Stewart had been down here, Mark, I'd have sued to quiet title, and I'd have held that ground, don't you know it?" And he sighed; and after ruminating a moment, he added, in a tone of withering contempt: "But these lawyers won't touch a case unless a man has some rights; humph! they haven't any more strategy into 'em than a clam. But Bill Stewart—thunder! Now, you just take that Ophir suit that's coming off in Virginia, for instance— why, God bless you, Bill Stewart'll worry the witnesses, and bully-rag the Judge, and buy up the jury and pay for 'em; and he'll prove things that never existed—hell! What won't he prove! That's the idea—what won't he prove, you know? Why, Mark, I'll tell you what he done when—"

The Unreliable was interrupted here by a messenger from the hotel office, who handed him several sheets of legal cap, very neatly folded. He took them and motioned the young man to retire. "Now," said he, confidentially, "do you know what that is, Sweetness?" I said I thought it was a wash bill, or a hotel bill, or something of that kind. His countenance beamed with admiration: "You've struck it, by the Lord; yes, sir, that's just what it is—it's another of them d——d assessments; they levied one on me last week, and I meant to go and see a lawyer about it, but"—The Unreliable simmered down into a profound reverie, and I waited in silence to see what species of villainy his fertile brain would bring forth. At last he started up exultingly, with a devilish light in his eye: "I've got them in the door, Mark! They've been trying all they knew how to freeze me out, but they can't win. This hotel ain't incorporated under the laws of the Territory, and they can't collect—they are only a lot of blasted tenants in common! O, certainly" (with bitter scorn), "they'll get rich playing *me* for a Chinaman, you know." I forbear to describe how he reveled in the prospect of swindling the Occidental out of his hotel bill—it is too much humiliation even to think of it.

This young man insisted upon taking me to a concert last night, and I refused to go at first, because I am naturally suspicious of him, but he assured me that the Bella Union Melodeon was such a chaste and high-toned establishment that he would not hesitate to take any lady there who would go with him. This remark banished my fears, of course, and we proceeded to the house of amusement. We were the first arrivals there. He purchased two pit-tickets for twenty-five cents apiece; I demurred at this kind of hospitality, and reminded him that orchestra seats were only fifty cents, and private boxes two dollars and a half. He bent on me a look of compassion, and muttered to himself that some people have no more sense than a boiled carrot—that some people's intellects were as dark as the inside of a cow. He walked into the pit, and then climbed over into the orchestra seats as coolly as if he had chartered the theatre. I followed, of course. Then he said, "Now, Mark, keep your eye skinned on that doorkeeper, and do as I do." I did as he did, and I am ashamed to say that he climbed a stanchion and took possession of a private box. In due course several gentlemen performers came on the stage, and with them half a dozen lovely and blooming damsels, with the largest ankles you ever saw. In fact, they were dressed like so many parasols—as it were. Their songs, and jokes, and conundrums were received with rapturous applause. The Unreliable said these things were all copyrighted; it is probably true—I never heard them anywhere else. He was well pleased with the performance, and every time one of the ladies sang, he testified his approbation by knocking some of her teeth out with a bouquet. The Bella Union, I am told, is supported entirely by Washoe patronage. There are forty-two single gentlemen here from Washoe, and twenty-six married ones; they were all at the concert last night except two—both unmarried. But if the Unreliable had not told me it was a moral, high-toned establishment, I would not have observed it.

Hon. Wm. H. Davenport, of Virginia, and Miss Mollie Spangler, of Cincinnati, Ohio, were married here on the 10th instant, at the residence of Colonel John A. Collins. Among the invited guests were Judge Noyes and lady, Messrs. Beecher and Franz, of Virginia, and Mr. Mark Twain; among the uninvited I noticed only the Unreliable. It will probably never be known what became of the spoons. The bridal party left yesterday for Sacramento, and may be expected in Virginia shortly. Old fat, jolly B. C. Howard, a Lyon county Commissioner, is here, at the Russ House, where he will linger a while and then depart for his old home in Vermont, to return again in the Fall. Col. Raymond, of the Zephyr-Flat mill, is in the city, also, and taking up a good deal of room in Montgomery street and the Bank Exchange; he has invested in some fast horses, and I shall probably take them over to Washoe shortly. There are multitudes of people from the Territory here at the three principal hotels—consequently provisions are scarce. If you will send a few more citizens down we can carry this election, and fill all these city offices with Carson and Virginia men.

There is not much doing in stocks just now, especially in the Boards. But I suspect it is the case here as it is in Virginia, that the Boards do precious little of the business. Many private sales of Union (Gold Hill) and Yellow Jacket have transpired here during the past week at much higher prices than you quote those stocks at. Three hundred feet of Golden Gate changed hands at $100 per foot, and fifty feet at $110; but a telegram from Virginia yesterday, announcing that they had "struck it"—and moderately rich—in the San Francisco, raised both stocks several figures, as also the Golden Eagle (first south extension of the Golden Gate), which had been offered the day before at $30 a foot. Two hundred feet of Oriental were sold at private sale to-day at $7 a foot. Now, you hear no talk in Virginia but the extraordinary dullness of the San Francisco market. Humbug! It may be dull in the Boards, but it is lively enough on the street. If you doubt it, say so, and I will move around a little and furnish you with all the statistics you want.

I meant to say something glowing and poetical about the weather, but the Unreliable has come in and driven away refined emotion from my breast. He says: "Say it's bully, you tallow-brained idiot! that's enough; anybody can understand that; don't write any of those infernal, sick platitudes about sweet flowers, and joyous butterflies, and worms and things, for people to read before breakfast. You make a fool of yourself that way; everybody gets disgusted with you; stuff! be a man or a mouse, can't you?"

I must go out now with this conceited ass—there is no other way to get rid of him.

MARK TWAIN

8.

Letter from Mark Twain

Steamboat Springs, Nevada Territory, [August 18, 1863]

☞ The letter is dated "Tuesday afternoon" and was published in the *Enterprise* on Wednesday, August 19, 1863. The last sentence indicates that Mark Twain got his manuscript aboard the stagecoach just as it left Steamboat Springs.

A burlesque biography of John Van Buren Perry by Mark Twain had been published in the *Enterprise* on an undetermined date, probably between January and April, 1863; it is printed in Rabb, *Wit and Humor of America*, V, 1809–1813. "Jack" Perry, in addition to being city marshal of Virginia, was foreman of the volunteer Hook and Ladder Company No. 1. According to Sam P. Davis, many of the volunteer firemen had come from New York, and they evidently arrived in Nevada surrounded by the nimbus that folklore and the theater had cast about the "Bowery B'hoys" in the 1850's. Mose, the mythical hero who led these fire laddies into action, had figured in more than twenty plays produced in New York and elsewhere 1848–1856. Francis S. Chanfrau had acted the role "some thousand times" from coast to coast. There had even been a *Mose in California* (by W. B. Chapman, 1849). Mose was a Bowery tough who loved a free-for-all, but "in the line of duty the daredevil fireboy combined matter-of-fact valor with a streak of sentiment and rude chivalry." He "is always found defending right against wrong."[1] Sam Davis' account of Perry and the other volunteer firemen of Virginia City suggests Buck Fanshaw in *Roughing It*[2] and demonstrates how easily folklore motives from the slums of New York could become naturalized in the Far West:

> Their original training in combat had been with fists, spanners and fire trumpets, but they quickly acquired the knack of knife and pistol, and were a formidable crowd to be reckoned with. Big, powerful, good-natured, these men, though rough, were not depraved or vicious, and they always arrayed themselves on the side of law and order whenever an issue was made with lawlessness and disorder. A spirit of comradeship and organization animated them at all times, and this solidarity made them a wholesome menace to the more humorous [numerous?] but less compacted criminal element.

When the news of the first battle of Bull Run reached Virginia City in August, 1861, continues Davis,

The *Enterprise* was getting out an extra containing the particulars of the disastrous defeat, about noon, when Jack Perry, who was an old pressman and therefore a privileged character, dropped into the office and asked to see the proofs. The giant fireman read the dispatches all through, how our army had been routed and the New York Fire Zouaves cut to pieces, without saying a word, but with the tears streaming like two great water courses down his cheeks. Then he got up, slid his pistol a little more to the front where it would be handier, and left the office, remarking simply:

"No damned secesh had better crow within my hearing today."

He must have infected every member of the Fire Department with his feeling; for an hour later when the extra was issued and the Southern sympathizers began to exult, one would have thought the battle of Bull Run itself had struck the Comstock, instead of a mere account of it. Not a rejoicing mouth opened but it was instantly closed by a massive fist. Not a head exhibiting a secession tendency showed itself but it was unmercifully hit. . . . When the sun sank behind Mount Davidson that afternoon it had looked for the last time on secession domination in Nevada Territory. The rough element of the Union spirit had asserted itself, and the timid, but more numerous part, quickly rallied to its support. Thereafter there was no open jubilation over Southern victories.[3]

Mark Twain's writing about the cold from which he was trying to recover at Steamboat Springs illustrates his impulse to verbalize every experience. In part, of course, what is at work here is simply the newspaper man's unceasing obligation to produce copy. But the impulse is deeper than this. It points toward a literary ideal that reached conscious formulation in the nineteenth century and has shaped much writing of our own day: the effort to use language as a medium for interpreting literally all of life.

The *Enterprise* had inaugurated a new steam-press—the first in Nevada—on July 31.[4] Myron Angel says that "The general mix-up on that occasion of new press, newspaper and bottles of wine, caused 'Mark Twain' to take among other things, a severe cold, 'that settled on his mind' . . ."[5] He was laid up for a couple of days early in August, and Clement T. Rice generously wrote his local items for him, including a spurious apology to men whom Mark Twain had abused in print.[6] He went back to work for a time, but the cold hung on, and he tried to cure it by a vacation at Lake Tahoe. When the social life at the Lake House proved too strenuous he came back down to Steamboat Springs to rest.[7] This illness gave rise to a letter entitled "How to Cure a Cold" that was reprinted in the San Francisco *Golden Era* on September 20ᵉ and was eventually included in *Sketches New and Old* in 1875 as "Curing a Cold."

EDS. ENTERPRISE: Never mind the date—I haven't known what day of the month it was since the fourth of July. In reality, I am not well enough to write, but am angry now, and like our old Methodist parson at home in Missouri, who started in to produce rain by a season of fervent prayer, "I'll do it or bust." I notice in this morning's ENTERPRISE a lame, impotent abortion of a biography of Marshal Perry, and I cannot understand what you mean by it. You either want to impose upon the public with an incorrect account of that monster's career (compiled from items furnished by himself, I'll warrant), or else you wish to bring into disrepute my own biography of him, which is the only correct and impartial one ever published. Which is it? If you really desired that the people should know the man they were expected to vote for, why did you not republish that history? By referring to it you will see that your own has not a word of truth in it. Jack Perry has made you believe he was born in New York, when in reality he was born in New Jersey; he has told you he was a pressman—on the contrary, he is by occupation a shoemaker,—by nature a poet, and by instinct a great moral humbug. If I chose, I could enumerate a dozen more instances to prove that, in his own vulgar phraseology, Jack Perry has successfully played you for a Chinaman. I suppose if he had told you the size of his boots was No. 5, you wouldn't have known enough to refrain from publishing the absurdity. Now the next time you want any facts about Jack Perry, perhaps you had better refer to the standard biography compiled by myself, or else let me hash them up for you. You have rushed into these biographies like a crazy man, and I suppose you have found out by this time that you are no more fitted for that sort of thing than I am for a circus rider (which painfully reminds me that my last horseback trip at Lake Bigler, on that razor-bladed beast of Tom Nye's, has lengthened my legs and shortened my body some). If I could devote more time to composition and less to coughing, I would write all those candidates' biographies over again, just to show you how little you know about it.

I must have led a gay life at Lake Bigler, for it seems a month since I flew up there on the Pioneer coach, alongside of Hank Monk, the king of stage drivers. But I couldn't cure my cold. I was too careless. I went to the lake (Lake Bigler I must beg leave to call it still, notwithstanding, if I recollect rightly, it is known among sentimental people as either Tahoe Lake or Yahoo Lake—however, one of the last will do as well as the other, since there is neither sense nor music in either of them), with a voice like a bullfrog, and by indulging industriously in reckless imprudence, I succeeded in toning it down to an impalpable whisper in the course of seven days. I left there in the Pioneer coach at half-past one on Monday morning, in company with Mayor Arick, Mr. Boruck and young Wilson (a nice party for a Christian to travel with, I admit), and arrived in Carson at five o'clock—three hours and a half out. As nearly as I can estimate it, we came down the grade at the rate of a hundred miles an hour; and if you do not know how frightfully deep those mountain gorges look, let me recommend that you go, also, and skim along their edges at the dead of night.

I left Carson at two o'clock with Dyer—Dyer, the polite—Dyer, the accommodating—Dyer, of the Carson and Steamboat stage line, and reached the Steamboat Springs Hotel at dusk, where all others who are weary and hungry are invited to come, and be handsomely provided for by Messrs. Holmes & Stowe. At Washoe we ate a supper of unimpeachable squareness at the Washoe Exchange, where I found Hon. J. K. Lovejoy, Dr. Bowman, and Captain Rawlings—there may have been other old acquaintances present, but the champagne that Lovejoy drank confused my vision so much that I cannot recollect whether there were or not. I learned here that the people who own ranches along Steamboat creek are very indignant at Judge Mott for granting an injunction to the Pleasant Valley Mill Company, whereby they are prohibited from using the water in the stream upon their lands. They say the mill company purchased the old Smith ranch and that portion of the creek which passes through it, and now they assume the right to deprive ranchmen owning property two or three miles above their lines from irrigating their lands with water which the mill company never before pretended to claim.

They further state that the mill men gave bonds in the trivial sum of $1,000, whereas the damage already done the crops by the withdrawal of the water amounts to more than $20,000. Again, the idea is that the mill men need the water to wet a new ditch which they have been digging, and after that is accomplished they will pay the amount of the bond and withdraw the injunction. Moreover—so the story runs—Judge Mott promised a decision in the case three weeks ago, and has not kept his word. The citizens of Galena, in mass meeting assembled, have drawn up a petition praying that the Judge will redress their grievances to-day, without further delay. If the prayer is unheeded, they will turn the water on their ranches to-morrow in defiance of the order of the court. I believe I have recounted all these facts just as I got them; but if I haven't, I can't help it, because I have lost my note-book again. I think I could lose a thousand note-books a week if I had them. And, moreover, if you can ferret out the justice of the above proceedings, you are a better lawyer than I am—and here comes Orrick Johnson's Virginia stage again, and I shall have to fling in my benediction before I sing the doxology, as usual. Somehow or other, I can never get through with what I have to say.

MARK TWAIN

9.

Letter from Mark Twain

Steamboat Springs, Nevada Territory, August 23, 1863

☞ Mark Twain begins with a puff for the Steamboat Springs Hotel which we may hope paid for his vacation. His lack of interest in what he is writing is revealed by the jumbled syntax in the second paragraph. This kind of carelessness is rare with him, from the very beginning of his work as a journalist. The remainder of the letter exploits the most obvious, and for twentieth-century readers the most dated, of Western humorous themes—physical discomfort.

THE SPRINGS

EDS. ENTERPRISE: I have overstepped my furlough a full week— but then this is a pleasant place to pass one's time. These springs are ten miles from Virginia, six or seven from Washoe City and twenty from Carson. They are natural—the devil boils the water, and the white steam puffs up out of crevices in the earth, along the summits of a series of low mounds extending in an irregular semi-circle for more than a mile. The water is impregnated with a dozen different minerals each one of which smells viler than its fellow, and the sides of the springs are embellished with very pretty parti-colored incrustations deposited by the water. From one spring the boiling water is ejected a foot or more by the infernal force at work below, and in the vicinity of all of them one can hear a constant rumbling and surging, somewhat resembling the noises peculiar to a steamboat in motion—hence the name.

THE HOTEL

The Steamboat Springs Hotel is very pleasantly situated on a grassy flat, a stone's throw from the hospital and the bath houses. It is capable of accommodating a great many guests. The rooms are large, "hard-finished" and handsomely furnished; an abundant supply of pure water, which can be carried to every part of the house, in case of fire, by means of hose; the table is furnished with fresh vegetables and meats from the numerous fine ranches in the valley, and lastly, Mr. Stowe is a pleasant and accommodating landlord, and is ably seconded by Messrs. Haines, Ellsworth and Bingham. These gentlemen will never allow you to get ill-humored for want of polite attention—as I gratefully remember, now, when I recall the stormy hours of Friday, when that accursed "Wake-up Jake" was in me. But I haven't got to that, yet. God bless us! it is a world of trouble, and we are born to sorrow and tribulation—yet, am I chiefest among sinners, that I should be prematurely damned with "Wake-up Jake," while others not of the elect go free? I am trying to go on with my letter, but this thing bothers me; verily, from having "Wake-up Jake" on the stomach for three days, I have finally got it on the brain. I am grateful for the change. But I digress.

THE HOSPITAL

Dr. Ellis, the proprietor of the Springs, has erected a large, tastefully designed, and comfortable and well ventilated hospital, close to the bath-houses, and it is constantly filled with patients afflicted with all manner of diseases. It would be a very profitable institution, but a great many who come to it half dead, and leave it again restored to robust health, forget to pay for the benefits they have received. Others, when they arrive, confess . . . that they are penniless, yet few men could look upon the sunken cheeks of these, and upon their attenuated forms and their pleading, faded eyes, and refuse them the shelter and assistance we all may need some day. Without expectation of reward, Dr. Ellis gives back life, hope, and health to many a despairing, poverty-stricken devil; and when I think of this, it seems so strange that he could have had the meanness to give me that "Wake-up Jake." However, I am wandering away from the subject again. All diseases (except confirmed consumption) are treated successfully here. A multitude of invalids have attended these baths during the past three years, yet only an insignificant number of deaths have occurred among them. I want to impress one thing upon you: it is a mistaken notion that these Springs were created solely for the salvation of persons suffering venereal diseases. True, the fame of the baths rests chiefly upon the miracles performed upon such patients, and upon others afflicted with rheumatism, erysipelas, etc., but then all ordinary ailments can be quickly and pleasantly cured here without a resort to deadly physic. More than two-thirds of the people who come here are afflicted with venereal diseases—fellows who know that if "Steamboat" fails with them they may as well go to trading feet with the undertaker for a box—yet all here agree that these baths are none the less potent where other diseases are concerned. I know lots of poor, feeble wretches in Virginia who could get a new lease of life by soaking their shadows in Steamboat Springs for a week or two. However, I must pass on to

THE BATHS

My friend Jim Miller has charge of these. Within a few days the new bath-house will be finished, and then twelve persons may bathe at once, or if they be sociable and choose to go on the double-bed principle, four times as many can enjoy the luxury at the same time. Persons afflicted with loathsome diseases use bath-rooms which are never entered by the other patients. You get up here about six o'clock in the morning and walk over to the bath-house; you undress in an ante-room and take a cold shower-bath—or let it alone, if you choose; then you step into a sort of little dark closet floored with a wooden grating, up through which come puffs and volumes of the hottest steam you ever performed to (because the awkwardest of us feel a hankering to waltz a little under such circumstances, you know), and then if you are alone, you resolve to have company thenceforward, since to swap comments upon your sensations with a friend, must render the dire heat less binding upon the human constitution. I had company always, and it was the pleasantest thing in the world to see a thin-skinned invalid cavorting around in the vapory obscurity, marveling at the rivers of sweat that coursed down his body, cursing the villainous smell of the steam and its bitter, salty taste—groping around meanwhile, for a cold corner, and backing finally into the hottest one, and darting out again in a second, only remarking "Outch!"—and repeating it when he sits down, and springs up the same moment off the hot bench. This was fun of the most comfortable character; but nothing could be more agreeable than to put your eye to the little square hole in the door, and see your boiled and smoking comrade writhing under the cold shower-bath, to see him shrink till his shoulders are level with the top of his head, and then shut his eyes and gasp and catch his breath, while the cruel rain pattered down on his back and sent a ghastly shiver through every fiber of his body. It will always be a comfort to me to recall these little incidents. After the shower-bath, you return to the ante-room and scrub yourself all over with coarse towels until your hide glows like a parlor carpet—after which, you feel as elastic and vigorous as an acrobat. Then if you are sensible, you take no exercise, but just eat your breakfast and go to bed—you will find that an hour's nap will not hurt you any.

THE "WAKE-UP JAKE"

A few days ago I fell a victim to my natural curiosity and my solicitude for the public weal. Everybody had something to say about "Wake-up Jake." If a man was low-spirited; if his appetite failed him; if he did not sleep well at night; if he were costive; if he were bilious; or in love; or in any other kind of trouble; or if he doubted the fidelity of his friends or the efficacy of his religion, there was always someone at his elbow to whisper, "Take a 'wake-up,' my boy." I sought to fathom the mystery, but all I could make out of it was that the "Wake-up Jake" was a medicine as powerful as "the servants of the lamp," the secret of whose decoction was hidden away in Dr. Ellis' breast. I was not aware that I had any use for the wonderful "wake-up," but then I felt it to be my duty to try it, in order that a suffering public might profit by my experience—and I would cheerfully see that public suffer perdition before I would try it again. I called upon Dr. Ellis with the air of a man who would create the impression that he is not so much of an ass as he looks, and demanded a "Wake-up Jake" as unostentatiously as if that species of refreshment were not at all new to me. The Doctor hesitated a moment, and then fixed up as repulsive a mixture as ever was stirred together in a table-spoon. I swallowed the nauseous mess, and that one meal sufficed me for the space of forty-eight hours. And during all that time, I could not have enjoyed a viler taste in my mouth if I had swallowed a slaughterhouse. I lay down with all my clothes on, and with an utter indifference to my fate here or hereafter, and slept like a statue from six o'clock until noon. I got up, then, the sickest man that ever yearned to vomit and couldn't. All the dead and decaying matter in nature seemed buried in my stomach, and I "heaved, and retched, and heaved again," but I could not compass a resurrection—my dead would not come forth. Finally, after rumbling, and growling, and producing agony and chaos within me for many hours, the dreadful dose began its work, and for the space of twelve hours it vomited me, and purged me, and likewise caused me to bleed at the nose.

I came out of that siege as weak as an infant, and went to the bath with Palmer, of Wells, Fargo & Co's., and it was well I had company, for it was about all he could do to keep me from boiling the remnant of my life out in the hot steam. I had reached that stage wherein a man experiences a solemn indifference as to whether school keeps or not. Since then, I have gradually regained my strength and my appetite, and am now animated by a higher degree of vigor than I have felt for many a day. 'Tis well. This result seduces many a man into taking a second, and even a third "Wake-up Jake," but I think I can worry along without any more of them. I am about as thoroughly waked up now as I care to be.

My stomach never had such a scouring out since I was born. I feel like a jug. If I could get young Wilson or the Unreliable to take a "Wake-up Jake," I would do it, of course, but I shall never swallow another myself—I would sooner have a locomotive travel through me. And besides, I never intend to experiment in physic any more, just out of idle curiosity. A "Wake-up Jake" will furbish a man's machinery up and give him a fresh start in the world—but I feel I shall never need anything of that sort any more. It would put robust health, and life and vim into young Wilson and the Unreliable—but then they always look with suspicion upon any suggestion that I make.

GOOD-BYE

Well, I am going home to Virginia to-day, though I dislike to part from the jolly boys (not to mention iced milk for breakfast, with eggs laid to order, and spiced oysters after midnight with the Reverend Jack Holmes and Bingham) at the Steamboat Springs Hotel. In conclusion, let me recommend to such of my fellow citizens as are in feeble health, or are wearied out with the cares of business, to come down and try the hotel, and the steam baths, and the facetious "Wake-up Jake." These will give them rest, and moving recreation—as it were.

MARK TWAIN

10.

Letter from Mark Twain

San Francisco, September 13, 1863

☞ The description of the stage driver in this letter is in Mark Twain's best early manner, and if one disregards the coyness about Adah Isaacs Menken's costume, the review of *Mazeppa* is equally good. Miss Menken played the part of Mazeppa in the play of that name in San Francisco at Tom Maguire's Opera House for sixty nights at $500.00 a night.[1] She brought her company to Virginia City the following February. Mark Twain met her and, according to Albert B. Paine, "became briefly fascinated" by her charms.[2] Mrs. H. A. Perry was an actress in the Menken troupe.[3] It is characteristic of Mark Twain that he dwells with such pleasure upon the horse used in the performance. He carried out his promise to review the current fashions seen at the Pioneer Ball in a letter to the *Golden Era* published on September 27.[4]

OVER THE MOUNTAINS

EDITORS ENTERPRISE: The trip from Virginia to Carson by Messrs. Carpenter & Hoog's stage is a pleasant one, and from thence over the mountains by the Pioneer would be another, if there were less of it. But you naturally want an outside seat in the day time, and you feel a good deal like riding inside when the cold night winds begin to blow; yet if you commence your journey on the outside, you will find that you will be allowed to enjoy the desire I speak of unmolested from twilight to sunrise. An outside seat is preferable, though, day or night. All you want to do is to prepare for it thoroughly. You should sleep forty-eight hours in succession before starting so that you may not have to do anything of that kind on the box. You should also take a heavy overcoat with you. I did neither. I left Carson feeling very miserable for want of sleep, and the voyage from there to Sacramento did not refresh me perceptibly. I took no overcoat and I almost shivered the shirt off myself during that long night ride from Strawberry Valley to Folsom. Our driver was a very companionable man, though, and this was a happy circumstance for me, because, being drowsy and worn out, I would have gone to sleep and fallen overboard if he had not enlivened the dreary hours with his conversation. Whenever I stopped coughing, and went to nodding, he always watched me out of the corner of his eye until I got to pitching in his direction, and then he would stir me up and inquire if I were asleep. If I said "No" (and I was apt to do that), he always said "it was a bully good thing for me that I warn't, you know," and then went on to relate cheerful anecdotes of people who had got to nodding by his side when he wasn't noticing, and had fallen off and broken their necks. He said he could see those fellows before him now, all jammed and bloody and quivering in death's agony—"G'lang! d——n that horse, he knows there's a parson and an old maid inside, and that's what makes him cut up so; I've saw him act jes' so more'n a thousand times!" The driver always lent an additional charm to his conversation by mixing his horrors and his general information together in this way. "Now," said he, after urging his team at a furious speed down the grade for a while, plunging into deep bends in the road brimming with a thick darkness almost palpable to the touch, and darting out again and again on the verge of what instinct told me was a precipice, "Now, I seen a poor cuss—but you're asleep again, you know, and you've rammed your head agin' my side-pocket and busted a bottle of nasty rotten medicine that I'm taking to the folks at the Thirty-five Mile House; do you notice that flavor? ain't it a ghastly old stench? The man that takes it down there don't live on anything else—it's vittles and drink to him; anybody that ain't used to him can't go a-near him; he'd stun 'em—he'd suffocate 'em; his breath smells like a graveyard after an earthquake—you Bob! I allow to skelp that ornery horse, yet, if he keeps on this way; you see he's been on the overland till about two weeks ago, and every stump he sees he cal'lates it's an Injun." I was awake by this time, holding on with both hands and bouncing up and down just as I do when I ride a horseback. The driver took up the thread of his discourse and proceeded to soothe me again: "As I was a saying, I see a poor cuss tumble off along here one night—he was monstrous drowsy, and went to sleep when I'd took my eye off of him for a moment—and he fetched up agin a boulder, and in a second there wasn't anything left of him but a promiscus pile of hash! It was moonlight, and when I got down and looked at him he was quivering like jelly, and sorter moaning to himself, like, and the bones of his legs was sticking out through his pantaloons every which way, like that." (Here the driver mixed his fingers up after the manner of a stack of muskets, and illuminated them with the ghostly light of his cigar.) "He warn't in misery long though. In a minute and a half he was deader'n a smelt—Bob! I say I'll cut that horse's throat if he stays on this route another week." In this way the genial driver caused the long hours to pass sleeplessly away, and if he drew upon his imagination for his fearful histories, I shall be the last to blame him for it, because if they had taken a milder form I might have yielded to the dullness that oppressed me, and got my own bones smashed out of my hide in such a way as to render me useless forever after—unless, perhaps, some one chose to turn me to account as an uncommon sort of hat-rack.

MR. BILLET IS COMPLIMENTED BY A STRANGER

Not a face in either stage was washed from the time we left Carson until we arrived in Sacramento; this will give you an idea of how deep the dust lay on those faces when we entered the latter town at eight o'clock on Monday morning. Mr. Billet, of Virginia, came in our coach, and brought his family with him—Mr. R. W. Billet of the great Washoe Stock and Exchange Board of Highwaymen—and instead of turning his complexion to a dirty cream color, as it generally serves white folks, the dust changed it to the meanest possible shade of black: however, Billet isn't particularly white, anyhow, even under the most favorable circumstances. He stepped into an office near the railroad depot, to write a note, and while he was at it, several lank, gawky, indolent immigrants, fresh from the plains, gathered around him. Missourians—Pikes—I can tell my brethren as far as I can see them. They seemed to admire Billet very much, and the faster he wrote the higher their admiration rose in their faces, until it finally boiled over in words, and one of my countrymen ejaculated in his neighbor's ear,—"Dang it, but he writes mighty well for a nigger!"

THE MENKEN—WRITTEN ESPECIALLY FOR GENTLEMEN

When I arrived in San Francisco, I found there was no one in town—at least there was no body in town but "the Menken"—or rather, that no one was being talked about except that manly young female. I went to see her play "Mazeppa," of course. They said she was dressed from head to foot in flesh-colored "tights," but I had no opera-glass, and I couldn't see it, to use the language of the inelegant rabble. She appeared to me to have but one garment on—a thin tight white linen one, of unimportant dimensions; I forget the name of the article, but it is indispensable to infants of tender age—I suppose any young mother can tell you what it is, if you have the moral courage to ask the question. With the exception of this superfluous rag, the Menken dresses like the Greek Slave; but some of her postures are not so modest as the suggestive attitude of the latter. She is a finely formed woman down to her knees; if she could be herself that far, and Mrs. H. A. Perry the rest of the way, she would pass for an unexceptionable Venus. Here every tongue sings the praises of her matchless grace, her supple gestures, her charming attitudes. Well, possibly, these tongues are right. In the first act, she rushes on the stage, and goes cavorting around after "Olinska"; she bends herself back like a bow; she pitches headforemost at the atmosphere like a battering-ram; she works her arms, and her legs, and her whole body like a dancing-jack: her every movement is as quick as thought; in a word, without any apparent reason for it, she carries on like a lunatic from the beginning of the act to the end of it. At other times she "whallops" herself down on the stage, and rolls over as does the sportive pack-mule after his burden is removed. If this be grace then the Menken is eminently graceful. After a while they proceed to strip her, and the high chief Pole calls for the "fiery untamed steed"; a subordinate Pole brings in the fierce brute, stirring him up occasionally to make him run away, and then hanging to him like death to keep him from doing it; the monster looks round pensively upon the brilliant audience in the theatre, and seems very willing to stand still—but a lot of those Poles grab him and hold on to him, so as to be prepared for him in case he changes his mind. They are posted as to his fiery untamed nature, you know, and they give him no chance to get loose and eat up the orchestra. They strap Mazeppa on his back, fore and aft, and face uppermost, and the horse goes cantering up-stairs over the painted mountains, through tinted clouds of theatrical mist, in a brisk exciting way, with the wretched victim he bears unconsciously digging her heels into his hams, in the agony of her sufferings, to make him go faster. Then a tempest of applause bursts forth, and the curtain falls. The fierce old circus horse carries his prisoner around through the back part of the theatre, behind the scenery, and although assailed at every step by the savage wolves of the desert, he makes his way at last to his dear old home in Tartary down by the footlights, and beholds once more, O, gods! the familiar faces of the fiddlers in the orchestra. The noble old steed is happy, then, but poor Mazeppa is insensible—"ginned out" by his trip, as it were. Before the act closes, however, he is restored to consciousness and his doting old father, the king of Tartary; and the next day, without taking time to dress—without even borrowing a shirt, or stealing a fresh horse—he starts off on the fiery untamed, at the head of the Tartar nation, to exterminate the Poles, and carry off his own sweet Olinska from the Polish court. He succeeds, and the curtain falls upon a bloody combat, in which the Tartars are victorious. "Mazeppa" proved a great card for Maguire here; he put it on the boards in first-class style, and crowded houses went crazy over it

every night it was played. But Virginians will soon have an opportunity of seeing it themselves, as "the Menken" will go direct from
our town there without stopping on the way. The "French Spy"
was played last night and the night before, and as this spy is a
frisky Frenchman, and as dumb as an oyster, Miss Menken's extravagant gesticulations do not seem so overdone in it as they do
in "Mazeppa." She don't talk well, and as she goes on her shape
and her acting, the character of a fidgety "dummy" is peculiarly
suited to her line of business. She plays the Spy, without words,
with more feeling than she does Mazeppa with them.

I am tired writing, now, so you will get no news in this letter. I
have got a note-book full of interesting hieroglyphics, but I am
afraid that by the time I am ready to write them out, I shall have
forgotten what they mean. The lady who asked me to furnish her
with the Lick House fashions, shall have them shortly—or if I ever
get time, I will dish up those displayed at the great Pioneer ball,
at Union Hall, last Wednesday night.

                                                        MARK TWAIN

11.

First Annual Fair of the Washoe Agricultural, Mining and Mechanical Society

Carson City, October 19, 1863

☞ This letter is attributed to "Our Special Reporter." Since "Mark
Twain" was a well-established pseudonym by this time, the by-line
might be taken as evidence that the piece was written by someone else.
But "Mark Twain" was used only for letters primarily personal and
humorous in intention; it was not signed to impersonal dispatches such
as those reporting the Constitutional Convention of 1863 or the sessions
of the third Territorial Legislature in 1864. Furthermore, there are affirmative reasons for believing that Mark Twain covered the fair for
the *Enterprise*. In a letter to the San Francisco *Call* early in August he
announced: "Perhaps it will increase the public confidence in this infant experiment [the Washoe fair] to know that by Legislative enactment I am Recording Secretary of it, at an exorbitant salary, payable
quarterly in Territorial scrip, subject to the mild discount of seventy-five
percent."[1] The appointment is confirmed by a news story in the Virginia

City *Daily Union* of October 14, 1863, which reveals further that the recording secretary's salary was to be three hundred dollars per annum, and that William M. Gillespie was corresponding secretary.[2] Finally, in *Roughing It* Mark Twain speaks of himself as having written dispatches about the fair. He says of his decision to leave Nevada: "There was no longer satisfying variety in going down to Carson to report the proceedings of the legislature once a year, and horse-races and pumpkin shows once in three months (they had got to raising pumpkins and potatoes in Washoe Valley, and of course one of the first achievements of the legislature was to institute a ten-thousand-dollar agricultural fair to show off forty dollars' worth of those pumpkins in—however, the territorial legislature was usually spoken of as the 'asylum')."[3]

The selection reprinted here comprises about one-half the dispatch preserved in the Scrapbook. The omitted first part is given over to a perfectly routine "notice of the stock on exhibition."

The roles of sports reporter, city planner, landscape architect, and Nevada booster in which Mark Twain appears in this dispatch are not usual with him, but the charming conceit of reporting a speech in dashes and marks of punctuation bears the stamp of authenticity.

The "former letter" mentioned in the last paragraph of the dispatch is not extant.

THE TRIUMPHAL PARADE

LATE ON Saturday afternoon, after the announcement of the awards in class A had been made, all the stock that had received premiums formed in a sort of triumphal procession, with the band at the head, and the stock following in the order of precedence to which they were entitled by the decision of the Judges, and marched down to the city, through the principal streets of which they paraded two or three times back and forth before final dismissal. The parade of so many fine animals in the streets was really a very fine sight, and was witnessed by everybody with much pleasure, being the first grand parade of the kind ever seen in the Territory.

GREAT PANTOMIME SPEECH

While waiting at the race course on Saturday for the arrival of some of the officers from the Pavilion, some of the boys belonging to the brass band in attendance concluded to do what they could for the amusement of those present, and so took possession of the platform from which the awards were to be made. One of the party was introduced to the audience as a very eloquent gentleman, who had volunteered to favor those present with a speech on the success of the Fair. The speaker took his position and made a polite bow to his audience, another of the musicians prepared to take down the speech and the third acted in the capacity of bottle-holder. The speaker soon launched forth, and in a few moments had worked himself up into a tremendous state of excitement. His lips worked convulsively, though no sound escaped them. He pointed toward the rocky peaks of the Sierras, then at the surrounding brown hills, finishing with a complacent wave of his hand toward the broad valley in which he stood. He was leaning far over the railing of the platform in the middle of a most eloquent appeal to the crowd, occasionally pointing heavenward, when his bottle-holder was suddenly overtaken by a violent fit of admiration, which he felt constrained to manifest by a most vigorous stamping upon the boards of the platform—so vigorous that he burst through one of the boards and hung suspended by the arms. A keg of nails was kicked over in the row, and the great oratorical effort came to an end amid the prolonged shouts and cheers of the crowd. I was favored with a look at the speech as taken down by the reporter, and give the following extract: "———! ———! ———? ———! (?)———††———; ———, ———, ———!!! ———." There were some ten pages in the same style, but as your readers will perhaps be better pleased with the extract I have given than with the whole speech, as taken down by the reporter, I will omit the balance.

RACES SATURDAY AFTERNOON

The challenge of "Deuces" against the field on Friday, for $300, catch-weights, barring "Breckinridge," was accepted by "Kate Mitchell," but to-day she was lame and forfeited. After the failure of these horses to run, a race was gotten up between three Spanish nags, for a purse of $27.50, single dash of a mile. In starting "Grey Dick" and the black nag, "Sheep," got off at the tap of the drum, but the sorrel horse "Split-ear," was held by his owner. "Sheep" and "Grey Dick" dashed forward, when the cry of "Come back!" was raised by several, also by a voice or two on the Judges' stand. "Grey Dick's" rider came back, but the rider of "Sheep" (Johnny Craddock), after riding back a short distance and ascertaining that the drum had tapped, turned about and rode leisurely around the track, winning the race and purse, according to the decision of the Judges and the rules of the Carson Racing Club. The decision was that once the drum was tapped, it was a go—the riders not being required to pay any attention to the calls to come back from anybody. Outside bets were declared drawn. A new race was now made up between the same nags. Theo. Winters paid the entrance fees for the three horses, amounting to $15; purse, $20; single dash of a mile. The horses got a very fair start; on the first quarter "Sheep" got the lead, "Grey Dick" came next, and "Split-ear" brought up the rear. "Sheep" still held his own on nearing the home-stretch, but "Grey Dick" soon began to gain on him, and they were soon head and head. Both riders used the whip freely on the home-stretch and the race was more stubbornly contested than any one that has taken place on the track this week. The betting had been very free on "Sheep" and "Grey Dick," "Sheep" seeming to be the favorite, and the excitement was intense. "Sheep" passed the score 6 inches ahead of "Grey Dick," winning the purse; time, 1:58. A purse of $16.25 was now made up, the same horses to run, single dash of one mile. "Grey Dick" had the track, "Split-ear" second, "Sheep" third. The horses got a very good start. "Grey Dick" led for the first half mile, "Sheep" following closely and "Split-ear" far behind. "Grey Dick" kept the lead down the home-stretch, the others following in about the same order in which they passed the half mile post, and came in three lengths ahead of "Sheep," "Split-ear" being three or four hundred yards behind. "Grey Dick" won the purse; time, 2:8. A purse of $25 was now made up for a slow race—the slowest horse of the three to win—riders to change horses. "Split-ear" had the track, "Sheep" second, "Grey Dick" third. "Sheep's" owners had given him all the water he could drink on the sly, and from the start he was behind and kept at least three hundred yards behind all the way round the track, "Grey Dick" came in first, "Split-ear" second and "Sheep" rolled along far behind. "Sheep" won the race and purse; time 2:17.

A HINT TO CARSON

There are some things that kept running through my mind while looking through the city of Carson, and considering the peculiarities of its site, that I cannot refrain from jotting down here, though not coming strictly under the head of the Fair. However, they were suggested by improvements made on the Plaza in preparing for the holding of the Fair, and may, therefore, be considered as one of its legitimate fruits. I think that every person who attended the Fair must have been most forcibly struck with the great improvement made in the appearance of the Plaza by the planting of evergreens on it in front of and about the Pavilion; this first led me to consider the site of the town and the many advantages its location afforded for making it one of the prettiest and pleasantest cities on the Eastern Slope. Situated on a wide, and almost level, plain, at but a short distance from the eastern base of the Sierras, with numerous fine mountain streams tumbling down the hills behind it, Carson might have every street as well supplied with ditches of water as are those of Salt Lake City. The water from these ditches might be made to cause a thousand gardens in the city to "bloom as the rose." At no very great expense, the water of one of the mountain streams near by might be brought upon the Plaza in pipes, and used to supply fountains in various parts of the grounds; about these fountains willows and plats of flowers might be planted, which, with a liberal sprinkling of cottonwood and other trees in various parts, would make it a far prettier place than the "Willows," near San Francisco. With some such improvements Carson would be apt to attract nearly all the wealthy men owning mines and mills, or doing business in this part of the Territory— they would all wish to reside in or near so pretty and pleasant a place. If the Plaza was turned into a park as pleasant and beautiful as it might be made, it would soon become a general place of resort on Saturdays and Sundays for all the young people, and pleasure seekers in general, of all the neighboring towns and cities. If the present Pavilion is allowed to stand where it is, it should be raised at least six to eight feet higher than it is by putting under it some kind of basement; then, with a broad flight of steps at the entrance of each wing, it would be a really imposing edifice, and one that would at once elicit the admiration of every stranger passing through the town. Mr. Curry, one of the most public-spirited men in Carson, has already put a beautiful and substantial fence around the Plaza, and has offered to build a fountain that will throw a stream some twenty-five feet high, provided the Water Company, now about supplying water to the city, would furnish the amount of water needed. The people of Carson have, as I remarked above, the foundations for the handsomest city on the Eastern Slope, and the fault will lie with themselves if they don't make it such.

THE FAIR A SUCCESS AND A VALUABLE LESSON

I have not yet been able to obtain the exact amount of all the receipts of the Fair, and will therefore defer all mention of sums. The receipts in full will shortly be obtained and published; I may, however, say that I heard it stated that the receipts would be much more than adequate to the liquidation of all outstanding liabilities of the Society, and that the $2,000 appropriated by the Legislature could be allowed to stand over untouched for the Fair of next year. A number of the members of the Society have acted most generously, and done much toward contributing to the financial success of the institution. Theodore Winters in the start donated the Society $200; afterwards he presented to the Society all his winnings, amounting to $225, and has in various other ways aided the institution to near the amount of $1,000. The owners of the Carson Race Course, as I took occasion to mention in a former letter, acted in the most liberal and handsome manner by the Society, in giving them the free use of all their grounds and buildings, to say nothing of the fact of their having worked all the week like Trojans for the success of the Fair. Mr. Gillespie, the Secretary, and many other officers of the Society, labored day and night during the progress of the exhibition, that nothing might be left undone that could further the plans or aid the triumphant result of an institution which too many had predicted would die in an inglorious fizzle. But we have no "fizzle" to chronicle. We have not, it is very true, made the grandest display of the kind ever seen on the Pacific Coast, but there have been much worse. We came to the exhibition, many of us, with a feeling of dubiousness in our hearts—half ashamed to tell where we were going, even when on the way. When we came away, we felt quite proud, held up our heads, and said we'd "been to the Fair!" We have most of us been dwellers in the mountains and delvers in the mines, and knew little of the agricultural capacity of our valleys; we had rather supposed that we should be obliged always to look to California for our supplies of such articles of farm produce as we might need; but we have now had a faint glimpse of what may be done upon our soil, and feel no hesitancy in calling upon all who wish to till the earth in a land where the soil yields a bountiful return, and the best market in the world is open at the door of the cultivator, to come and occupy the land lying ready and free for all settlers. All who are now engaged in the cultivation of the soil of Washoe, and were present at the exhibition—and even those who only hear of it from the reports going forth—will now go to work in greater earnestness and with more confidence. Especially will this be the case with those contemplating fruit culture; and we shall expect soon to see orchards in all our valleys and vineyards gracing the slopes of all our hills.

12.

Letter from Mark Twain

Carson City, November 7, 1863

☞ The first convention called to frame a state constitution for Nevada was in session November 2—December 11, 1863.[1] The constitution which it wrote was rejected by the voters of the Territory on January 19, 1864, largely because William M. Stewart and other spokesmen for mining interests attacked a clause allowing taxation of undeveloped mining properties. The slate of nominees for state offices submitted with the constitution also aroused opposition.[2] Mark Twain and the *Enterprise* supported the constitution before the election, but he himself grew cool toward it as the campaign developed.[3] A second constitution, prepared by a later convention in the summer of 1864, which omitted the clause allowing taxation of undeveloped mining properties, was adopted September 7, 1864.[4]

The "thing which appeared recently . . . concerning an occurrence . . . in the great pine forest down there at Empire" was Mark Twain's celebrated "Empire City massacre" hoax, published in the *Enterprise* on October 28, 1863.[5] Mark Twain named Abraham Curry as the source of the fictitious information in this story, and gave to the supposed insane murderer and suicide the name "P. Hopkins, or Philip Hopkins." He also declared that this Hopkins, having cut his own throat, died in front of the Magnolia Saloon. The sly reference to the Gold Hill *News* has point because that paper was at first taken in by the hoax and then ribbed Mark Twain over the indignation his story had aroused.⁶

EDS. ENTERPRISE: This has been a busy week—a notable and a historical week—and the only one which has yet passed over this region, perhaps, whose deeds will make any important stir in the outside world. Some dozens of people in America have heard of Nevada Territory (which they vaguely understand to be in Virginia City, though they have no definite idea as to where Virginia City is) as the place which sends silver bricks to the Sanitary fund; and some other dozens have heard of Washoe, without exactly knowing whether the name refers to the Northwest passage or to the source of the Nile—but when it is shouted abroad through the land that a new star has risen on the flag—a new State born to the Union—then the nation will wake up for a moment and ask who we are and where we came from. They will also ascertain that the new acquisition is called Nevada; they will find out its place on the map, and always recollect afterwards, in a general way, that it is in North America; they will see at a glance that Nevada is not in Virginia City and be surprised at it; they will behold that neither is it in California, and will be unable to comprehend it; they will learn that our soil is alkali flats and our shrubbery sage-brush, and be as wise as they were before; their mouths will water over statistics of our silver bricks, and verily they will believe that God createth silver in that form. This week's work is the first step toward giving the world a knowledge of Nevada, and it is a giant stride, too, for it will provoke earnest inquiry. Immigration will follow, and wild-cat advance.

This Convention of ours is well worth being proud of. There is not another commonwealth in the world, of equal population, perhaps, that could furnish the stuff for its fellow. I doubt if any Constitutional Convention ever officiated at the birth of any State in the Union which could boast of such a large proportion of men of distinguished ability, according to the number of its members, as is the case with ours. There are thirty-six delegates here, and among them I could point out fifteen who would rank high in any community, and the balance would not be second rate in most

Legislatures. There are men in this body whose reputations are not local, by any means—such as Governor Johnson, Wm. M. Stewart, Judge Bryan, John A. Collins, N. A. H. Ball, General North and James Stark, the tragedian. Such a constellation as that ought to shed living light upon our Constitution. General North is President of the Convention; Governor Johnson is Chairman of the Legislative Committee—one of the most important among the Standing Committees, and one which has to aid in the construction of every department of the Constitution; Mr. Ball occupies his proper place as Chairman of the Committee on Finance, State Debt, etc.; the Judiciary Committee is built of sound timber, and is hard to surpass; it is composed of Messrs. Stewart, Johnson, Larrowe and Bryan.

We shall have a Constitution that we need not be ashamed of, rest assured; but it will not be framed in a week. Every article in it will be well considered and freely debated upon.

And just here I would like to know if it would not be as well to get up a constitutional silver brick or so, and let the Sanitary fund rest a while. It would cost at least ten thousand dollars to put this Convention through in anything approaching a respectable style; yet the sum appropriated by the Legislature for its use was only $3,000, and the scrip for it will not yield $1,500. The new State will have to shoulder the present Territorial debt of $90,000, but it seems to me we might usher her into the world without adding to this an accouchement fee—so to speak—of ten or fifteen thousand more. Why, the Convention is so poor that it cannot even furnish newspapers for its members to read; kerosene merchants hesitate to afford it light; unfeeling draymen who haul wood to the people, scorn its custom; it elected official reporters, and for two days could negotiate no desks for them to write on: it confers upon them no spittoons, to this day; in fact, there is only one spittoon to every 7 members and they furnish their own fine-cut into the bargain; in my opinion there are not inkstands enough to go around, or pens either, for that matter; Col. Youngs, Chairman of the Committee on Ways and Means (to pay expenses), has gone blind and baldheaded, and is degenerating into a melancholy lunatic; this is all on account of his financial troubles; it all comes of his tireless efforts to bullyrag a precarious livelihood for the Convention out of Territorial scrip at forty-one cents on the dollar. Will ye see him die, when fifty-nine cents would save him? I wish I could move the Convention up to Virginia, that you might see the Delegates worried, and business delayed or brought to a standstill every hour in the day by the eternal emptiness of the Treasury. Then would you grow sick, as I have done, of hearing members caution each other against breeding expense. I begin to think I don't want the Capital at Virginia if this financial distress is always going to haunt us. Now, I had forgotten until this moment that all these secrets about the poverty of the Convention treasury, and the inoffensive character of Territorial scrip, were revealed to the house yesterday by Colonel Youngs, with a feeling request that the reporters would keep silent upon the subject, lest people abroad should smile at us. I clearly forgot it—but it is too late to mend the matter now.

Hon. Gordon N. Mott is in town, and leaves with his family for San Francisco to-morrow. He proposes to start to Washington by the steamer of the 13th.

Mr. Lemmon's little girl, two years old, had her thigh bone broken in two places this afternoon; she was run over by a wagon. Dr. Tjader set the limb, and the little sufferer is doing as well as could be expected under the circumstances.

I used to hear Governor Johnson frequently mentioned in Virginia as a candidate for the United States Senate from this budding State of ours. He is not a candidate for that or any other office, and will not become one. I make this correction on his own authority, and, therefore, the various Senatorial aspirants need not be afraid to give it full credence.

Messrs. Pete Hopkins and A. Curry have compromised with me, and there is no longer any animosity existing on either side. They were a little worried at first, you recollect, about that thing which appeared recently (I think it was in the Gold Hill News), concerning an occurrence which has happened in the great pine forest down there at Empire.

We sent our last report to you by our stirring official, Gillespie, Secretary of the Convention. I thought that might account for your not getting it, in case you didn't get it, you know.

MARK TWAIN

13.

Letter from Mark Twain
Carson City, November 15, 1863

🖙 The "Homographic Record of the Constitutional Convention" should not be confused with the "phonographic" (i.e., shorthand) reports of the deliberations; it was a tabular chart listing the delegates with various items of biographical information.[1]

The write-up of Samson's slaughter of the Philistines is a further effort to reply to the numerous critics of the Empire City massacre hoax (see headnote to § 12). Since no file of the San Francisco *Evening Journal* for the relevant period seems to be extant, Mark Twain's allusion to that newspaper can not be more precisely explained.

EDITORS ENTERPRISE: "Compiled by our own Reporter!" Thus the Virginia Union of this morning gobbles up the labors of another man. That "Homographic Record of the Constitutional Convention" was compiled by Mr. Gillespie, Secretary of the Convention, at odd moments snatched from the incessant duties of his position, and unassisted by "our own reporter" or anybody else. Now this isn't fair, you know. Give the devil his due—by which metaphor I refer to Gillespie, but in an entirely inoffensive manner, I trust; and do not go and give the credit of this work to one who is not entitled to it. I copied that chart myself, and sent it to you yesterday, and I don't see why you couldn't have come out and done the complimentary thing, by claiming its paternity for me. In that case, I should not have mentioned this matter at all. But the main object of the present letter is to furnish you with the revolting details of—

ANOTHER BLOODY MASSACRE!

A massacre, in which no less than a thousand human beings were deprived of life without a moment's warning of the terrible fate that was in store for them. This ghastly tragedy was the work of a single individual—a man whose character was gifted with many strong points, among which were great benevolence and generosity, and a kindness of heart which rendered him susceptible of being persuaded to do things which were really, at times, injurious to himself, and which noble trait in his nature made him a very slave to those whom he loved—a man whose disposition was a model of mildness until a fancied wrong drove him mad and impelled him to the commission of this monstrous crime—this wholesale offering of blood to the angry spirit of revenge which rankled in his bosom. It is said that some of his victims were so gashed, and torn, and mutilated, that they scarcely retained a semblance of human shape. As nearly as I can get at the facts in the case—and I have taken unusual pains in collecting them—the dire misfortune occurred about as follows: It seems that certain enemies ill-treated this man, and in revenge he burned a large amount of property belonging to them. They arrested him, and bound him hand and foot, and brought him down to Lehi, the county seat, for trial. And the Spirit of the Lord came mightily upon him, and the cords that were upon his arms became as flax that was burnt with fire, and his bands loosed from off his hands. And he found a new jaw-bone of an ass, and put forth his hand and took it, and slew a thousand men therewith. When he had finished his terrible tragedy, the desperado, criminal (whose name is Samson), deliberately wiped his bloody weapon upon the leg of his pantaloons, and then tried its edge upon his thumb, as a barber would a razor, simply remarking, "With the jaw-bone of an ass, heaps upon heaps, with the jaw of an ass have I slain a thousand men." He even seemed to reflect with satisfaction upon what he had done, and to derive great comfort from it—as if he would say, "ONLY a mere thousand—Oh, no I ain't on it, I reckon."

I am sorry that it was necessary for me to furnish you with a narrative of this nature, because my efforts in this line have lately been received with some degree of suspicion; yet it is my inexorable duty to keep your readers posted, and I will not be recreant to the trust, even though the very people whom I try to serve, upbraid me.

MARK TWAIN

P.S.—Now keep dark, will you? I am hatching a deep plot. I am "laying," as it were, for the editor of that San Francisco Evening Journal. The massacre I have related above is all true, but it occurred a good while ago. Do you see my drift? I shall catch that

fool. He will look carefully through his Gold Hill and Virginia ex-
changes, and when he finds nothing in them about Samson killing
a thousand men, he will think it is another hoax, and come out on
me again, in his feeble way, as he did before. I shall have him foul,
then, and I will never let up on him in the world (as we say in
Virginia). I expect it will worry him some, to find out at last, that
one Samson actually did kill a thousand men with the jaw-bone of
one of his ancestors, and he never heard of it before.

MARK

14.

Letter from Mark Twain
Carson City, December 5, 1863

☞ "The church in Carson" was the First Presbyterian Church, of
which Orion Clemens had been a trustee since soon after his arrival in
Nevada in 1861.[1] In January, 1864, Mark Twain was to deliver a humorous speech before the Third House of the Legislature for the benefit of
the church (§ 26, below).

EDITORS ENTERPRISE: The church in Carson prospereth. A fine
edifice will soon be completed here, wherein the gospel may be
comfortably preached, and listened to in comfort likewise. A complimentary benefit to this enterprise was given at the theatre last
night by Hon. James Stark and Mrs. Cutler, the profits of which
amounted to upwards of two hundred dollars. Mrs. Cutler recited
several poems, and sang a few choice songs with such grace and
excellence as won for her the compliment of repeated and enthusiastic encores. Mr. Stark's readings were well selected and admirably delivered. His recital of the speech of Sergeant Buzfuz, in
the great breach of promise case of Bardell vs. Pickwick, was a
very miracle of declamation. If all men could read it like him, that
speech would live after Cicero's very creditable efforts had been
forgotten; yet heretofore I had looked upon that as the tamest of
Mr. Dickens' performances.

And just here, I am constrained, in behalf of the community, to
do justice to Charley Parker's liberality and good citizenship. He

prepared his theatre for this church benefit, put a stove in the green room, and had the house duly cleaned and lighted—all at his own expense. It was a good action, and gracefully and unostentatiously performed.

The Convention will probably complete its labors about Wednesday. The members are growing restive and impatient under this long exile from their private business, and are anxious to finish their work and get back home. Three of the Esmeralda delegation— Messrs. Stark, Conner and Bechtel, being imperatively called away by the necessity of attending to their private affairs, have been granted indefinite leave of absence. These gentlemen have been constantly at their posts, and unremitting in the discharge of their duties, and well deserved this kindness at the hands of the Convention. And between you and me, if there were no ladies in Carson, my estimable old fossil, Colonel Youngs, would ask permission to go home, also. Now, why will a man, when he gets to be a thousand years old, go on hanging around the women, and taking chances on fire and brimstone, instead of joining the church and endeavoring, with humble spirit and contrite heart, to ring in at the eleventh hour, like the thief on the cross? Why will he?

QUESTIONS OF PRIVILEGE

Mr. STERNS rose to a question of privilege again, to-day, and requested that the reporters would publish his speeches *verbatim* or not at all. The fact is, they ought to be reported *verbatim*, but then we work eighteen hours a day, and still have not time to give more than the merest skeletons of the speeches made in the Convention. Johnson and Stewart, and Larrowe, and Bryan, and others, complain not, however, although we condense their remarks fearfully. Even Judge Brosnan's stately eloquence, adorned with beautiful imagery and embellished with classic quotations, hath been reported by us thus tersely: "Mr. Brosnan opposed the motion." Only that, and nothing more. But we had taste enough not to mar a noble speech with the deadly engines of reduction and the third person.

Now, in condensing the following speech, the other day, we were necessarily obliged to leave out some of its most salient points, and I acknowledge that my friend Sterns had ample cause for being annoyed at its mutilation. I hope he will find the present report all right, though (albeit the chances are infernally against that result). I have got his style verbatim, whether I have the substance or not.

MR. STERNS' SPEECH

The question being on the amendment offered in Committee of the Whole, to Mr. Stewart's proposed substitute for Section 1 of the Article entitled "Taxation," as reported from the Standing Committee:

Mr. STERNS said—Mr. President, I am opposed, I am hostile, I am uncompromisingly against this proposition to tax the mines. I will go further, sir. I will openly assert, sir, that I am not in favor of this proposition. It is wrong—entirely wrong, sir (as the gentleman from Washoe has already said); I fully agree (with the gentleman who has just taken his seat) that it is unjust and unrighteous. I do think, Mr. President, that (as has been suggested by the gentleman from Ormsby) we owe it to our constituents to defeat this pernicious measure. Incorporate it into your Constitution, sir, and (as was eloquently and beautifully set forth in the speech of the gentleman from Storey) the gaunt forms of want, and poverty, and starvation, and despair will shortly walk in the high places of this once happy and beautiful land. Add it to your fundamental law, sir, and (as was stated yesterday by the gentleman from Lander) God will cease to smile upon your labors. In the language (of my colleague), I entreat you, sir, and gentlemen, inflict not this mighty iniquity upon generations yet unborn! Heed the prayers of the people and be merciful! Ah, sir, the quality of mercy is not strained, so to speak (as has been aptly suggested heretofore), but droppeth like the gentle dew from Heaven, as it were. The gentleman from Douglas has said this law would be unconstitutional, and I cordially agree with him. Therefore, let its corse to the ramparts be hurried—let the flames that shook the battle's wreck, shine round it o'er the dead— let it go hence to that undiscovered country from whose bourne no traveler returns (as hath been remarked by the gentleman from Washoe, Mr. Shamp), and in thus guarding and protecting the poor miner, let us endeavor to do unto others as we would that others should do unto us (as was very justly and properly observed by Jesus Christ upon a former occasion).

After which, the Convention not knowing of any good reason why they should not tax the miners, they went to work and taxed them.

Now, that is *verbatim,* as nearly as I could come at it. I took it from my own mysterious short-hand notes, which are mighty shaky, I am willing to admit; but then, I guarded against inaccuracy by consulting the several authorities quoted in the speech, and from them I have the assurance that my report of Mr. Sterns' comprehensive declamation is eminently correct. I cannot bet on it, though, nevertheless—I cannot possibly bet on it.

I think I have hit upon the right plan, now. It is better to report a member *verbatim,* occasionally, and keep him pacified, than have him rising to these uncomfortable questions of privilege every now and then. I hope to be able to report Bill Stewart *verbatim* in the course of a day or two, if he will hold on a spell.

MARK TWAIN

15.

Letter from Mark Twain
Carson City, December 12, 1863

☞ Mark Twain is again apparently paying his hotel bill with a little favorable publicity.

William M. Stewart's position with respect to the proposed constitution is not easy to make out. He spoke "fervently and eloquently" in favor of its adoption, at a public meeting in Virginia City on December 19, 1863.[1] An editorial in the *Union* on January 8 indicated that Stewart still believed the constitution could be construed in such a way as not to be harmful to mining interests: "Stewart & Co. say that our Legislature, if we adopt the Constitution, can frame a revenue law exempting the mines from taxation."[2] As late as January 12, "Carl" wrote to the *Union* from Carson City that Stewart was supporting ratification as a means of getting rid of Judge John W. North of the territorial Supreme Court.[3] Editorials in the *Union* down to the election (on January 19) and even afterward continued to assume that Stewart supported the proposed constitution.[4] Yet Myron Angel and H. H. Bancroft both assert that Stewart opposed ratification, and indeed that his opposition had great effect.[5] No doubt there were complex political negotiations in back rooms during the last days of the campaign.

Angel says that Joseph T. Goodman of the *Enterprise* and John Church of the *Union* were rivals for the position of state printer, but George W. Bloor was the man actually nominated by the Union convention—the only party which put up a slate of candidates. The *Enterprise* nevertheless supported both the adoption of the constitution and the election of the Union candidates; the *Union*, after supporting ratification for a time, changed its policy and opposed the constitution, mainly because of its dissatisfaction with the slate of candidates put up by the Union party at the same election.[6]

The anecdote commemorated in the inscription on the watch presented to Hank Monk, stage driver, is told and retold in *Roughing It.*[7]

The "Third House" of the Constitutional Convention is explained in section 16.

THE LOGAN HOTEL

Such is my destination. Thither I go to recuperate. I take with me a broken spirit, blighted hopes and a busted constitution. Also some gin. I shall return again, after many days, restored to vigorous health; restored to original purity; free from sin, and prepared to accept any lucrative office the people can be induced to force upon me. If elected, I shall donate my salary to charitable institutions. I will finish building this chronic brick church here, and lease a high-priced parson to run it. Also, an exorbitant choir. Everything connected with the church shall be conducted in the bulliest manner. The Logan Hotel is situated on the banks of Lake Bigler—or Lake Tahoe, which signifieth "grasshopper" in the Digger tongue. I am not going with any of the numerous pleasure parties which go daily to the lake and infest the Logan Hotel. I shall travel like Baxter's hog—in a gang by myself. I am weary of the gay world, and I pine for an hour of solitude. The hotel is new, handsomely furnished, and commodious; it stands within fifty feet of the water's edge, and commands a view of all the grand scenery thereabout; its table is furnished with the best the market affords, and behold they eat trout there every day; fifteen miles over the new King's Canyon road is all the journey it is necessary to take—after which the worn pilgrim may rest in peace in the bosom of Logan & Stewart. That is as good a thing as I want, as long as I am not married.

NO MORE MINES

A year from now, there will not be a mine left in this Territory. This is an appalling statement, but it is a true one. I guessed it from remarks made by that disreputable old cottonhead, Bill Stewart, who as good as promised me ten feet in the "Justis," and then backed down again when the stock went up to $80 a foot. That was a villainous way to treat me, who have gone on juries for him, and held my grip through all the monstrous fabrications he chose to present in his eloquent sophistry, and then brought in a verdict for him, when it seemed morally certain that Providence would interfere and stop the nefarious business. I said, the last time, that I would never serve on one of Bill Stewart's juries again, until they put a lightning rod on the Court House. I said it, and my word is good. I am not going to take any more chances like that. But what I commenced to tell about was, that last night, after the Convention adjourned, and the political meeting was called together, Bill Stewart went to work with his characteristic indecent haste (just a parallel case with that Justis affair), to *construe* the Constitution!—construe and determine the species of the new-laid egg from which is to be hatched our future power and greatness, while the tender thing was warm yet! Bill Stewart is always construing something—eternally distorting facts and principles. He would climb out of his coffin and construe the burial service. He is a long-legged, bull-headed, whopper-jawed, constructionary monomaniac. Give him a chance to construe the sacred law, and there wouldn't be a damned soul in perdition in a month. I have my own opinion of Bill Stewart, and if it would not appear as if I were a little put out about that Justis (that was an almighty mean thing), I would as soon express it as not. He construed the Constitution, last night, as I remarked before. He gave the public to understand that the clause providing for the taxation of the mines meant nothing in particular; that he wanted the privilege of construing that section to suit himself; that a mere hole in the ground was not a mine, and it wasn't property (he slung that in because he has a costly well on his premises in Virginia); and that it would be a difficult matter to determine in our courts what does really constitute a mine. Do you see his *drift?* Well, I do. He will prove to the satisfaction of the courts that there are only two definite kinds of mine; that one of these is an excavation from which metallic ores or other mineral substances are "dug" (which is the dictionary phrase). Then of course, the miners will know enough to stop "digging" and go to blasting. Bill Stewart will then show, easily enough, that these fellows' claims are not "mines" according to the dictionary, and consequently they cannot be taxed. He will show that the only other species of "mine" is a "pronominal adjective," and proceed to prove that there is nothing in the Constitution that will permit the State to tax English grammar. He will demonstrate that a mere hole in the ground is not a mine, and is not liable to taxation. The end will be that a year from now we shall all own in these holes in the ground, but no man will acknowledge that he owns in a "mine"; and about that time custom, and policy, and construction, combined, will have taught us to speak of the staunch old bulwark of the State as "The Great Gould & Curry Hole-in-the-Ground." Bill Stewart will put them up to it. In one short year, sir, from this date, I feel within me that Bill Stewart will have succeeded in construing the last vestige of a mine out of this country.

STATE PRINTER

This subject worried the Convention some. In the first place, the Standing Committee reported an article providing for the election of a State Printer, whose compensation was to be fixed by law, etc. The members, without even showing the Committee the courtesy of discussing the matter, snubbed them very pointedly, by pitching the bill overboard without offering the semblance of an apology for their conduct. They substituted an article providing for printing State work by contract. That was debated to death, and duly buried with its still-born predecessor. Then they tried a Superintendent of Public Printing. That plan appeared to suit them. They adopted it, and looked upon the work of their hands and pronounced it good. There the matter rested until last night, when Governor Johnson got up and asked unanimous consent to substitute the original State Printer article for the Superintendent. He pointed out to the Convention that the office of Superintendent would be turned into a mere sinecure, and its incumbent would accomplish no good to the State—and behold, without a word of objection, the change was made! Verily, it is vastly better to yield to wisdom at last, than not at all.

SCHOOL FUND

Speaking of State Printer, reminds me that we made a mistake in the report published this morning. We said the school moneys were to be invested only in United States bonds—whereas, the truth is, it was decided that they might be invested in either United States or State bonds.

HANK MONK

A superb gold watch, worth five or six hundred dollars, was presented to Hank Monk, here, night before last. The donors were John S. Henning, Joe Clark, H. H. Raymond, Alex. O'Neil, William Thompson, Jr., John O. Earl, W. M. Lent and three others. The ceremonies were conducted at Frank Ludlow's daguerrean rooms. Judge Turner made the presentation speech, and Judge Hardy replied on behalf of the defendant. Champagne flowed freely. The watch is gorgeously embellished with coaches and horses, and with charms and seals in keeping with the same, and bears for a motto Hank's famous remark to Horace Greeley: "KEEP YOUR SEAT, HORACE—I'LL GET YOU THERE ON TIME!"

"THE OLD PAH-UTAH"

Lovejoy has issued the first number of his paper at Washoe City, and the above is its name. It is as pretty as a sweetheart, and as readable as a love-letter—and in my experience, these similes express a good deal. But why should Lovejoy spell it Pah-Utah? That isn't right—it should be Pi-Uty, or Pi-Ute. I speak by authority. Because I have carefully noted the little speeches of self-gratulation of our noble red brother, and he always delivers himself in this wise: "Pi-Uty boy heepy work—Washoe heep lazy." But if you question his nationality, he remarks, with oppressive dignity: "Me no dam Washoe—me Pi-Ute!" Wherefore, my researches have satisfied me that one of these, or both, is right. Lovejoy ought to know this, even better than me; he came here before May, 1860, and is, consequently, a blooded Pi-Ute, while I am only an ignorant half-breed.

CARSON CITY

Call your Constitutioners home. They do nothing but sing the praises of Carson City, and Carson society, and Carson climate. Hite, and Brosnan, and Youngs, and Sterns, and half the balance of them, are more than half inclined to stay here. It is absurd. Pipe to quarters!
FINAL REPORT

The Third House of the Constitutional Convention met in solemn grandeur, at 11 o'clock last night. To-morrow or next day I shall compile a *verbatim* report of its proceedings for the forthcoming volume of official reports of the Convention, and if you think you can afford to pay enough for it I will allow you to publish it in advance of that volume.
MARK TWAIN
President Constitutional Convention (Third House)

16.

Nevada State Constitutional Convention; Third House
Carson City, December 13, 1863

☞ This dispatch, except for the part dealing with the second session of the Third House, is reprinted in Angel, *History of Nevada*, pp. 82–84, and (with further omissions) in Mack, *Mark Twain in Nevada*, pp. 273–276. The scrapbook of Mark Twain items in the Morse-Frear Collection, Yale University Library, contains another clipping of this piece from the *Enterprise,* with three annotations in Mark Twain's hand which were evidently made at a time when he was planning to bring out a volume of his newspaper articles in the East. One of the penciled notes identifies Stewart as "present U. S. Senator" (which indicates that the notation was made between 1864 and 1875); another reads: "Conventions & legislatures are a good deal alike, all America over—which fact may excuse the insertion of this burlesque." The third note corrects "question" to "quotation" in J. J. Musser's reference to Hamlet's soliloquy.[1] The reference to phonographic reporting by Mark Twain is, of course, facetious.

Richard G. Lillard, in his unpublished dissertation "Studies in Washoe Journalism and Humor," says of the Third House:

This strange institution of Carson City appeared in 1862 [during the session of the second Territorial Legislature] and lasted at least seven years. It is, apparently, without a parallel in American history. Intended by its prankster founders to burlesque the processes and results of popular legislation, it met informally, in rear rooms, saloons, the schoolhouse, the Presbyterian Church, the Assembly itself. Legislators, lawyers, hangers-on, and townsmen made up the membership. . . . it made fun of governors' messages, proposed absurd bills, told lies, punned, played tricks, baited prominent politicians, and "elected" state officials.[2]

A reporter for the Sacramento *Union* wrote on November 15, 1862, that the Third House "meets every evening in a rear building, as Mrs. Malaprop would say, 'contagious to' a drinking saloon." He quotes a paragraph from the "Annual Message of Captain Jim, Chief of the Washoes, and Governor (de facto) of Nevada, Delivered before the Third House of the Territorial Legislature, Friday, November Fourteenth, One Thousand Eight Hundred and Sixty-Two."[3] This address, a burlesque of Governor James W. Nye's message to the legislature, was circulated as a broadside.[4] Under cover of a ponderous irony, it is critical of the national administration, and of California capitalists (against whom the Incorporation Law passed later in the session was supposedly directed). Since these views are known to have been held by Hal Clayton, the Carson attorney who presided over the early sessions of the Third House, the "Annual Message of Captain Jim" was probably his work.[5] On December 17 the Third House met in the street under the windows of the hotel where the legislature was in session, and with bonfires and a brass band undertook "to make Councilman [Gavin D.] Hall [of Ormsby County] vote right on the Corporation Bill." This outdoor meeting was addressed by Clayton, Thomas Hannah, John J. Musser, and John D. Winters. The Corporation bill was passed by both houses.[6]

During this session of the legislature the meetings of the Third House seem to have been open to the public, at least to males. Dr. Charles L. Anderson, a newly arrived immigrant, wrote to his wife from Carson on November 16: "The 'Third House,' a mock legislature is the only place of amusement. I have attended two evenings. It is a poor entertainment."[7]

The term "Third House" was of course illogical with reference to the unicameral Constitutional Convention, but the name was inherited from the Third House of the earlier sessions of the bicameral legislature. For Mark Twain's participation in meetings of the Third House during the session of the third Territorial Legislature, see headnote to section 26, below.

The oath of office prescribed for all officials in the proposed state constitution included the words,

> ... I do ... solemnly swear (or affirm) that I have not fought a duel, nor sent or accepted a challenge to fight a duel, nor been a second to either party, nor in any manner aided or assisted in such duel, nor been knowingly the bearer of such challenge or acceptance, since the adoption of the Constitution of the State of Nevada, and that I will not be so engaged or concerned, directly or indirectly, in or about any such duel, during my continuance in office.[8]

The reader will recognize that Mark Twain is parodying the forensic mannerisms of prominent speakers in the Convention. He probably mimicked their voices and gestures when he delivered his message orally.

[REPORTED IN PHONOGRAPHIC SHORT-HAND BY MARK TWAIN]

THE Third House met in the Hall of the Convention at 11 P. M., Friday, immediately after the final adjournment of the First House.

On motion of Mr. Nightingill, the rules were suspended and the usual prayer dispensed with, on the ground that it was never listened to by the members of the First House, which was composed chiefly of the same gentlemen which constitute the Third, and was consequently merely ornamental and entirely unnecessary.

Mr. Mark Twain was elected President of the Convention, and Messrs. Small and Hickok appointed to conduct him to the Chair, which they did amid a dense and respectful silence on the part of the house, Mr. Small stepping grandly over the desks, and Mr. Hickok walking under them.

The President addressed the house as follows, taking his remarks down in short-hand as he proceeded.

Gentlemen—This is the proudest moment of my life. I shall always think so. I think so still. I shall ponder over it with unspeakable emotion down to the latest syllable of recorded time. It shall be my earnest endeavor to give entire satisfaction in the high and bully position to which you have elevated me. [Applause.]

The President appointed Mr. Small, Secretary, Mr. Gibson official reporter, and Mr. Pete Hopkins, Chief Page, and Uncle Billy Patterson, First Assistant Page. These officers came forward and took the following oath:

"We do solemnly affirm that we have never seen a duel, never been connected with a duel, never heard of a duel, never sent or received a challenge, never fought a duel, and don't want to. Furthermore, we will support, protect and defend this constitution which we are about to frame, until we can't rest, and will take our pay in scrip."

Mr. Youngs—"Mr. President: I, ah — I — that is —"

The President—"Mr. Youngs, if you have got anything to say, say it; and don't stand there and shake your head and gasp 'I — ah, I — ah,' as you have been in the habit of doing in the former Convention."

Mr. Youngs—"Well, sir, I was only going to say that I liked your inaugural, and I perfectly agree with the sentiments you appeared to express in it, but I didn't rightly understand what —"

The President—"You have been sitting there for thirty days, like a bump on a log, and you never rightly understand anything. Take your seat, sir, you are out of order. You rose for information? Well, you'll not get it — sit down. You will appeal from the decision of the Chair? Take your seat, sir, the Chair will entertain no appeals from its decisions. And I would suggest to you, sir, that you will not be permitted, here, to growl in your seat, and make malicious side remarks in an undertone, for fifteen minutes after you have been called to order, as you have habitually done in the other house."

The President—"The subject before the house is as follows. The Secretary will read:"

Secretary—"A–r, ar, — t–i, ti — arti, c–l–e, cle, —article—"

The President—"What are you trying to do, sir?"

Secretary—"Well, I am only a helpless orphan, and I can't read writing."

The Chair appointed Mr. Hickok to assist Mr. Small, and discharged Mr. Gibson, the official reporter, because he did not know how to write.

Mr. Youngs—(singing)—"For the lady I love will soon be a bride, with the diadem on her brow-ow-ow."

President—"Order, you snuffling old granny!"

Mr. Youngs—"I AM in order, sir."

The President—"You are not, sir — sit down."

Mr. Youngs—"I won't, sir! I appeal to —."

The President—"Take—your—seat!"

Mr. Youngs—"But I insist that Jefferson's Manual —."

The President—"D——n Jefferson's Manual! The Chair will transact its own business in its own way, sir."

Mr. Chapin—"Mr. President: I do hope the amendment will not pass. I do beg of gentlemen—I do beseech of gentlemen—that they will examine this matter carefully, and earnestly, and seriously, and with a sincere desire to do the people all the good, and all the justice, and all the benefit it is in their power to do. I do hope, Mr. President —."

The President—"Now, there YOU go! What are you trying to get through your head?—there's nothing before the house."

The question being on Section 4, Article 1 (free exercise of religious liberty):

Mr. Stewart said—"Mr. President: I insist upon it, that if you tax the mines, you impose a burden upon the people which will be heavier than they can bear. And when you tax the poor miner's shafts, and drifts, and bed-rock tunnels, you are NOT taxing his property; you are NOT taxing his substance; you are NOT taxing his wealth—no, but you are taxing what may become property some day, or may not; you are taxing the shadow from which the substance may eventually issue or may not; you are taxing the visions of Alnaschar; which may turn to minted gold, or only prove the forerunners of poverty and misfortune; in a word, sir, you are taxing his hopes; taxing the aspirations of his soul; taxing the yearnings of his heart of hearts! Yes, sir, I insist upon it, that if you tax the mines, you will impose a burden upon the people which will be heavier than they can bear. And when you tax the poor miner's shafts, and drifts, and bed-rock tunnels, you are NOT taxing his property; you are NOT taxing his substance; you are NOT taxing his wealth—no, but you are taxing what may become property some day, or may not; you are taxing the shadow from which the substance may eventually issue or may not; you are taxing the visions of Alnaschar, which may turn to minted gold, or merely prove the forerunners of poverty and misfortune; in a word, sir, you are taxing his hopes! taxing the aspirations of his soul!—taxing the yearnings of his heart of hearts! Ah, sir, I do insist upon it that if you tax the mines, you will impose a burden upon the people which will be heavier than they can bear. And when you tax the poor miner's shafts, and drifts, and bed-rock tunnels —"

The President—"Take your seat, Bill Stewart! I am not going to sit here and listen to that same old song over and over again. I have been reporting and re-reporting that infernal speech for the last thirty days, and want you to understand that you can't play it off on this Convention any more. When I want it, I will repeat it myself—I know it by heart, anyhow. You and your bed-rock tunnels, and blighted miners' blasted hopes, have gotten to be a sort of nightmare to me, and I won't put up with it any longer. I don't wish to be too hard on your speech, but if you can't add something fresh to it, or say it backwards, or sing it to a new tune, you have simply got to simmer down for awhile."

Mr. Johnson—"Mr. President: I wish it distinctly understood that I am not a candidate for the Senate, or any other office, and have no intention of becoming one. And I wish to call the attention of the Convention to the fact, sir, that outside influences have been brought to bear, here, that ——"

The President—"Governor Johnson, there is no necessity of your putting in your shovel here, until you are called upon to make a statement. And if you allude to the engrossing clerk as an outside influence, I must inform you, sir, that his battery has been silenced with Territorial scrip at forty cents on the dollar."

Mr. Sterns—"Mr. President, I cordially agree with the gentleman from Storey county, that if we tax the mines we shall impose a burden upon the people that will be heavier than they can bear. I agree with him, sir, that in taxing the poor miner's shafts, and drifts, and bed-rock tunnels, we would not be taxing his property, or his wealth, or his substance, but only that which may become such at some future day—an Alnascharean vision, which might turn to coin or might only result in disaster and disappointment to the defendant—in a word, sir, I coincide with him in the opinion that it would be equivalent to taxing the hopes of the poor miner— his aspirations—the dear yearnings of his —"

The President—"Yearnings of his grandmother! I'll slam this mallet at the next man that attempts to impose that tiresome old speech on this body. SET DOWN! You have been pretty regular about re-hashing other people's platitudes heretofore, Mr. Sterns, but you have got to be a little original in the Third House. Your sacri-legious lips will be marring the speeches of the Chair, next."

Mr. Ralston—"Mr. President: I have but a word to say, and I do not wish to occupy the attention of the house any longer than I can help; although I could, perhaps, throw more light upon the matter of our eastern boundary than those who have not visited that interesting but comparatively unknown section of our budding commonwealth. It is growing late, and I do not feel as if I had a right to tax the patience —"

The President—"Tax! Take your seat, sir, take your seat. I will NOT be bullyragged to death with this threadbare subject of taxation. You are out of order, anyhow. How do you suppose anybody can listen in any comfort to your speech, when you are fumbling with your coat all the time you are talking, and trying to button it with your left hand, when you know you can't do it? I have never seen you succeed yet, until just as you got the last word out. And then the moment you sit down, you always unbutton it again. You may speak, hereafter, Mr. Ralston, but I want you to understand that you have got to button your coat before you get up. I do not mean to be kept in hot water all the time by your little oratorical eccentricities."

Mr. Larrowe—"Mr. President: There are nine mills in Lander county already — let me see — there is Dobson's, five stamp; Thompson's, eight stamp; Johnson's, three stamp — well, I cannot give the names of all of them, but there are nine, sir—NINE splendid, steam-power quartz-mills, disturbing with their ceaseless thunder the dead silence of centuries! Nine noble quartz-mills, sir, cheering with the music of their batteries the desponding hearts of pilgrims from every land!—nine miraculous quartz-mills, sir, from whose steam-pipes and chimneys ascends a grateful incense to the god of Labor and Progress!—nine sceptred and anointed quartz-mills, sir, whose mission it is to establish the power, and the greatness, and the glory of Nevada, and place her high along the —"

The President—"Now will you just take your seat, and hold your clatter until somebody asks you for your confounded Reese River quartz-mill statistics? What has Reese River got to do with religious freedom?—and what have quartz-mills got to do with it—

and what have you to do with it yourself? You are out of order, sir—plant yourself. And moreover, when you get up here to make a speech, I don't want you to yell at me as if you thought I were in San Francisco—I'm not hard of hearing. I don't see why President North didn't tone you down long ago."

Mr. Larrowe—"I think I am in order, Mr. President. It was a rule in the other Convention that no member could speak when there was no question before the house; but after the question had been announced by the Chair, members could then go on and speak on any subject they pleased—or rather, that was the custom, sir—the ordinary custom."

The President—"Yes, sir, I know it has been the custom for thirty days and thirty nights in the other Convention, but I will let gentlemen know that they can't ring in three-stamp Reese River quartz-mills on the third house when I am considering the question of religious liberty—the same being dear to every American heart. Plant yourself, sir—plant yourself. I don't want any more yowling out of you, now."

Mr. Small—"The Secretary would beg leave to state, for the information of the Con——"

The President—"There, now, that's enough of that. You learned that from Gillespie, I won't have any of that kind of nonsense here. When you have got anything to say, talk it right out; and see that you use the personal pronoun 'I,' also, and drop that presumptuous third person. 'The Secretary would beg leave to state!' The devil he would. Now suppose you take a back seat, and wait until somebody asks you to state something. Mr. Chapin, you will please stop catching flies while the Chair is considering the subject of religious toleration."

Mr. Ball—"Mr. President: The Finance Committee, of which I have the honor to be chairman, have arrived at the conclusion that it is a hundred and thirty miles from here to Folsom; that it will take two hundred and thirty miles of railroad iron to build a road that distance, without counting the switches; this would figure up as follows: Bars, 14 feet 3 inches long; weight, 800 pounds; 1,000 bars to the mile, 800,000 pounds; 130,000 bars for the whole distance, weight, 104,000,000 pounds; original cost of the iron, with insurance and transportation to Folsom from St. Louis, via Salt

Lake City, added, say three dollars and a half a pound, would amount to a fraction over or under $312,722,239.42. Three hundred and twelve million, seven hundred and twenty-two thousand, two hundred and thirty-nine dollars and forty-two cents, sir. That is the estimate of the Committee, sir, for prime cost of one class of material, without counting labor and other expenses. In view of these facts, sir, it is the opinion of the Committee that we had better not build the road. I did not think it necessary to submit a written report, because —"

The President—"Take your seat, Mr. Ball—take your seat, sir. Your evil eye never lights upon this Chair but the spirit moves you to confuse its intellect with some of your villainous algebraical monstrosities. I will not entertain them, sir; I don't know anything about them. You needn't mind bringing in any written reports here—or verbal ones either, unless you can confine yourself to a reasonable number of figures at a time, so that I can understand what you are driving at. No, sir, the Third House will not build the railroad. The other Convention's donation of $3,000,000 in bonds, worth forty cents on the dollar, will buy enough of one of those bars to make a breastpin, and that will have to satisfy this commonwealth for the present. I observe that Messrs. Wasson and Gibson and Noteware and Kennedy have their feet on their desks. The chief page will proceed to remove those relics of ancient conventional barbarism from sight."

Mr. Musser—"Mr. President: To be, or not to be—that is the question —"

The President—"No, sir! The question is, shall we tolerate religious indifference in this community; or the rights of conscience; or the right of suffrage; or the freedom of the press; or free speech, or free schools, or free niggers. The Chair trusts it knows what it is about, without any instructions from the members."

Mr. Musser—"But, sir, it was only a quotation from —"

The President—"Well, I don't care, I want you to sit down. The Chair don't consider that you know much about religion anyhow, and consequently the subject will suffer no detriment from your letting it alone. You and Judge Hardy can subside, and study over the preamble until you are wanted."

Mr. Brosnan—"Mr. President, these proceedings have all been

irregular, extremely and customarily irregular. I will move, sir, that the question be passed, for the present, and that we take up the next section."

Mr. Mitchell—"I object to that, Mr. President. I move that we go into Committee of the Whole on it."

Mr. Wasson—"I move that it be referred back to the Standing Committee."

Mr. North—"I move that the rules be suspended and the whole article placed upon its final passage."

The President—"Gentlemen, those of you who are in favor of adopting the original proposition, together with the various motions now pending before the house, will signify the same by saying 'aye.'"

No one voting in the negative, the chair decided the vote to be unanimous in the affirmative.

The President—"Gentlemen, your proceedings have been exactly similar to those of the convention which preceded you. You have considered a subject which you knew nothing about; spoken on every subject but the one before the house, and voted without knowing what you were voting for or having any idea what would be the general result of your action. I will adjourn the Convention for an hour, on account of my cold, to the end that I may apply the remedy prescribed for it by Dr. Tjader—the same being gin and molasses. The Chief Page is hereby instructed to provide a spoonful of molasses and a gallon of gin, for the use of the President."

OUR CARSON DISPATCH—SECOND SESSION
[BY TELEGRAPH]

Third House met after recess, and transacted the following business:

Secretary read Section 15, Legislative Department:

"SECTION 15. The doors of each house shall be kept open during the session."

Kinkead moved to amend by adding the words "and the windows also, if the weather will permit."

Secretary read Section 32, Legislative Department:

"SECTION 32. No law shall be passed authorizing married women to carry on business as sole traders."

On motion of Sterns, construed to mean that married women shall not preach.

Secretary read Section 6, Declaration of Rights:

"SECTION 6. Excessive bail shall not be required, nor excessive fines imposed."

Youngs moved to amend by striking out the word "bail" and inserting the word "board." Adopted, unanimously.

SECTION 1. Miscellaneous Provisions, was amended so as to read as follows:

"SECTION 1. The seat of government shall be at Carson, and the Legislature shall hold its session in the plaza during the first six years."

Section added empowering the President of the Third House of the Convention to convene, by proclamation, the Third House of the State Legislature, for the purpose of electing two United States Senators, within thirty days after the Constitution shall have been ratified.

Name of the State changed to "Washoe," in conformity with the law which called the Convention together.

New section added, as follows:

"SECTION —. No Sheriff or other officer shall be expected to arrest any assassin or other criminal on strong presumptive evidence, merely, nor any other evidence, unless such assassin or other criminal shall insist upon his privilege of being arrested."

The hour having arrived for the President to take his regular gin and molasses, the Convention adjourned.

Last night, about 12 o'clock—[here the telegraph ceased working.—BLOOMER, operator.]

17.

Christmas Presents

Virginia City, published December 29, 1863

☞ This article is unsigned, but the author refers to himself as Mark Twain. The phrase "Be-he-mi-soi-vin," despite or perhaps because of Mark Twain's slang translation, has defied the editor's efforts at explication. Artemus Ward (Charles F. Browne, the celebrated newspaper humorist and lecturer) had arrived in Virginia City on December 18 and had almost at once become a boon companion of the *Enterprise* staff.[1] The "Mrs. Cutter" mentioned as an associate in Miss Clapp's school is apparently the Mrs. W. K. Cutler who signed the open letter to the *Enterprise* protesting against Mark Twain's "How Is It?" editorial concerning disposition of funds intended for the Sanitary Commission (§38, below) and also the Mrs. Cutler who recited poems and sang songs in the evening performance for the benefit of the First Presbyterian Church at Carson City on December 4, 1863 (§14, above). D. K. Sessions says that "Mrs. E. G. Cutler (now [1881] Mrs. Haydon) celebrated as a singer and elocutionist" was associated with Miss Clapp in the Sierra Seminary.[2] It was indubitably W. K. Cutler to whom Mark Twain sent a defiant note on May 28, 1864 (the manuscript, in Mark Twain's handwriting, is among the Dan De Quille Papers in the Bancroft Library, University of California, Berkeley).

Mark Twain's proposed design for a state seal is discussed in Part One.

WE received from Carson, Saturday, a long yellow box, of suspicious appearance, with the following inscription upon it: "Mark Twain, ENTERPRISE Office, Virginia—Free—Politeness Langton's Pioneer Express—*Be-hi-me-soi-vin*." That last phrase is Greek, and means "Bully for you!" We are not sure that it was written by Mrs. H. F. R., of Carson, and there was no evidence accompanying the box to show that it was. This is what makes us so obstinate in the opinion that it might have been written by somebody else. The box contained a toy rabbit, of the jackass persuasion, gifted with ears of aggravated dimensions, and swathed in sage-brush; an Indian chief—a mere human creation—made of raisins, strung on a skeleton formed of a single knitting-needle, with a solitary fig for a body, and a chicken feather driven into the head of the effigy, to denote its high official character. One more present remained—the same being a toy watchman's rattle, made of pine and tastefully painted. We are glad to have that rattle now, but when we asked for such a thing at a certain convivial party in Carson, it will be remembered that we meant to bestow it upon another young man who was present, and whose absent mind, we imagined, might be collected together and concentrated by means of such an instrument. We have presented the rabbit to Artemus Ward, to be preserved as a specimen of our resources; the other presents we shall always wear near our heart. The following report of the committee, accompanying the box, has been received, accepted, adopted, and the same referred to the Committee of the Whole—people:

CARSON CITY, *December 25, 1863.*

Mr. MARK TWAIN—*Sir:* The undersigned has the honor to be selected by the gay company of ladies and gentlemen and boys and girls and Santa Claus, who came in person with Judge Dixson's wolf-skin cap, coat, pants and a mask, and sleigh bells around his waist, and dashed in the room just after Mrs. Cutter and two long rows of children had sung a pretty piece, and read a letter from Santa Claus, when that individual immediately dashed into the room to the terror of some of the children, thirty-six in all, and climbed the Christmas tree, all covered with presents, and little lighted candles, and handed down things for everybody, and afterwards danced with the now reconciled children, and then dashed out; after which there was supper and dancing by the ladies and gentlemen; and the school which was thus made to enjoy themselves last night till midnight, was Miss H. K. Clapp and Mrs. Cutter's Seminary, which is one of the best there is, and instructed me to send you these things, which I do by Langton's Express, handed down from the Christmas tree by Santa Claus, marked "Mark Twain," to wit: One rabbit under a sage brush, to represent your design for a seal in the Constitutional Convention; one rattle, presented by a lady of whom you begged for one when you were here last, and a Pi-Ute to be eaten, being a chief with a chicken feather in his hat, composed of a fig for his body and otherwise raisins, sent to you by request of a lady of the medical profession, all of which is submitted by WILLIAM A. TRINITY, Committee

18.

The Bolters in Convention
Virginia City, published December 30, 1863

☞ This editorial, also unsigned, is identified as Mark Twain's work by the author's reference to himself as one of the reporters at the Constitutional Convention: no other member of the *Enterprise* staff served in that capacity. "The Babes in the Wood" was the wildly inappropriate title given by Artemus Ward to many of his humorous lectures.

As the tone of the article indicates, the *Enterprise* supported the regular Union delegation from Storey County (and later supported the slate of state officers nominated by the state convention for submission to the voters along with the proposed constitution). The bolters' delegation from Storey County was unanimously rejected by the state nominating convention of the Union party at Carson City, December 31, 1863.[1]

Although the bolters' meeting gave groans for William M. Stewart and A. W. Baldwin, by the time of the election (January 19, 1864) both Stewart and Baldwin had turned against the proposed constitution. They joined hands with the bolters from the Union party and the Democrats to help defeat it.[2] Eventually the newspapers which had opposed the first constitution, most important among them the Virginia City *Union* (of which Fitch was an editor), went over to the Democratic party. But Stewart remained in the Republican party.[3]

AT 7 o'clock last night a large number of citizens met at the Court House for the purpose of selecting sixteen new delegates, which they hoped might prove more acceptable to the State Convention than those elected by the regular County Convention day before yesterday. There appeared to be some discord in this Convention as well as in that which preceded it, but of course the manner in which it was constituted prevented the possibility of any one's bolting from it in the regular and recognized way. It was a gorgeous sight to behold those two hundred fearless spirits of Storey— those noble human soda-bottles, so to speak effervescing with the holy gas of pure unselfish patriotism, rising in their might to bust out, as it were, the infamous action of 3,000 voters of Storey county, as done in the County Convention by their chosen representatives. But we are fearfully and wonderfully made, and we glorious Americans will occasionally astonish the God that created us when we get a fair start.

The proceedings opened with three cheers and a tiger for the stars and stripes.

Mr. Corson moved that Dr. Minneer be elected chairman of the meetings. Carried.

Mr. Barclay nominated Wm. H. Davenport and James Phelan as Secretaries. They were elected without opposition.

The following Vice Presidents were then elected: James Brannon, Dighton Corson, Judge Leconey, J. W. Noyes, Thos. Lynch, Judge Ferris, John A. Collins, A. B. Elliott, E. Bond, W. H. Young, J. S. Black, Thos. G. Taylor, S. A. Kellogg, Judge Frizell, J. H. Heilshorn, P. Quigley, J. T. Sage, John Church, W. R. Warnock and R. H. Rider. [Several of these gentlemen were said to be present.]

The Chairman reviewed the action of the County Convention, and said it was not satisfactory to the majority of the community; therefore the people had met now to improve upon that action in their sovereign capacity as fountain-head of power in the land. He said the present Convention would nominate sixteen delegates, and hoped they would be accepted by the State Convention in preference to the delegates elected by the late packed Convention.

[A voice—"Three cheers!" No response.]

A committee previously and mysteriously appointed immediately brought in a report containing the following names. There was no suspicion of packing about it, however. The report reads as follows:

Report of the committee appointed by a meeting of citizens held at the Court House on Monday evening, December 29th, to select the names of sixteen citizens to be presented to the mass meeting this evening as suitable persons to represent Storey county in the Union State Convention, to be held at Carson on the 31st inst., beg leave to submit the following names: Dr. Geiger, John Dohle, Thomas Lynch, Captain White, Joseph Loryea, J. L. Black, George E. Brickett, Thomas Hannah, J. D. Meagher, Augustus Ash.

Mr. Corson moved that the report be accepted, and the committee discharged. Carried.

Mr. Fitch was called for and addressed the Convention at great length, re-hashing, adding to and improving his most recent editorials in the Virginia *Union.* He was heard with interest and was frequently applauded.

Judge Brosnan was next called for, very enthusiastically. As is always his custom, Mr. Brosnan spoke eloquently and feelingly, and was repeatedly and loudly cheered. Public speakers are not given to adhering strictly to the truth as a general thing, but we know Judge Brosnan is. However, he stood up there last night and misrepresented old Nestor—a poor devil who has been dead hundreds and hundreds of years. And Judge Brosnan knew perfectly well that he was departing from the record when he unblushingly abused old Nestor's wardrobe and said he wore a poisoned shirt. Now why couldn't he confine himself to living convention-packers and let dead foreigners alone? That's it—we are down on that kind of thing, you know.

[Cries, "Hannah! Hannah!" "Gentlemen, wait a moment!" "I call for the adoption of the report before we have any speaking!"]

However, Mr. Hannah came forward and said that "As had been remarked by both gentlemen who have preceded me," and then went on and made both gentlemen's speeches over again, in such a pleasant way, and with such vehemence of manner that "the people"—that mighty lever being present, and filling very nearly three-fourths of the house—"the people" applauded each familiar argument as it fell upon their ears, and felt really comfortable over it. He touched us very agreeably by speaking of us as "those intelligent reporters who officiated at the late Constitutional Convention." [The word "intelligent" is our own. We had an idea it would make the sentence read better.] Toward the last, Mr. Hannah soared into originality, and touched upon a multitude of subjects on his own hook. Notwithstanding its apparent originality, however, we shall always be haunted by the dreadful suspicion that the fag-end of Tom Hannah's speech was gobbled out of the Babes in the Wood.

Mr. Brosnan moved that a committee of five be appointed to draft resolutions.

Mr. Pepper suggested that there was already a question before the house. [A voice—"Sit down."]

The Chairman remarked that there was a question before the house, and proceeded to state it as being on the adoption of the report of the Committee on Nominations.

The house refused to entertain the report in its entirety, and demanded, in great confusion, that the candidates should be voted for separately, which was done, and the following gentlemen elected:

Messrs. Geiger, Dohle, Lynch, White, Black, Hannah, Warnock, Ash, Phillips, G. H. [sic], J. Y. Paul, Doak (?), Frizell, Burke, Knox, Brickett.

Messrs. Loryea and Meagher were voted for and rejected, and confusion grew worse confounded in the meantime.

Mr. Warnock moved the appointment of a Nominating Committee of ten, to present names to the next mass meeting, as candidates for Legislators, Judges, etc. Carried.

The Committee on Resolutions was appointed as follows: Messrs. Brosnan, Frizell, Hannah, Corson, Bond.

The committee created by Mr. Warnock's resolution was then nominated and elected, as follows: Messrs. Warnock, Jas. Campbell, Hannah, Jacob Young, Manning, Lackey, Dimock, Carey, Van Vliet and Flood.

Mr. Corson moved to add five to the committee, and take them from Gold Hill and Flowery. Carried.

The following gentlemen were nominated and elected: Messrs. Phillips, La Flower and Bishop.

[Here great trouble arose about a suggestion that the Convention might possibly be electing people who were opposed to them. It was a wise and bully idea. Mr. James Campbell called at our office after the Convention adjourned, and requested us to remove his name from the nominating committee.]

After which, with remarkable unanimity, the Convention struck off the names of the Gold Hill members from the nominating committee, and left it to the President to fill up with other Gold Hill men.

Mr. Frizell submitted the following names, which he said had been selected by a mass meeting in Gold Hill: Wm. C. Derall, E. R. Burke, Ed. C. Morse, Sam Doak, and J. W. Phillips.

They were unanimously elected.

Chas. H. Knox of Flowery was added to the committee.

The Committee on Resolutions then reported as follows:

Resolved, That as subjects of a Government, yet free, we rejoice at the inestimable right and privilege to publicly assemble and approve or condemn, when the general good requires it, the manner in which our representatives may have discharged the duties assigned them by the suffrages of the people.

2. As the sense of this large assemblage of citizens which may justly be denominated a spontaneous uprising of an outraged and insulted constituency, that the action of the County Nominating Convention, held in Virginia on the 28th day of December, instant,

has been unjust, unfair, arbitrary, and without precedent in the history of conventional legislation.

3. That the resolutions adopted, and the other proceedings had by the said Convention, fail to express the true sentiments of the people of this county, and only proclaim the sentiments of a few interested individuals. Regarding them as such, we unanimously repudiate them, and declare that those resolutions and proceedings ought not to have, and have not, any binding force upon the political action of the free, independent and Union-loving electors of Storey county.

4. That copies of the proceedings of this meeting be transmitted to the members of the ensuing State Nominating Convention, from other counties, accompanied with a respectful request that they will do justice to the great majority of the people of Storey county, and rebuke the odious and unjust system of "packing" conventions by admitting the nominees of this meeting to seats in the Convention, as the true delegates and representatives of the people of Storey.

The resolutions were unanimously adopted.

A County Central Committee was elected, as follows: J. L. Black, Chas. Knox, Jas. Phelan, E. R. Burke, Samuel Doak, T. R. P. Dimock, Thos. Barclay, Dighton Corson, W. D. [sic] Warnock, Jacob Young.

Motion that the delegates elected be instructed to go to Carson to-morrow (Wednesday) and that no proxies be allowed except in extreme cases, and that such extreme cases be attended to by the delegates, themselves. Carried.

A motion that the Central Committee meet in the District Court room to-morrow (Wednesday) evening, prevailed.

Also, a motion that the Convention adjourn until next Monday evening—to meet then at the District Court room.

The meeting broke up with cheers for the Convention, the Union, the old flag, and groans for Stewart and Baldwin.

It was a dusty, a very dusty, Convention, and as has been previously remarked in America, we are a great people.

CARD

EDS. ENTERPRISE.—The gentleman who reported the proceedings of the Union mass meeting last evening for the ENTERPRISE, unintentionally misquotes. He says Mr. Brosnan slandered the defunct "Nestor." Not so—Mr. B—— made no allusion to that hair-brained, crazy old fool, "Nestor," nor to his "wardrobe." But Mr. B—— did mention *that* other jealous and wicked "cuss," Nessus, and his historical, villainous "shirt."

Now, if that facetious sinner, blunderer and *sage-brush painter*, "Mark Twain," had thus libelled me, I could forgive him; but to be thus misrepresented (though undesignedly) by the "intelligent" reporter of the ENTERPRISE is, as Mrs. Partington would say, absolutely inseparable.

C. M. Brosnan

Virginia, Dec. 30th

19.

A Gorgeous Swindle
Virginia City, published December 30, 1863

☞ This article is unsigned, and the only evidence that Mark Twain wrote it is its style. But this evidence is convincing. Such phrases as "untechnical, leather-headed thieves" and "probably in time for the resurrection"; the unusual superlatives "soothingest" and "most refreshingest"; and the imaginary "denizen of some obscure western town walking with stately mien to the express office to get his regular monthly dividends," amid awed whispers from the bystanders—these sound enough like Mark Twain to warrant ascribing the article to him. The rise and fall of the duped Westerner provide an embryonic plot for a story like "The Man That Corrupted Hadleyburg."

The text of the fraudulent pamphlet, quoted in full at the end of the article in the *Territorial Enterprise,* is omitted here because of its great length.

Dr. MAY, of the International Hotel, has put into our hands the following documents, which will afford an idea of how infinitely mean some people can become when they get a chance. This firm of Read & Co., Bankers, 42 South Third street, Philadelphia, will do to travel—but not in Washoe, if we understand the peculiar notions of this people. The accompanying letter, circular, and certificate of stock were sent by Read & Co. to Dr. May's nephew, Theodore E. Clapp, Esq., Postmaster at White Pigeon, Michigan. Through the Doctor, Mr. Clapp had learned a good deal about Washoe, and saw at a glance, of course, that a swindle was on foot which would not only cheat multitudes of the poorest classes of men in the States, but would go far toward destroying confidence in our mines and our citizens if permitted to succeed. He lost no time, therefore, in forwarding the villainous papers to Dr. May, and we are sure the people of the Territory are right heartily thankful to him for doing so.

The certificate of stock is a curiosity in the way of unblushing rascality. It does not state how many shares there are in the company, or what a share is represented by. It is a comprehensive arrangement—the company propose to mine all over "Nevada Territory, adjoining California"! They are not partial to any particular mining district. They are going to "carry on" a general "gold and silver mining business"!—the untechnical, leather-headed thieves! The company is "TO BE" organized—at some indefinite period in the future—probably in time for the resurrection. The company is "to be" incorporated "for the purpose of purchasing machinery"— they only organize a company in order to purchase machinery— the inference is, that they calculate to steal the mine. And only to think—a man has only got to peddle forty or fifty of these certificates of stock for Messrs. Read & Co. in order to become fearfully and wonderfully wealthy!—or, as they eloquently put it, "By taking hold now, and assisting to raise the capital stock of this company, you have it within your grasp to place yourself [in] a way to receive a large income annually without spending one cent!" Oh, who wouldn't take hold now? Breathes there a man with soul so dead that he wouldn't take hold under such seductive circumstances? Scasely. Read & Co. want to get money—rather than miss, they will even grab at a paltry two-and-a-half piece—thus: "You can send in $2.50 at a time." Two and a half at a time, to buy shares in another Gould & Curry!

But the coolest, the soothingest, the most refreshingest paragraph (to speak strongly) is that one which is stuck in at the bottom of the circular, with an air about it which mutely says, "it's of no consequence, and scarcely worth mentioning, but then it will do to fill out the page with." The paragraph reads as follows: "N.B.— Subscribers can receive their dividends, as they fall due, at Messrs. Read & Co's Banking House, No. 42 South Third street, Philadelphia, or have them forwarded by express, of which all will be regularly notified!" We imagine we can see a denizen of some obscure western town walking with stately mien to the express office to get his regular monthly dividend; we imagine less fortunate people making way for him, and whispering together, "There goes old Thompson—owns ten shares in the People's Gold and Silver Mining Company—Lord! but he's rich!—he's going after his dividends now." And we imagine we see old Thompson and his regular dividends fail to connect. And finally, we imagine we see the envied Thompson jeered at by his same old neighbors as "the old fool who got taken in by the most palpable humbug of the century."

Who is "Wm. Heffly, Esq., of San Francisco," who knows it all, and who has calmly waited for three years without once swerving from his purpose of "starting a mining company" as soon as he could become satisfied that quartz-mining was a permanent thing? Cautious scoundrel! You couldn't fool him into going into a highway robbery like the "People's Gold and Silver Mining Company," until he was certain he could make the thing look plausible. But if he wrote those circulars and things, he was never a week in Washoe in his life, because we don't talk about "cap rock" in this country— that's a Pike's Peak phrase; and when we talk about "cab-rock," we never say it pays "$24 to the ton," or any other price; we don't crush wall-rock, as a general thing. There is no "Washoe Mining District" in this Territory, and the President of the People's Company did a bully good thing when he "reserved the right to change the location" of operations whenever he pleased. Mr. Heffly's knowledge of the prices of leading stocks here borders on the marvelous. He says Gould & Curry is worth "$5,000 per share." A "share" is three inches; but Gould & Curry don't sell at $20,000 a foot; he puts Ophir at $2,400 "per share"; now a "share" of Ophir is one inch. All the other prices mentioned by Mr. Heffly are wrong, and never were right at any time, perhaps. In the items written by Mr. Heffly, and pretended to be clipped from the *Bulletin* and the *Standard,* he uses mining technicalities never uttered either by miners or newspaper men in this part of America. The only true statement in these documents is the one which reads—"Therefore, in subscribing to the capital stock of this company, you are acting on a certainty, and taking no risk whatever." That is eminently so. You are acting on a certainty of being swindled, and so far from there being any risk about that result, it is the deadest "open and shut" thing in the world.

Now this swindle ought to be well ventilated by the newspapers—not that sound business men will ever be swindled by it, but the unsuspecting multitude, who yearn to grow suddenly rich, will assuredly have their slender purses drained by it. . . .

20.

Doings in Nevada
Carson City, January 4, 1864

☞ This article, first published in the "Town Topics" department of the New York *Sunday Mercury* (February 7, 1864, p. 3), may seem out of place in a volume devoted primarily to Mark Twain's work for the *Territorial Enterprise.*[1] It is included because it is closely related in subject matter to other pieces in the volume, and because of its intrinsic interest. Until the clipping turned up in the Moffett scrapbooks, it had been supposed that the earliest writing by Mark Twain to appear in an Eastern periodical (except for a couple of juvenilia in the Boston *Carpet-Bag*) was "Those Blasted Children," published in the *Mercury* on February 21, 1864.[2] An unpublished letter from Mark Twain to his mother and sister, written from Carson City on January 9, 1864, says that he had written an article for the *Mercury* the night before which can be identified as "Those Blasted Children." The incident on which the sketch is based probably occurred during Mark Twain's visit to San Francisco in September, 1863, but his letter fixes the date of composition as January 8, 1864. The present article was therefore written, as well as published, earlier than "Those Blasted Children." Both articles represent Mark Twain's effort to find a metropolitan market for his writing in consequence of the advice and encouragement of Artemus Ward during Ward's visit to Virginia City in December, 1863.³

It is interesting that opposition to the proposed constitution had reached such a stage by January 4 that Mark Twain took an aloof and even hostile attitude toward it.

The account of how the act authorizing the calling of a constitutional convention was passed by the legislature even though the blanks had not been filled in closely parallels a passage in a letter from Mark Twain to his mother written in January, 1864.⁴

OUR lively correspondent, Mark Twain, sends us his "opinions and reflections" upon recent political movements in Nevada Territory, which will be found interesting:

CARSON CITY, NEVADA TERRITORY,
January 4, 1864

EDITOR T. T.: The concentrated wisdom of Nevada Territory (known unto and respected by the nations of the earth as "Washoe") assembled in convention at Carson recently, and framed a constitution. It was an excellent piece of work in some respects, but it had one or two unfortunate defects which debarred it from assuming to be an immaculate conception. The chief of these was a clause authorizing the taxing of the mines. The people will not stand that. There are some 30,000 gold and silver mining incorporations here, or mines, or claims, or which you please, or all, if it suits you better. Very little of the kind of property thus represented is improved yet, or "developed" as we call it; it will take two or three years to get it in a developed and paying condition, and will require an enormous outlay of capital to accomplish such a result. And until it does begin to pay dividends, the people will not consent that it shall be burdened and hindered by taxation. Therefore, I am satisfied they will refuse to ratify our new constitution on the 19th inst.

It had an amusing feature in it, also. That was the Great Seal of the State. It had snow-capped mountains in it; and tunnels, and shafts, and pickaxes, and quartz-mills, and pack-trains, and mule-teams. These things were good; what there were of them. And it has railroads in it, and telegraphs, and stars, and suspension-bridges, and other romantic fictions foreign to sand and sage-brush. But the richest of it was the motto. It took them thirty days to decide whether it should be *"Volens et Potens"* (which they said meant "Able and Willing"), or "The Union Must and Shall be Preserved." Either would have been presumptuous enough, and surpassingly absurd just at present. Because we are not able and willing, thus far, to do a great deal more than locate wild-cat mining-claims and reluctantly sell them to confiding strangers at a ruinous sacrifice—of conscience. And if it were left to us to preserve the Union, in case the balance of the country failed in the attempt, I seriously believe we couldn't do it. Possibly, we might make it mighty warm for the Confederacy if it came prowling around here, but ultimately we would have to forsake our high trust, and quit preserving the Union. I am confident of it. And I have thought the matter over a good deal, off and on, as we say in Paris. We have an animal here whose surname is the "jackass rabbit." It is three feet long, has legs like a counting-house stool, ears of monstrous length, and no tail to speak of. It is swifter than a greyhound, and as meek and harmless as an infant. I might mention, also, that it is as handsome as most infants: however, it would be foreign to the subject, and I do not know that a remark of that kind would be popular in all circles. Let it pass, then—I will say nothing about it, though it would be a great comfort to me to do it, if people would consider the source and overlook it. Well, somebody proposed as a substitute for that pictorial Great Seal, a figure of a jackass-rabbit reposing in the shade of his native sage-brush, with the motto *"Volens* enough, but not so d——d *Potens."* Possibly that had something to do with the rejection of one of the proposed mottoes by the Convention.

STATE NOMINATING CONVENTION

We do not fool away much time in this country. As soon as the Constitution was duly framed and ready for ratification or rejection by the people, a convention to nominate candidates for State offices met at Carson. It finished its labors day before yesterday. The following nominations were made: For Governor, M. N. Mitchell; Lieutenant-Governor, M. S. Thompson; Secretary of State, Orion Clemens; Treasurer, Wm. B. Hickok; Member of Congress, John B. Winters; Superintendent of Public Instruction, Rev. A. F. White. Now, that ticket will be elected, but the Constitution won't. In that case, what are we to do with these fellows? We cannot let them starve. They are on our hands, and are entitled to our charity and protection. It is different with them from what it is with other people, because, although the Almighty created them, and used to care for and watch over them, no doubt it was long, long ago, and he may not recollect them now. And I think it is our duty to look after them, and see that they do not suffer. Besides, they all owe me something for traducing and vilifying them in the public prints, and thus exciting sympathy for them on the score of persecution, and securing their nomination; and I do not think it right or just that I should be expected to do people favors without being paid for it, merely because those favors failed to produce marketable fruit. No, Sir; I elected those fellows, and I shall take care that I am fairly remunerated for it. Now, if you know any small State, lying around anywhere, that I could get a contract on for the running of it, you will oblige me by mentioning it in your next. You can say that I have all the machinery on hand necessary to the carrying on of a third-rate State; say, also, that it is comparatively new, portions of it never having been used at all; also, that I will part with it on pretty nearly any terms, as my constitution is prostrated, and I am anxious to go into some other business. And say my various State officers are honest and capable—however, don't say that—just leave that out—let us not jest on a serious matter like this. But you might put in a little advertisement for me in the following shape, for instance. And it would be a real kindness to me if you would be so good as to call attention to it in your editorial columns. You see I am a sort of an orphan, away out here, struggling along on my own hook, as it were. My mother lives in St. Louis. She is sixty years of age, and a member of the Presbyterian Church. She takes no pride in being gay; in fact, she don't rush around much in society, now. However, I do not ask any man's sympathy on that account. I was simply going to offer my little advertisement.

FOR SALE OR RENT

One Governor, entirely new. Attended Sunday-school in his youth, and still remembers it. Never drinks. In other respects, however, his habits are good. As Commander-in-Chief of the Militia, he would be an ornament. Most Governors are.

One Lieutenant-Governor—also new. He has other merits, of minor importance, beside. No objection to going into the country—or elsewhere.

One Secretary of State. An old, experienced hand at the business. Has edited a newspaper, and been Secretary and Governor of Nevada Territory—consequently, is capable; and also consequently, will bear watching; is not bigoted—has no particular set of religious principles—or any other kind.

One small Treasurer—(second-hand). Will make a good officer. Was Treasurer once before, in [the] States. Took excellent care of the funds—has them yet.

One Member of Congress—new, but smart, sometimes called "Old Smarty, from Mud Springs." Has read every newspaper printed in Nevada Territory for two years, and knows all about the war. Would be a good hand to advise the President. Is young, ardent, ambitious, and on it. No objection to traveling, provided his mileage is paid.

One Superintendent of Public Instruction—good as new. Understands all the different systems of teaching, and does not approve of them. It is his laudable boast that he is a self-made man. It has been said of him by his admirers that God Almighty never made such a man. It is probably so. He is the soul of honor, and is willing to take greenbacks at par. No objection to making himself generally useful; can preach, if required.

Also, a large and well-selected assortment of State Legislators, Supreme Judges, Comptrollers, and such gimcracks, handy to have about a State Government, all of which are for sale or rent on the mildest possible terms, as, under present circumstances, they are of no earthly use to the subscriber.

For further particulars, address

MARK TWAIN. Carson, N.T.

OUR CONSTITUTION ILLEGAL

Now, joking aside, these are all good, honest, capable men, and would reflect credit upon the several positions for which they have been nominated; but then the people are not going to ratify the Constitution; and, consequently, they will never get a chance. I am glad that such is the case. In the Legislature, last year, I was wielding the weapon which, under just such circumstances, is mightier than the sword, at the time that the Act authorizing the calling together of a Convention to form a State Constitution was passed; and I know the secret history of that document. It was reported back from the Committee with a lot of blanks in it (for dates, apportionment, and number of members, amount of money appropriated to defray expenses of the Convention, etc.). Both Houses passed the Bill without filling those blanks; it was duly enrolled, brought back, and signed by the presiding officers of the Legislature, and then transmitted, a worthless, meaningless, and intentionally powerless instrument—to Gov. Nye for his signature—at night. And lo! a miracle. When the bill reached the Governor, there was not a solitary blank in it! Who filled them, is—is a great moral question for instance; but the enrolling clerk did not do it at any rate, since the emendations are in an unknown and atrocious handwriting. Therefore, the bill was a fraud; the convention created by it was a fraud; the fruit of the convention was an illegitimate infant constitution and a dead one at that; a State reared upon such a responsibility would be a fraudulent and impotent institution, and the result would be that we should ultimately be kicked back into a territorial condition again on account of it. Wherefore, when men say, "Let our constitution slide for the present," we say Amen.

21.

Letter from Mark Twain
Carson City, January 10, 1864

☞ On January 11, "Carl" (Clement T. Rice) commented on this piece in his "Letter from Carson" to the *Daily Union*:

"Mark Twain" is at his good natured joking again. Yesterday's letter of his, in the Enterprise, half way threatened to move the capital from this pleasant city, if Ormsby county did not repent herself and give a majority for the State and its manifold scenes of plunder. Of course Mark was joking; he only got up that little bit of romance to hide his own "indifference" to the State movement. Carson City will be the capital long after the proposed Constitution is voted down and forgotten.[1]

Mark Twain's implication that only those possessing taxable property or desiring to hold public office have a "tangible right to take an interest in the Constitution" resembles the "stake-in-society" theory of political representation that was defended by the Whigs and attacked by the Democrats in the early nineteenth century.[2]

"Dan" is of course Dan De Quille, Mark Twain's colleague and roommate in Virginia City.

For a description of Theodore Winters' house in Washoe Valley, see section 27.

Artemus Ward (Charles Farrar Browne) had arrived in Virginia City December 18 on a lecture tour.[3] Although he had intended to stay only a few days, he did not leave until near the end of December—probably the thirtieth.[4] He made the *Enterprise* office his headquarters, and his visit was "a period of continuous celebration" with Mark Twain, Dan De Quille, Joe Goodman, and others.[5] The letter of Artemus Ward from which Mark Twain quotes passages is in the Mark Twain Papers.[6]

For identification of Kettle-Belly Brown, see the Biographical Directory.

POLITICS

EDITORS ENTERPRISE: Well, how are you and the *News* and the *Bulletin* making out for the Constitution in Storey? I suppose it will be voted down here. I said so to a Virginia man yesterday. "Well," says he, "that reminds me of a circumstance. A good old practical Dutchman once contributed liberally toward the building of a church. By and by they wanted a lightning rod for it, and they came to the Dutchman again. 'Not a dam cent,' says he, 'not a dam cent! I helps to puild a house for te Lord, und if he joose to dunder on it and knock it down, he must do it at his own risk!' Now in the Constitution, we have placed the Capital here for several years; Carson has always fared well at our hands in the legislature, and finally, we have tacitly consented to say nothing more about the Mint being built in this inconvenient locality. This is the house that has been built for Carson—and now if she chooses to go and dunder on it and knock it down, by the Lord she'll have to take the consequences! The fact is all our bullion is silver, and we don't want the country flooded with silver coin; therefore, we can save the Government a heavy expense, and do the Territory a real kindness, by showing the authorities that we don't need a mint, and don't want one. And as to that Capital, we'll move it up to Storey, where it belongs."

So spake the Virginian. I listened as one having no taxable property and never likely to have; as one being out of office and willing to stay out; as one having no tangible right to take an interest in the Constitution, and consequently not caring a straw whether it carried or not. The man spoke words of wisdom, though. I am aware that the capital could have been removed last session, and from the complexion of the new Territorial Assembly, I suppose it can be done this year. Notwithstanding these things though, and notwithstanding I am a free white male citizen of Storey county, I conjecture that I have a right to my private opinion that Carson is the proper place for the seat of Government and it ought to remain here so long as I don't try to make capital out of that opinion. Nobody has a right to arrest me for being disorderly on such ground as that.

BAGGAGE

Dan, will you send my baggage down here, or have I got to go on borrowing clothes from Pete Hopkins through all eternity?

YOUNG GILLESPIE

Young Gillespie is down here in my employ. On a small salary. I have got him figuring with the Legislators for extra compensation for the reporters.

THE LEGISLATURE

The Territorial Legislature will meet here next Tuesday at noon. The rooms used last year in the county buildings, have been let by the County Commissioners for the use of the two Houses, at $500 for the session of forty days, payable in greenbacks. The halls are now being fitted up, and will be ready at the proper time.

HOUSE-WARMING

All Carson went out to warm Theodore Winters' new house, in Washoe Valley, on Friday evening, and had a pleasant time of it. The house and its furniture together, cost $50,000.

WARREN ENGINE COMPANY

The Warren boys brought out their superb machine for practice yesterday. She threw a heavy stream entirely over the tall flag-staff in the Plaza.

RELIGIOUS

Religious matters are booming along in Carson. Mrs. Wiley, who is an unusually talented vocalist, has been requested to give a concert for the benefit of my old regular chronic brick church, and will probably do so shortly.

THE SQUAIRES TRIAL

A jury has finally been empaneled in this murder case, or manslaughter case, or justifiable homicide, or whatever it is, and the trial set for to-morrow.

MARSH CHILDREN

Concerning the Marsh troupe, R. G. Marsh sends the following note to Major Dallam, of the *Independent:*

"—Please insert enclosed corrected advertisement, and make such flourish and announcement as your local feeling will admit of, consistent with a kleer konshuns.

Yours till we meat and drink."

The Company will appear at the Carson Theatre on Monday, Tuesday and Wednesday evenings of the present week. Billy O'Neil comes along, too.

ARTEMUS

I received a letter from Artemus Ward, to-day, dated "Austin, January 1." It has been sloshing around between Virginia and Carson for awhile. I hope there is no impropriety in publishing extracts from a private letter—if there be, I ought not to copy the following paragraph of his:

"I arrived here yesterday morning at 2 o'clock. It is a wild, untamable place, but full of lion-hearted boys. I speak tonight. See small bills. * * * I hope, some time, to see you and Kettle-belly Brown in New York. My grandmother—my sweet grandmother—she, thank God, is too far advanced in life to be affected by your hellish wiles. My aunt—she might fall. But didn't Warren fall, at Bunker Hill? [The old woman's safe. And so is the old girl, for that matter.—MARK.] Do not sir, do not, sir, do not flatter yourself that you are the only chastely-humorous writer onto the Pacific slopes. * * * I shall always remember Virginia as a bright spot in my existence, and all others must or rather cannot be, 'as it were.' "

I am glad that old basket-covered jug holds out. I don't know that it does, but I have an impression that way. At least I can't make anything out of that last sentence. But I wish him well, and a safe journey, drunk or sober.

MARK TWAIN

22.

Legislative Proceedings
Carson City, January 12, 1864

☞ For a discussion of Mark Twain's work in reporting the third Territorial Legislature (January 12—February 20, 1864) see "Sam Clemens and Mark Twain" and "Political Reporting" in Part One.

HOUSE OF REPRESENTATIVES,
CARSON, 11 A.M., *January 12, 1864.*

THE Constitution pot boils. Gentlemen from the different sections of the Territory—visiting brethren of the Legislature—agree in the opinion that the Constitution will carry by a very respectable vote on the 19th. This will have its effect upon Ormsby county, which, strangely enough, considering the advantages she would derive from having the Capital permanently located at Carson, a mint built here, and the number of resident officials increased, has heretofore been opposed to the establishment of a State Government.

And speaking of the mint, I have an item of news relating to that subject. Mr. Lockhart, the Indian Agent, has just received a letter from Commissioner Bennet, in which he says he has been informed by Secretary Chase that no further steps will be taken toward building a mint in this region until our *State Representatives* arrive in Washington! This is in consequence of efforts now being made by Mr. Conness to have the mint located at Virginia. The authorities want advice from representatives direct from the people. As I said before, the people of Ormsby will oppose the Constitution.

O, certainly they will! They will if they are sick—or sentimental—or consumptive—or don't know their own interests—or can't see when God Almighty smiles upon them, and don't care anyhow. Now if Ormsby votes against the Constitution, let us clothe ourselves in sackcloth and put ashes on our heads; for in that hour religious liberty will be at an end here—her next step will be to vote against her eternal salvation. However the anti-Constitutional sentiment here is growing weak in the knees.

Most of the members have arrived, and the wheels of government will begin to churn at 12 M.

MARK TWAIN

23.

Legislative Proceedings
Carson City, January 13, 1864

☞ R. G. Marsh's Juvenile Comedians, composed of girls and boys six to sixteen years of age, toured the West Coast in 1860 and again in the winter of 1863–1864. "The performances of this juvenile troupe were a saccharine variation of the new theatrical modes; the repertoire was made up of farces, fairy extravaganzas, sensation plays, and burlesque."[1] *The Toodles,* adapted by William E. Burton from "an old sentimental piece called The Broken Heart, or, The Farmer's Daughter," had been first performed at Burton's Chambers Street Theatre in New York on October 2, 1848. The role of Timothy Toodles became one of Burton's "undying successes."[2] The Marsh troupe had played *The Toodles* at Laura Keene's Varieties in New York in 1857.[3] *The Limerick Boy* was a favorite on the New York stage in the early 1860's, and William M. ("Billy") O'Neil was a celebrated actor in Irish farces.[4]

BEFORE the Legislature begins its labors, I will just mention that the Marsh Troupe will perform in Virginia to-morrow night (Thursday)—at the Opera House of course—for the benefit of Engine Company No. 2. They played here last night—"Toodles," you know. Young George Marsh—whose theatrical costumes are ungainly enough, but not funny—took the part of Toodles, and performed it well—performed it as only cultivated talent, or genius, or which you please, or both, could enable him to do it. Little

Jenny Arnot (she with the hideous—I mean affected—voice) appeared as Mrs. Toodles. Jenny is pretty—very pretty; but by the usual sign, common to all those of her sex similarly gifted, I perceive she knows it. Therefore, let us not speak of it. Jenny is smart—but she knows that too, and I grant you it is natural that she should. And behold you, when she does forget herself and make use of her own natural voice, and drop her borrowed one, it is the pleasantest thing in life to see her play. The other ladies—however, I neglected to preserve a theatre bill, and I do not know what characters they personified. However, one was a handsome sailor boy, and the other was a lovely, confiding girl with auburn hair—the same being stuck after each other. Alexander was gotten up in considerable taste as a ratty old gentleman—the father of one of the stuck—the auburn one, I think. Beatty was one of those dear reformed pirates, who comes in at the finale with a bandaged head and a broken heart, and leans up against the side-scenes and slobbers over his past sins, and is *so* interesting. Billy O'Neil was so successful in keeping the house in a roar as the Limerick Boy, and especially as the Irish Schoolmaster, that he was frequently driven from his own masterly gravity. After the performance was over, he said, "Those girls on the front seats knew where the laugh came in, didn't they?" I said they did. I further observed that if there was any place where the laugh didn't come in, those girls on the front seats didn't know it. Wherefore, if so, he had them there. My head was level. I think I am not transcending the limits of truth, when I assert that my head was eminently level. I would not flatter Billy O'Neil, yet I cannot help thinking that as "Barney the Baron," night before last, he was the drunkest white man that ever crossed the mountains. George Boulden, assisted by Mr. Alexander, sang "When this Cruel War is Over, as it Were," and was thrice encored.

A circumstance happened to an acquaintance of mine this week, which I promised to say nothing about. A young man from one of the neighboring counties, took a good deal of silk dress, with a moderate amount of girl in it, home from the theatre, and on his way back to his constituents he jammed his leg into a suburban post-hole, and remained anchored out there in the dark until considerably after midnight. He wept, and he prayed, and he cussed. He continued to cuss. He cussed himself, and the Board of Aldermen, and the County Commissioners. He even cussed his own relations, and more particularly his grandmother, which was innocent. It seemed a good deal mixed as to whether he was ever going to get loose or not; but the coyotes got to skirmishing around him and grabbing at his independent leg, and made him uncommon lively. Whereat, he put on his strength, and tugged and cussed, and kicked at the coyotes, and cussed again, and tugged, and finally, out he came—but he pulled the post-hole up by the roots in doing of it. It was funny—exceedingly funny. However, I don't mind it; I slept all the same, and just as well.

I have received that carpet-sack of mine at last. It contained two shirts and six empty champagne bottles. Also one garrote collar, with a note from Dan written on it in pencil, accounting for the bottles under the plea that "voluminous baggage maketh a man to be respected." It was an airy and graceful thought, and a credit to his great mind. The shirts were marked respectively "R. M. Daggett" and "Sandy Baldwin," from which I perceive that Dan has been foraging again.

We organized yesterday. "We" is the House of Representatives, you understand. Simmons will make a good Speaker; and, besides, I shall be near by to volunteer a little of my Third House experience, occasionally. The Council did not expend half an hour in getting very thoroughly and permanently organized. The regular joint committees were appointed to wait on the Governor, and that Body will be produced in Court this morning to testify concerning the condition of the country. N.B.—The several departments of the law-making power are called Bodies. The Governor is one of them, by law—therefore it is disrespectful to speak of him otherwise than as a Body—a jolly, unctuous, oleaginous old Body. That's it. I do not consider that we are entirely organized yet, either. You see, we are entitled to a Chaplain. The Organic Act vouchsafes unto us the consolations of religion—payable in Greenbacks at three dollars a day. We roped in the Rev. Mr. White, yesterday, and gouged him out of a prayer, for which, of course, we never intend to pay him. We go in for ministers looking to Providence in little matters of this kind. Well, there is no harm in us, and we calculate to run this institution without a Chaplain. In accordance with a motion of Mr. Nightingill, we dispensed with the services of Chaplain in the

Third House, and it is a matter of no little pride to me to observe that this Aggregation of Wisdom manifests a disposition, not only in this but in many other respects, to send Jefferson's Manual and the Organic Act to the d——l and take the published proceedings of that Body as its parliamentary gospel—its guide to temporal glory and ultimate salvation.

The House will proceed to business now in a few minutes.

MARK TWAIN

24.

Letter from Mark Twain
Carson City, January 14, 1864

☞ Miss Hannah K. Clapp's residence, which in 1863 was situated on the southwest corner of Proctor and Nevada streets,[1] may possibly have housed the Sierra Seminary also. At this time Carson City had one public school (conducted by "Misses Hart and Mulligan"[2]) and two private schools—Miss Clapp's, and William B. Lawlor's, which Mark Twain describes in section 27, below, as the best school in the Territory.

MISS CLAPP'S SCHOOL

By authority of an invitation from Hon. Wm. M. Gillespie, member of the House Committee on Colleges and Common Schools, I accompanied that statesman on an unofficial visit to the excellent school of Miss Clapp and Mrs. Cutler, this afternoon. The air was soft and balmy—the sky was cloudless and serene—the odor of flowers floated upon the idle breeze—the glory of the sun descended like a benediction upon mountain and meadow and plain— the wind blew like the very devil, and the day was generally disagreeable.

The school— however, I will mention first that a charter for an educational institution to be called the Sierra Seminary, was granted to Miss Clapp during the Legislative session of 1861, and a bill will be introduced while the present Assembly is in session, asking an appropriation of $20,000 to aid the enterprise. Such a sum of money could not be more judiciously expended, and I doubt not the bill will pass.

The present school is a credit both to the teachers and the town. It now numbers about forty pupils, I should think, and is well and systematically conducted. The exercises this afternoon were of a character not likely to be unfamiliar to the free American citizen who has a fair recollection of how he used to pass his Friday afternoons in the days of his youth. The tactics have undergone some changes, but these variations are not important. In former times a fellow took his place in the luminous spelling class in the full consciousness that if he spelled cat with a "k," or indulged in any other little orthographical eccentricities of a similar nature, he would be degraded to the foot or sent to his seat; whereas, he keeps his place in the ranks now, in such cases, and his punishment is simply to " 'bout face." Johnny Eaves stuck to his first position, to-day, long after the balance of the class had rounded to, but he subsequently succumbed to the word "nape," which he persisted in ravishing of its final vowel. There was nothing irregular about that. Your rightly constructed schoolboy will spell a multitude of hard words without hesitating once, and then lose his grip and miss fire on the easiest one in the book.

The fashion of reading selections of prose and poetry remains the same; and so does the youthful manner of doing that sort of thing. Some pupils read poetry with graceful ease and correct expression, and others place the rising and falling inflection at measured intervals, as if they had learned the lesson on a "see-saw"; but then they go undulating through a stanza with such an air of unctuous satisfaction, that it is a comfort to be around when they are at it.

> "The boy—stoo–dawn—the bur—ning deck—
> When–sawl—but *him* had fled—
> The flames—that shook—the battle—zreck—
> Shone round—him *o'er*—the dead."

That is the old-fashioned *impressive* style—stately, slow-moving and solemn. It is in vogue yet among scholars of tender age. It always will be. Ever since Mrs. Hemans wrote that verse, it has suited the pleasure of juveniles to emphasize the word "him," and lay atrocious stress upon that other word "o'er," whether she liked it or not; and I am prepared to believe that they will continue this practice unto the end of time, and with the same indifference to Mrs. Hemans' opinions about it, or any body's else.

They sing in school, now-a-days, which is an improvement upon the ancient regime; and they don't catch flies and throw spit-balls at the teacher, as they used to do in my time—which is another improvement, in a general way. Neither do the boys and girls keep a sharp look-out on each other's shortcomings and report the same at headquarters, as was a custom of by-gone centuries. And this reminds me of Gov. Nye's last anecdote, fulminated since the delivery of his message, and consequently not to be found in that document. The company were swapping old school reminiscences, and in due season they got to talking about that extinct species of tell-tales that were once to be found in all minor educational establishments, and who never failed to detect and impartially denounce every infraction of the rules that occurred among their mates. The Governor said that he threw a casual glance at a pretty girl on the next bench one day, and she complained to the teacher—which was entirely characteristic, you know. Says she, "Mister Jones, Warren Nye's looking at me." Whereupon, without a suggestion from anybody, up jumped an infamous, lisping, tow-headed young miscreant, and says he, "Yeth, thir, I *thee* him do it!" I doubt if the old original boy got off that ejaculation with more gusto than the Governor throws into it.

The "compositions" read to-day were as exactly like the compositions I used to hear read in our school as one baby's nose is exactly like all other babies' noses. I mean the old principal earmarks were all there: the cutting to the bone of the subject with the very first gash, without any preliminary foolishness in the way of a gorgeous introductory; the inevitable and persevering tautology; the brief, monosyllabic sentences (beginning, as a very general thing, with the pronoun "I"); the penchant for presenting rigid, uncompromising facts for the consideration of the hearer, rather than ornamental fancies; the depending for the success of the composition upon its general merits, without tacking artificial aids to the end of it, in the shape of deductions or conclusions, or clap-trap climaxes, albeit their absence sometimes imparts to these essays the semblance of having come to an end before they were finished—of arriving at full speed at a jumping-off place and going

suddenly overboard, as it were, leaving a sensation such as one feels
when he stumbles without previous warning upon that infernal
"To be Continued" in the midst of a thrilling magazine story. I
know there are other styles of school compositions, but these are
the characteristics of the style which I have in my eye at present.
I do not know why this one has particularly suggested itself to my
mind, unless the literary effort of one of the boys there to-day left
with me an unusually vivid impression. It ran something in this
wise:

COMPOSITION

"I like horses. Where we lived before we came here, we used to
have a cutter and horses. We used to ride in it. I like winter. I like
snow. I used to have a pony all to myself, where I used to live
before I came here. Once it drifted a good deal—very deep—and
when it stopped I went out and got in it."

That was all. There was no climax to it, except the spasmodic
bow which the tautological little student jerked at the school as
he closed his labors.

Two remarkably good compositions were read. Miss P.'s was
much the best of these—but aside from its marked literary excellence, it possessed another merit which was peculiarly gratifying
to my feelings just at that time. Because it took the conceit out of
young Gillespie as completely as perspiration takes the starch out
of a shirt-collar. In his insufferable vanity, that feeble member of
the House of Representatives had been assuming imposing attitudes, and beaming upon the pupils with an expression of be-
nignant imbecility which was calculated to inspire them with the
conviction that there was only one guest of any consequence in the
house. Therefore, it was an unspeakable relief to me to see him
forced to shed his dignity. Concerning the composition, however.
After detailing the countless pleasures which had fallen to her lot
during the holidays, the authoress finished with a proviso, in substance as follows—I have forgotten the precise language: "But I
have no cheerful reminiscences of Christmas. It was dreary,
monotonous and insipid to the last degree. Mr. Gillespie called
early, and remained the greater part of the day!" You should have
seen the blooming Gillespie wilt when that literary bombshell fell
in his camp! The charm of the thing lay in the fact that the last

naive sentence was the only suggestion offered in the way of accounting for the dismal character of the occasion. However, to my mind it was sufficient—entirely sufficient.

Since writing the above, I have seen the architectural plans and specifications for Miss Clapp and Mrs. Cutler's proposed "Sierra Seminary" building. It will be a handsome two-story edifice, one hundred feet square, and will accommodate forty "boarders" and any number of pupils beside, who may board elsewhere. Constructed of wood, it will cost $12,000; or of stone, $18,000. Miss Clapp has devoted ten acres of ground to the use and benefit of the institution.

I sat down intending to write a dozen pages of variegated news. I have about accomplished the task—all except the "variegated." I have economised in the matter of current news of the day, considerably more than I purposed to do, for every item of that nature remains stored away in my mind in a very unwritten state, and will afford unnecessarily ample material for another letter. It is useless material, though, I suspect, because, inasmuch as I have failed to incorporate it into this, I fear I shall not feel industrious enough to weave out of it another letter until it has become too stale to be interesting. Well, never mind—we must learn to take an absorbing delight in educational gossip; nine-tenths of the revenues of the Territory go into the bottomless gullet of that ravenous school fund, you must bear in mind.   Mark Twain

25.

Legislative Proceedings
Carson City, January 14–27, 1864

☞ The reader should be reminded that the dispatches reprinted here were the joint responsibility of Mark Twain and Clement T. Rice of the *Daily Union;* but Mark Twain covered the House while his colleague covered the Council. He certainly wrote the notes included within square brackets and signed "Mark" or "Mark Twain." He very probably also wrote most if not all of the interpolated notes signed "Rep."

The selections below from the proceedings of the House consist mainly of passages which have been given flavor by Mark Twain's comments.

A letter by Mark Twain ridiculing the great number of applications for notaries' commissions was published in the *Territorial Enterprise* on February 9, 1864, and reprinted in the San Francisco *Golden Era* on February 28.[1]

The "one secesh in Lander" expelled from office by Acting Governor Orion Clemens was Probate Judge Parish B. Ladd.[2]

HOUSE—THIRD DAY

CARSON, *January 14*

Say—you have got a compositor up there who is too rotten particular, it seems to me. When I spell "devil" in my usual frank and open manner, he puts it "d——l"! Now, Lord love his conceited and accommodating soul, if I choose to use the language of the vulgar, the low-flung and the sinful, and such as will shock the ears of the highly civilized, I don't want him to appoint himself an editorial critic and proceed to tone me down and save me from the consequences of my conduct; that is, unless I pay him for it, which I won't. I expect I could spell "devil" before that fastidious cuss was born.—MARK TWAIN.]

The Speaker called the House to order at 10 A.M.

RESOLUTIONS

Mr. Heaton introduced a concurrent resolution, that when the Legislative Assembly adjourn to-morrow, it be to meet again on Wednesday, 21st, at 12 M.

A motion to suspend the rules was put to a vote and carried—ayes 15; noes, Messrs. Clagett, Curley, Gillespie, Gove, Hess, Hunter, Jones and Trask.

Mr. Gillespie moved to amend by making the hour 1 P.M.

[More skirmishing about parliamentary usage—but the Chair is not in fault.—REPORTER.]

Mr. Fisher offered an amendment, to read "the House of Representatives and Council concurring." [Mr. Fisher got his notion from—well—say inspiration, for instance.—REPORTER.]

Mr. Clagett finally got up and straightened the blasted resolution.

The Speaker made a suggestion concerning the wording of the document. [Half an hour more will get it all right, you know. The parliamentary skirmishing still goes on, with unabated intelligence. This Aggregation of Wisdom *can* frame a concurrent resolution, but we must have time—we must have a reasonable length of time to do it in. I could have furnished all the amendments offered to this document, and all the transmogrifications it has passed through—but then you don't want a column of that kind of information. I don't consider it important.—REP.]

The resolution as infinitely amended and improved, was voted upon at last, and carried—ayes 18, noes 5—Messrs. Clagett, Gillespie, Gove, Hunter and Phillips. [I asked the Clerk what the resolution proposed to do now? And he said he'd be d——d if he knew.—REP.]

Mr. Clagett offered a resolution that the regular daily sessions of the House commence at 10 A.M.

Mr. Fisher moved to insert "except when otherwise ordered."

On a division the motion was lost—14 to 6.

The resolution was then adopted.

HOUSE—FOURTH DAY

CARSON, *January 15*

[The Committee on Rules for the Government of the House, reported yesterday the good old-fashioned and entirely proper rule that members and officers should keep their seats at adjournment until the Speaker had declared the House adjourned and left the Chair. Well, sir, the House debated it and voted it down. I can prove it by the Clerk's Journal. Now, considering that it was a harmless measure, and a customary one, and a mark of respect to the Chair; and considering that it is very seldom enforced, and also, that it was a little disrespectful to the Chair to vote it down, the action of the House in the matter seems somewhat strained. But I will interrupt you just here, if you please, and suggest to you that it is none of your business, and I want to know what you are putting in *your* lip about it for? I expect we can attend to our own affairs. And didn't they bullyrag that concurrent resolution yesterday? I reckon not. I do not admire the taste of the lobby members, though, in letting on as if they knew so much more about it, when the House is being rent with the mortal agonies of an effort to adjourn itself over for a week without adjourning the Council at the same time. The House did not wish to adjourn the Council without being asked to do so by that body, and if the House found it very nearly impossible to word the resolution so as not to adjourn the Council aforesaid, I do not conceive that it was dignified on the part of the lobby members to express by their countenances that they had their own opinions concerning the House. But didn't the House worry that concurrent resolution for a few hours or so? You bet you. However, we had better let "parliamentary usage" alone for the present, until our former knowledge on the knotty subject returns to our memories. Because Providence is not going to put up with this sort of thing much longer, you know. I observe there is no lightning rod on these county buildings.—MARK TWAIN.]

HOUSE—NINTH DAY
Afternoon Session

CARSON, *January 20*

Mr. Dean offered a resolution to employ a copying clerk.

Mr. Gillespie offered an amendment requiring the Engrossing and Enrolling Clerks to do this proposed officer's work. [These two officers are strictly ornamental—have been under wages since the first day of the session—haven't had anything to do, and won't for two weeks yet—and now by the eternal, they want some more useless clerical jewelry to dangle to the Legislature. If the House would discharge its extra scribblers, and let the Chief Clerk hire assistance only when he wants it, it seems to me it would be better. —REP.]

Without considering the appointment of a new jimcrack ornament, and starting his pay six weeks before he goes to work (only thirteen dollars a day), the House adjourned.

HOUSE—TENTH DAY

CARSON, *January 21*

An officer of the House—Charles Carter, Messenger—is lying at the point of death this morning. He ruptured a blood vessel of the brain, night before last, previous to which time he was in robust health. He was a youth of great promise, and was respected and esteemed by all who knew him. He held the position of Messenger of the House during the session of 1862, and his faithful attention to the duties of the office then was endorsed by his re-election the present session.

The chief portion of the population of Carson spent last night in feasting and dancing at the Warm Springs. Such of them as are out of bed at this hour, declare the occasion to have been one of unmitigated felicity.

The House met at 10 A.M.

LEAVE OF ABSENCE

Mr. Calder asked and obtained leave for one day for Mr. Clagett who was engaged in drafting a bill.

QUESTION OF PRIVILEGE

Mr. Stewart rose to a question of privilege, and said the ENTERPRISE and *Union* reporters had been moving Ellen Redman's toll-bridge from its proper position on the Carson Slough to an illegal one on the Humboldt Slough. [I did that. If Ellen Redman don't like it, I can move her little bridge back again—but under protest. I waded that Humboldt Slough once, and I have always had a hankering to see a bridge over it since.—MARK.]

HOUSE—TENTH DAY

Carson, *January 21*

. . . . . .

Mr. Phillips moved to amend Mr. Gillespie's resolution by striking out that portion which puts the Enrolling and Engrossing Clerks under the sole control of the Chief Clerk. Lost.

A warm debate sprung up on the subject. Mr. Gillespie manfully contended for the justness and expediency of adopting his resolution, and stated several propositions which were eminently correct, to-wit: that these subordinate officers ought to be under the control of the Chief Clerk; that they were under the pay of the House, and had been for some time, and yet had nothing to do; and finally, that copying being within the scope of their duties, they ought to be put at it and afforded an opportunity of rendering an equivalent for their salaries. Messrs. Stewart, Dixson and others were very fearful of discommoding the subordinate clerks, and very anxious to embellish the House with some more fellows calculated to swing a sinecure gracefully. The Chief Clerk stated that Mr. Powell, the

Enrolling Clerk, had labored assiduously, from the first, in rendering any and all assistance asked at his hands, but nobody coming forward to say how much Captain Murphy had done, and nobody being supplied with a pile of estimates [sufficient] to portray how much he hadn't done, it became the general impression that Captain Murphy had been considerably more ornamental than useful to the House of Representatives. But I am here only during the courtesy of the House—on my good behavior, as it were—and I am a little afraid that if I say this aggregation of Wisdom elected Captain Murphy more out of regard for his military services than respect for the nasty manner in which he can sling a pen, I shall get notice to quit.—MARK.

Mr. Gillespie, on leave, amended his resolution by adding "Provided said clerks shall not be interfered with in the discharge of their respective duties"—and had the resolution not been furnished with this loophole—if it had not been thus emasculated, it would not have passed. By a scratch it carried, though, and here are the voters' names:

AYES—Messrs. Calder, Elliott, Gillespie, Gove, Hess, Hunter, McDonald, Nelson, Requa, Trask, Ungar, Speaker—12.

NOES—Messrs. Barclay, Curler, Dean, Dixson, Fisher, Heaton, Jones, Phillips, Stewart, Tennant—10.

HOUSE—SIXTEENTH DAY

CARSON CITY, *January 27*

GENERAL ORDERS

The House resolved itself into Committee of the Whole, Mr. Fisher in the chair, upon the unfinished business of the general orders, and occupied the remainder of the forenoon session in the consideration of the Act providing for the appointment of Notaries Public and defining their duties. [This is a most important bill, and if passed will secure clearer and more comprehensible records hereafter. It will leave Storey county twelve Notaries in place of the fifteen hundred we have at present, and these twelve will have to be men of solid reputation, since they will have to give heavier bonds than all the fifteen hundred combined do at present; they must give bail in the sum of $5,000 each—$60,000 altogether. Mr. Fisher said three would be sufficient for Douglas county—he didn't want *all* the property there tied up in Notary's bonds. Mr. Clagett said there was scarcely a valid deed on the Humboldt records, because the certificates attached to them by ignorant Notaries were worthless, and he supposed property worth millions had already been jeopardized in the Territory by this kind of officers. He said one really splendid ignoramus out there who forwarded a bond in the sum of $10, had it returned with a notification that it must be increased to $500; he couldn't straddle the blind, and had to give up his commission. Besides, Mr. Clagett said, the passage of this Act would oust from office some twenty-five rabid Secessionists in Humboldt county alone! [Sensation.] If you could just see the official bonds drawn up and sent to the office of the Secretary of the Territory by some of these mentally deaf, dumb and blind Notaries, you would wonder, as I do, what they have been and gone and done, that Heaven should be down on them so. They never use revenue stamps—they don't subscribe the oath, they—well, they don't do anything that could lay them liable to an accusation of knowing it all, or even any fraction of it.

[Mr. Tennant said some few secesh had been appointed in Lander, but not so many as in Humboldt—they found one secesh in Lander last spring, and Acting-Governor Clemens captured him. I send you a copy of the bill, as they have just finished amending it in the Committee of the Whole, and suggest that you publish it.—MARK.]

26.

Legislative Proceedings

Carson City, January 28, 1864

☞ It will be recalled that Mark Twain had been chosen to deliver the Governor's Message to the Third House of the Constitutional Convention on December 11, 1863.[1] When the time drew near for the meeting of this burlesque assembly during the third Territorial Legislature, two trustees of the First Presbyterian Church of Carson addressed a public letter to him asking that the affair might be turned to the benefit of the Church "by charging toll-road franchises, and other persons, a dollar apiece for the privilege of listening to your communication." Mark Twain gave his consent in a letter that was also made public. He wrote:

"... although I am not a very dusty Christian myself, I take an absorbing interest in religious affairs, and would willingly inflict my annual message upon the church itself if it might derive benefit thereby."² The address was delivered on January 27, 1864, in the district courtroom of the Ormsby County Courthouse.³

The text of this address is unfortunately not extant. In fact, it may never have been published. Writing to his sister Pamela on March 18, 1864, Mark Twain encloses a photograph of "his Excellency Gov. Mark Twain, of the Third House, Hon. Wm. H. Clagett of the House of Representatives, and Hon. A. J. Simmons, Speaker of the same," but adds:

> I can't send you my Message. It was written to be *spoken*—to write it so that it would *read* well, would be too much trouble, & I shall probably never publish it. It was terribly severe on Gov. Nye, too, & since he has conferred on me one of the coveted Notarial appointments (without the formality of a *petition* from the people), it would be a mean return to print it now. If he had refused the appointment, though, I'd have delivered it in Virginia (I could have got the whole community at a dollar a head), & published it afterward.

Mark Twain goes on to describe the occasion—then almost two months in the past:

> I got my satisfaction out of it, though—a larger audience than Artemus had—the comfort of knowing that the slow-going, careless population of Carson *could* be induced to fill a house *once*,—the gratification of hearing good judges say it was the best thing of the kind they had ever listened to—& finally, a present of [a] handsome $225.00 gold watch, from Theodore Winters & Hon. A. W. Baldwin, inscribed 'To Gov. Mark Twain,' &c. &c. I am ahead on the Message, anyhow.⁴

"Carl" (Clement T. Rice) mentioned the speech in a letter from Carson City to the Virginia City *Daily Union* dated January 29, 1864:

> Last night a large and fashionable audience was called out to hear a message delivered by the Mark Two—otherwise called Twain. Indeed, this was the resuscitation of the celebrated Third House, or rip-snorting gymnasium, prepared for the benefit of outsiders who must orate or bust. Hal. Clayton assumed the chair, and the levities spread spontaneously. Mark Two's message only helped to keep up the effervescing spirit of the good work in behalf of that

same, ever-present, gaping skeleton of a church. The benefit on this occasion was large—perhaps $200—which will take the institution in out of the weather and hasten its completion very materially.[5]

Mark Twain's statement that he had never talked to a crowd before seems odd in view of his previous appearances before the Third House. Apparently the earlier sessions had been restricted to a few members of the Legislature or the Constitutional Convention. If the delivery of the "message" mentioned here was indeed Mark Twain's first appearance on what seemed to him a public occasion, it is noteworthy as the beginning of a long and brilliant career as a platform artist.

The speaker's pleasure in the occasion was marred by one mishap. He had invited Carrie, daughter of F. M. Pixley, one of the trustees of the church, to be his guest. She was very young, perhaps only eleven or twelve: she had worn her first long dress when Sam Clemens escorted her to the Ormsby-Wayman wedding on February 5, 1863.[6] Forty years later Carrie remembered that for the public session of the Third House she "had a wonderful dress made, and her father had bought her a lovely white fur opera cloak lined with blue satin . . ." Since Sam was not able to call for her before the performance, it was arranged he should send a hack for her. During his speech he noticed that she was not in the seat reserved for her, and made gestures of inquiry to her father, who failed to comprehend their meaning. When Clemens and Pixley drove to the Pixley house after the speech they found "Carrie with even the white opera cloak on, lying on the bed weeping. Morsiline, the colored girl that . . . always knew what to do, was making molasses candy to cheer her up." Sam had forgotten to order the hack for her. "Carrie tried and pretended to accept the apologies that Sam made, but from that day nothing could induce her to go out with him."[7]

HOUSE—SEVENTEENTH DAY

CARSON, *January 28*

I DELIVERED that message last night, but I didn't talk loud enough—people in the far end of the hall could not hear me. They said "Louder—louder," occasionally, but I thought that was a way they had—a joke, as it were. I had never talked to a crowd before, and knew none of the tactics of the public speaker. I suppose I spoke loud enough for some houses, but not for that District Court room, which is about seventy-five feet from floor to roof, and has no ceiling. I hope the people will deal as mildly with me, however, as

I did with the public officers in the annual message. Some folks heard the entire document, though—there is some comfort in that. Hon. Mr. Clagett, Speaker Simmons of the inferior House, Hon. Hal Clayton, Speaker of the Third House, Judge Haydon, Dr. Alban, and others whose opinions are entitled to weight, said they would travel several miles to hear that message again. It affords me a good deal of satisfaction to mention it. It serves to show that if the audience could have heard me distinctly, they would have appreciated the wisdom thus conferred upon them. They seemed to appreciate what they did hear though, pretty thoroughly. After the first quarter of an hour I ceased to whisper, and became audible. One of these days, when I get time, I will correct, amend and publish the message, in accordance with a resolution of the Third House ordering 300,000 copies in the various languages spoken at the present day.

P.S.—Sandy Baldwin and Theodore Winters heard that message, anyhow, and by thunder they appreciated it, too. They have sent a hundred dollars apiece to San Francisco this morning, to purchase a watch chain for His Excellency Governor Twain. I guess that is a pretty good result for an incipient oratorical slouch like me, isn't it? I don't know that anybody tendered the other Governor a testimonial of any kind. MARK TWAIN.]

27.

Letter from Mark Twain
Carson City, February 5, 1864

☞ Theodore Winters' house near Carson City attracted much attention. While it was still under construction, it was described in detail in the Virginia City *Daily Union* on October 16, 1863.[1] Since nowadays in California the term "ranch" designates a parcel of land of almost any size that is used for agricultural purposes, it is interesting that Mark Twain refers to Winters' holding of land—which had amounted to 732 acres in October—as a "farm" rather than as a "ranch." Had the Far Western usage not yet been established?

The reference to "one of our Miss Nancy 'Meriden' Prosecuting Attorneys" is obscure, but is probably an allusion to the writer who, signing himself "Meriden," had a few days before published in the Virginia City *Daily Union* a letter bitterly attacking Mark Twain.[2]

The attack on undertakers may well have been motivated by personal experience. Jennie Clemens, the eight-year-old daughter of Orion and Mollie Clemens, had died on February 1.[3]

WINTERS' NEW HOUSE

EDITORS ENTERPRISE: Theodore Winters' handsome dwelling in Washoe Valley, is an eloquent witness in behalf of Mr. Steele's architectural skill. The basement story is built of brick, and the spacious court which surrounds it, and whose columns support the verandah above, is paved with large, old-fashioned tiles. On this floor is the kitchen, dining-room, bath-room, bed-chambers for servants, and a commodious store-room, with shelves laden with all manner of substantials and luxuries for the table. All these apartments are arranged in the most convenient manner, and are fitted and furnished handsomely and plainly, but expensively. Water pipes are numerous in this part of the house, and the fluid they carry is very pure, and cold and clear. On the next floor above, are two unusually large drawing-rooms, richly furnished, and gotten up in every respect with faultless taste—which is a remark one is seldom enabled to apply to parlors and drawing-rooms on this coast. The colors in the carpets, curtains, etc., are of a warm and cheerful nature, but there is nothing gaudy about them. The ceilings are decorated with pure, white mouldings of graceful pattern. Two large bed-chambers adjoin the parlors, and are supplied with elaborately carved black walnut four-hundred-dollar bedsteads, similar to those used by Dan and myself in Virginia; the remainder of the furniture of these chambers is correspondingly sumptuous and expensive. On the floor above are half a dozen comfortable bedrooms for the accommodation of visitors; also a spacious billiard-room which will shortly be graced by a table of superb workmanship. The windows of the house are of the "Gothic" style, and set with stained glass; the chandeliers are of bronze; the stair railings of polished black walnut, and the principal doors of some kind of dark-colored wood—mahogany, I suppose. There are two peculiarly pleasant features about this house—the ceilings are high, and the halls of unusual width. The building—above the basement story—is of wood, and strongly and compactly put together. It stands upon tolerably high ground, and from its handsome verandah, Mr. Winters can see every portion of his vast farm. From the stables to the parlors, the house and its belongings is a model of comfort, convenience and substantial elegance; everything is of the best that could be had, and there is no circus flummery visible about the establishment.

I went out there to a party a short time ago, in the night, behind a pair of Cormack's fast horses, with John James. On account of losing the trail of the telegraph poles, we wandered out among the shingle machines in the Sierras, and were delayed several hours. We arrived in time, however, to take a large share in the festivities which were being indulged in by the Governor and the Supreme Court and some twenty other guests. The party was given by Messrs. Joe Winters and Pete Hopkins (at Theodore Winters' expense) as a slight testimonial of their regard for the friends they invited to be present. There was nothing to detract from the pleasure of the occasion, except Lovejoy, who detracted most of the wines and liquors from it.

AN EXCELLENT SCHOOL

I expect Mr. Lawlor keeps the best private school in the Territory—or the best school of any kind, for that matter. I attended one of his monthly examinations a week ago, or such a matter, with Mr. Clagett, and we arrived at the conclusion that one might acquire a good college education there within the space of six months. Mr. Lawlor's is a little crib of a school-house, papered from door to ceiling with black-boards adorned with impossible mathematical propositions done in white chalk. The effect is bewildering, to the stranger, but otherwise he will find the place comfortable enough. When we arrived, the teacher was talking in a rambling way upon a great many subjects, like a member of the House speaking to a point of order, and three boys were making verbatim reports of his remarks in Graham's phonographic short-hand on the walls of the school-room. These pupils had devoted half an hour to the study and practice of this accomplishment every day for the past four or five months, and the result was a proficiency usually attained only after eighteen months of application. It was amazing. Mr. Lawlor has so simplified the art of teaching in every department of instruction, that I am confident he could impart a thorough education in a short time to any individual who has as much as a spoonful of brains to work upon. It is in no spirit of extravagance that I set it down here as my serious conviction that Mr. Lawlor could even take one of our Miss Nancy "Meriden" Prosecuting Attorneys and post him up so in a month or two that he could tell his own witnesses from those of the defense in nine cases out of ten. Mind, I do not give this as an absolute certainty, but merely as an opinion of mine—and one which is open to grave doubts, too, I am willing to confess, now, when I come to think calmly and dispassionately about it. No—the truth is, the more I think of it, the more I weaken. I expect I spoke too soon—went off before I was primed, as it were. With your permission, I will take it all back. I know two or three prosecuting attorneys, and I am satisfied the foul density of their intellects would put out any intellectual candle that Mr. Lawlor could lower into them. I do not say that a Higher Power could not miraculously illuminate them. No, I only say I would rather see it first. A man always has more confidence in a thing after he has seen it, you know; at least that is the way with me. But to proceed with that school. Mr. Clagett invited one of those phonographic boys—Master Barry Ashim—to come and practice his short-hand in the House of Representatives. He accepted the invitation, and in accordance with resolutions offered by Messrs. Clagett and Stewart, he was tendered the compliment of a seat on the floor of the House during the session, and the Sergeant-at-Arms instructed to furnish him with a desk and such stationery as he might require. He has already become a reporter of no small pretensions. There is a class in Mr. Lawlor's school composed of children three months old and upwards, who know the spelling book by heart. If you ask them what the first word is, in any given lesson, they will tell you in a moment, and then go on and spell every word (thirty-five) in the lesson, without once referring to the book or making a mistake. Again, you may mention a word and they will tell you which particular lesson it is in, and what words precede it and follow it. Then, again, you may propound an abstruse grammatical enigma, and the school will solve it in chorus—will tell you what language is correct, and what isn't; and why and wherefore; and

quote rules and illustrations until you wish you hadn't said anything. Two or three doses of this kind will convince a man that
there are youngsters in this school who know everything about
grammar that can be learned, and what is just as important, can
explain what they know so that other people can understand it.
But when those fellows get to figuring, let second-rate mathemati-
cians stand from under! For behold, it is their strong suit. They
work miracles on a black-board with a piece of chalk. Witchcraft
and sleight-of-hand, and all that sort of thing is foolishness to the
facility with which they can figure a moral impossibility down to
an infallible result. They only require about a dozen figures to do
a sum which by all ordinary methods would consume a hundred
and fifty. These fellows could cypher a week on a sheet of foolscap.
They can find out anything they want to with figures, and they are
very quick about it, too. You tell them, for instance, that you were
born in such and such a place, on such and such a day of the month,
in such and such a year, and they will tell you in an instant how
old your grandmother is. I have never seen any banker's clerks who
could begin to cypher with those boys. It has been Virginia's unchristian policy to grab everything that was of any account that
ever came into the Territory—Virginia could do many a worse
thing than to grab this school and move it into the shadow of
Mount Davidson, teacher and all.

CONCERNING UNDERTAKERS

There is a system of extortion going on here which is absolutely
terrific, and I wonder the Carson *Independent* has never ventilated
the subject. There seems to be only one undertaker in the town,
and he owns the only graveyard in which it is at all high-toned
or aristocratic to be buried. Consequently, when a man loses his
wife or his child, or his mother, this undertaker makes him sweat
for it. I appeal to those whose firesides death has made desolate
during the few fatal weeks just past, if I am not speaking the truth.
Does not this undertaker take advantage of that unfortunate deli-
cacy which prevents a man from disputing an unjust bill for services rendered in burying the dead, to extort ten-fold more than his
labors are worth? I have conversed with a good many citizens on
this subject, and they all say the same thing: that they know it is

wrong that a man should be unmercifully fleeced under such circumstances, but, according to the solemn etiquette above referred to, he cannot help himself. All that sounds very absurd to me. I have a human distaste for death, as applied to myself, but I see nothing very solemn about it as applied to anybody—it is more to be dreaded than a birth or a marriage, perhaps, but it is really not as solemn a matter as either of these, when you come to take a rational, practical view of the case. Therefore I would prefer to know

that an undertaker's bill was a just one before I paid it; and I would rather see it go clear to the Supreme Court of the United States, if I could afford the luxury, than pay it if it were distinguished for its unjustness. A great many people in the world do not think as I do about these things. But I care nothing for that. The knowledge that I am right is sufficient for me. This undertaker charges a hundred and fifty dollars for a pine coffin that cost him twenty or thirty, and fifty dollars for a grave that did not cost him ten—and this at a time when his ghastly services are required at least seven times a week. I gather these facts from some of the best citizens of Carson, and I can publish their names at any moment if you want them. What Carson needs is a few more undertakers—there is vacant land enough here for a thousand cemeteries.

MARK TWAIN

28.

Legislative Proceedings
Carson City, February 8–15, 1864

☞ The eight short passages brought together here, like those grouped in section 25, are a sample of the notes interpolated by Mark Twain in the dispatches sent by him and Clement T. Rice to the *Territorial Enterprise* and the *Daily Union*. As has been indicated earlier, the editorial and typographical handling of the dispatches was not entirely consistent. Mark Twain certainly wrote the notes signed "Mark" or "Mark Twain" enclosed within brackets, and these are omitted from the text published by the *Daily Union*. He also very probably wrote the notes signed "Rep." and those left unsigned, including the one (not enclosed within brackets) at the beginning of the dispatch of February 9. Yet many of these were published by the *Union* as well as by the *Enterprise*.

The "pet bill" mentioned just after the five-o'clock adjournment on February 11 cannot be identified.

HOUSE—TWENTY-EIGHTH DAY
CARSON, *February 8, 1864*

. . . . .

THIS bill appears—to a man up a tree—to be a bill of sale of Nevada Territory to the California State Telegraph Company. They never print this kind of bills—wherefore I shall have to copy it myself for you. It flashed through the House under a suspension of the rules, before you could wink, they tell me. It provides that Mr. Watson (his other name is the California State Telegraph Company) shall have the exclusive right to connect Star, Unionville, Austin, Virginia, Gold Hill, Carson, etc., etc., with Sacramento and San Francisco, and nobody else shall be permitted to do likewise, for five years *after* this line is completed, and with a liberal length of time allowed Mr. Watson in which to get ready to begin to commence completing it. To have all the telegraph lines in the hands of one Company, makes it a little binding on newspapers and other people.—MARK.]

HOUSE—TWENTY-NINTH DAY

CARSON, *February 9*

I see you want the ayes and noes on all important measures. Long ago I got a batch of roll-calls and prepared to post the people concerning the final action of this body upon the various bills presented. But I got tired of it. I found the House too unanimous; they always voted aye, and I discovered that the list of noes was a useless incumbrance to the roll-call. Now when an important measure passes this House, and I neglect the roll-call, that need be no excuse for your doing the same thing; just publish the list of members and say they voted "aye"—you'll be about right. The thing is done thus: When a bill is on its final passage, and a member hears his name called, he rouses up and asks what's going on? The Speaker says, by way of information, "Third reading of a bill, sir." The member says, "Oh!—well, I vote aye," and becomes torpid again at once. Now, concerning that infamous telegraph monstrosity, it passed to its third reading in this House on the 4th of February. Messrs. Babcock, Dixson, Gray and Stewart were absent, and had no opportunity of voting aye—but all the balance voted affirmatively, of course, as follows:

AYES—Messrs. Barclay, Brumfield, Calder, Clagett, Curler, Deane, Elliott, Fisher, Gillespie, Gove, Heaton, Hess, Hunter, Jones, McDonald, Nelson, Phillips, Requa, Tennant, Trask, Ungar and Mr. Speaker.

NOES—None.

HOUSE—TUESDAY AFTERNOON

CARSON, *February 10*

The House then went into Committee of the Whole on the special order—Mr. Fisher in the Chair—and took up the first bill on the list. [Some seventy-five ladies have swarmed into the House, and the process of swarming still continues. I have a presentiment that I am to have an exhaustless stream of weak platitudes inflicted upon me by Young Gillespie and other unmarried members.—MARK.]   .   .   .   .   .   .

HOUSE—THIRTY-FIRST DAY

CARSON, *February 11*

The House met at 10 A.M. Present, 18. Absent, Messrs. Clagett, Dixson, Gillespie, Phillips, Stewart and Ungar.

QUESTIONS OF PRIVILEGE

Mr. Heaton rose to a question of privilege, and said he was reported in the ENTERPRISE as having moved that the Committee of the Whole recommend the rejection of Miss Clapp's Seminary bill. That was a mistake. He said his motion was to refer the bill back to the Standing Committee on Colleges and Common Schools. [I suppose that is true; I do not consider myself responsible for mistakes made when the House is full of beautiful women, who are writing tender notes to me all the time and expecting me to answer them. In cases of this kind, I would just as soon misrepresent a member as any other way.—MARK] Mr. Heaton was easy on the reporters, but he was very severe on Mr. Gillespie. He said it would appear from the report that Mr. Gillespie included him among those members who had dodged the issue on the telegraph bill—whereas he was absent from the House, by permission of the Speaker, with the Prison Committee.

The Speaker said there was nothing incorrect about the report—that Mr. Heaton was shielded from Mr. Gillespie's insinuation by a preceding paragraph, which stated the fact that he had been excused from attendance.

Whereupon Jefferson's Manual arose—the same being known on the credit accounts of the several saloons as "Young Gillespie"—and proceeded to waste the time of the House, as usual, in dilating upon some trivial distinction without a difference. [He was after the reporter of the ENTERPRISE, in the first place, but before I could catch his drift, he fell a victim to his old regular "parliamentary usage" dysentery,—passed his brains, and became a smiling, sociable, driveling lunatic. Consequently, I failed to find out what I had been doing to young Gillespie, after all.—MARK TWAIN.]

HOUSE—AFTERNOON SESSION
MESSAGE

A message was received from the Council, transmitting the following bills:

Council bill incorporating the Austin Christian Association. [The Speaker was at a loss to know what committee to refer a bill of such an unusual nature to—wherein his head was level. He finally referred it to the Lander delegation, two of the most faithful and consistent supporters of the Devil there are in the House.—MARK.]

Council bill for the relief of certain parties. Referred to the Committee on Claims.

At 5 P.M. the House adjourned until 6:30 P.M.

[While I was absent a moment, yesterday, on important business, taking a drink, the House, with its accustomed engaging unanimity, knocked one of my pet bills higher than a kite, without a dissenting voice. I convened the members in extra session last night, and deluged them with blasphemy, after which I entered into a solemn compact with them, whereby, in consideration of their re-instating my bill, I was to make an ample apology for all the mean things I had said about them for passing that infamous, unchristian, infernal telegraph bill the other day. I also promised to apologize for all the mean things that other people had published against them for their depraved action aforesaid. They re-instated my pet to-day, unanimously, thus fulfilling their contract to the letter, and in conformity with my promise above referred to, I hereby solemnly apologize for their rascally conduct in passing the infamous telegraph bill above mentioned. Under ordinary circumstances, they never would have done such a thing—but upon that occasion I think they had been fraternizing with Clagett and Simmons at the White House, and were under the vicious influence of Humboldt whisky. Consequently, they were not responsible, Sir—they were not responsible, either to anybody on earth or in heaven.—MARK TWAIN.]

HOUSE—FRIDAY AFTERNOON
CARSON, *February 12*

. . . . . .

An Act to amend an Act relating to game and fish. The passage of this bill was also recommended. [It provides that trout shall neither be caught in this Territory, nor exposed for sale, between the first of January and the first of April, under a penalty of $25 for each fish caught, killed or destroyed, or bought, sold or exposed for sale. The Act goes into effect on the first of the coming March, and therefore it would be well to publish it for the information of the people. It is a good law, and calls our lake by its right name—Lake Bigler—and rejects the spooney appellation of "Tahoe," which signifieth "grasshopper" in the Digger tongue, and "breechclout" in the Washoe lingo. Bigler is the legitimate name of the Lake, and it will be retained until some name less flat, insipid and spooney than "Tahoe" is invented for it. I am sorry, myself, that it was not called in the first place by some cognomen that could be persuaded to rhyme with something, because, you see, every sentimental cuss who goes up there and becomes pregnant with a poem invariably miscarries because of the unfortunate difficulty I have just mentioned. I speak of the matter lightly, but it is not a frivolous one, for all that. A very beautiful thing was once written by a distinguished English poet about our royal river at home, but the loveliness was all mashed out of it by the stress of weather to which he was obliged to succumb in order to gouge a rhyme out of its name. He had to call it "Mississip"!—MARK.]

HOUSE—SATURDAY AFTERNOON
CARSON, *February 13*

. . . . . .

An Act to incorporate the Virginia, Gold Hill, Washoe and Carson railroad.

[More railroads, you observe. The Council killed the Virginia and Dayton Railroad bill the other day. That franchise was well guarded, and the road would have been built. Will this, or any of the others?—REP.]

Mr. Barclay moved to lay the bill on the table. Lost.

The bill then passed by the following vote: [ayes 11, noes 9].

HOUSE—THIRTY-FIFTH DAY
CARSON, *February 15*

[At one o'clock this morning, as Mr. Gray, barkeeper at Bingham's, was leaving the saloon with his cash box in his hand, two men jumped out from the shadow of a door, enveloped him in a blanket, and seized the box. Gray held on to the property until the handle came off, and then, having no pistol, shouted with good enough effect to attract the attention of two foot passengers who had. These gentlemen opened a brisk fire on the retreating highwaymen—sent eight or ten navy balls after them—caused them to observe, plaintively, "O God!" and drop the box. All the dogs in town woke up and barked—they always do on such occasions, but they never bite, and they are opposed to chasing highwaymen—so the same escaped. Mr. Gray recovered the box, of course, which contained about one thousand dollars.—MARK.]

. . . . . .

[You have got a mighty responsible delegation here from Storey county. As Mr. Curler remarked the other day, "When you put your finger on that delegation, as a general thing, they ain't there." I believe you. In the face of a notice given last Saturday by Mr. Clagett, of the introduction of a little bill to remove the Capital to Virginia—in the face of it, I say, only one member from Storey, out of eight, was present when the proper time arrived this morning for the introduction of the bill. Mr. Elliott was present—he always is, for that matter, and always awake. It has been a good thing for the whole Territory, on more than one occasion, that he was at his post in this House. One member was present—seven were absent: Messrs. Gillespie, Heaton, Nelson, Phillips, Requa, Ungar and Barclay. Several of these gentlemen arrived an hour after the order for the introduction of bills had been passed. Now if the people of Storey do not want the Capital, it was the duty of these members, since they knew the question was before the House, to be on hand to use their best efforts to kill the bill—and if the people do want the Capital, then it was the duty of those members to be here and do what they could toward securing it. Above all things, they had no business to be absent at such a time. They knew what was going on, and they knew, moreover, that the fact that they have been pretty regular in their attendance when toll-roads were to be voted on, will indifferently palliate the offense of being absent upon this occasion. Last session Storey offered an immense price for the capital, and nothing in the world could have kept her from getting it but her own delegation. They kept her from it, though. Mr. Burke was absent. His vote, at the proper time, would have moved the Capital—and in the meantime, Mr. Tuttle, of Douglas, was brought from a sick bed to vote no. I suppose this bill will be introduced to-morrow (Tuesday) morning, at 10 o'clock—and I suppose some of the Storey delegation will be absent again. But if you want the roll-call to-morrow, you can have it. I have made a mistake. Mr. Gillespie came in this morning before the introduction of bills, though he was absent at an earlier hour, when the roll was called.— MARK.]

29.

Letter from Mark Twain
Carson City, February 13, 1864

☞ The peculiar violence of this attack on the Carson *Independent* shows that criticism of Mark Twain's Empire City massacre hoax more than a year earlier still rankled in him (see the headnote to §12).

The *Independent* was apparently, as Mark Twain suggests, having difficulties. On February 28, Israel Crawford, the proprietor, sold it to an association of printers, who were not able to revive it. Crawford took back possession of the paper a month later. It ceased publication in October, 1864.[1]

THE CARSON UNDERTAKER—CONTINUED

EDITORS ENTERPRISE: The *Independent* takes hold of a wretched public evil and shakes it and bullyrags it in the following determined and spirited manner this morning:

"Our friend, Mark Twain, is such a joker that we cannot tell when he is really in earnest. He says in his last letter to the ENTERPRISE, that our undertaker charges exorbitantly for his services—as much as $150 for a pine coffin, and $50 for a grave—and is astonished that the *Independent* has not, ere this, said something about this extortion. As yet we have had no occasion for a coffin or a bit of ground for grave purposes, and therefore know nothing about the price of such things. If any of our citizens think they have been imposed upon in this particular, it is their duty to ventilate the matter. We have heard no complaints."

That first sentence is false, and that clause in the second, which refers to the *Independent*, is false, also. I knew better than to be astonished when I wrote it. Unfortunately for the public of Carson, both propositions in the third sentence are true. Having had no use for a coffin himself, the editor "therefore knows nothing about the price of such things." It is my unsolicited opinion that he knows very little about anything. And anybody who will read his paper calmly and dispassionately for a week will endorse that opinion. And more especially his knowing nothing about Carson, is not surprising; he seldom mentions that town in his paper. If the Second Advent were to occur here, you would hear of it first in some other newspaper. He says, "If any of our citizens think they have been imposed upon in this particular, it is their duty to ventilate the matter." It is their duty—the duty of the citizens—to ferret out abuses and correct them, is it? Correct them through your advertising columns and pay for it—is that it? And then turn to your second page and find one of your insipid chalk-milk editorials, defending the abuse and apologizing for the perpetrator of it; or when public sentiment is too well established on the subject, pretending, as in the above case, that you are the only man in the community who don't know anything about it. Where did you get your notion of the duties of a journalist from? Any editor in the world will say it is *your* duty to ferret out these abuses, and *your* duty to correct them. What are you paid for? what use are you to the community? what are you fit for as conductor of a newspaper, if you cannot do these things? Are you paid to know nothing, and keep on writing about it every day? How long do you suppose such a jack-legged newspaper as yours would be supported or tolerated in Carson, if you had a rival no larger than a foolscap sheet, but with something in it, and whose editor would know, or at least have energy enough to find out, whether a neighboring paper abused one of the citizens justly or unjustly? That paragraph which I have copied, seems to mean one thing, while in reality it means another. Its true translation is, for instance: "Our name is *Independent*— that is, in different phrase, Opinionless. We have no opinions on any subject—we reside permanently on the fence. In order to have no opinions, it is necessary that we should know nothing—therefore, if this undertaker is fleecing the people, we will not know it, and then we shall not offend him. We have heard no complaints, and we shall make no inquiries, lest we do hear some."

Now, when I published a sarcasm upon the San Francisco Water Company, and the iniquity of "cooking dividends," some time ago, in the attractive form of a massacre at Dutch Nick's, by an irresponsible crazy man, this lively *Independent* came after me with the spirit of Old Hopkins strong upon him, and launched at me the red bolts of its virtuous wrath for bringing the high mission of journalism into disrepute—for leading the citizens of California to believe that the murderous proclivities of this people were more extensive than they really were, or, in other words, creating the impression abroad that we were all lunatics and liable to slay and destroy one another upon the slightest provocation. I did not reply to that, because I took it to be the fellow's honest opinion; and being his honest opinion, it was his duty to express it, whether it galled me or not. But he has permitted so many greater wrongs to pass unnoticed since then, that I have arrived at the conclusion that he only did it to modify the circulation of the ENTERPRISE hereabouts. I should be sorry to think he did it to procure my discharge. He would not, if he knew I was an orphan. Yet the same eyes that saw a great public wrong in that article on the massacre, wilfully see no wrong in this undertaker's impoverishing charges for burying people—charges which are made simply because, from the nature of the service rendered, a man dare not demur to their payment, lest the fact be talked of around town and he be disgraced. Oh, your *Independent* is a consistent, harmless, non-committal sheet. I never saw a paper of that non-committal name that wasn't. Even the religious papers bearing it give a decided, whole-souled support to neither the Almighty nor the Devil.

The editor of the *Independent* says he don't know anything about this undertaker business. If he would go and report a while for some responsible newspaper, he would learn the knack of finding out things. Now if he wants to know that the undertaker charged three or four prices for a coffin (the late Mr. Nash's) upon one occasion, and then refused to let it go out of his hands, when the funeral was waiting, until it was paid for, although the estate was good for it, being worth $20,000—let him go and ask Jack Harris. If he wants any amount of information, let him inquire of Curry, or Pete Hopkins, or Judge Wright. Stuff! let him ask any man he meets in the street—the matter is as universal a topic of conversation here as is the subject of "feet" in Virginia. But I don't suppose you want to know anything about it. I want to shed one more unsolicited opinion, which is that your *Independent* is the deadest, flattest, [most] worthless thing I know—and I imagine my cold, unsmiling undertaker has his hungry eye upon it.

Mr. Curry says if the people will come forward and take hold of the matter, a city cemetery can be prepared and fenced in a week, and at a trivial cost—a cemetery from which a man can set out for Paradise or perdition just as respectably as he can from the undertaker's private grounds at present. Another undertaker can then be invited to come and take charge of the business. Mr. Curry is right—and no man can move in the matter with greater effect than himself. Let the reform be instituted.

MARK TWAIN

30.

The Removal of the Capital
[Virginia City], February 16, 1864

☞ "A Looker-On," who signs this letter, was almost certainly Mark Twain. He probably wrote it during a week-end trip back to Virginia City (it was published on February 16, a Tuesday). Like the author of the letter, Mark Twain had been in Carson City as an observer of the proceedings of the Legislature, and he had discussed removal of the capital, although without strong feeling either for or against the measure. The contention that in Carson City the Legislature is "beyond the pale of newspaper criticism" echoes ideas expressed in section 29. The vivid description of how the Legislature operates bespeaks an author with precisely Mark Twain's recent and prolonged contact with the legislative process.

The implied criticism of the proposal to subsidize the Sierra Seminary may indicate bad feeling between Mark Twain and Mrs. W. K. Cutler, and thus may have some bearing on his subsequent attack on her and other women of Carson City in connection with the activities of the Sanitary Commission (see Part Three). It is noteworthy that despite William M. Stewart's close association with the *Territorial Enterprise*, Mark Twain criticizes his effort to secure an appropriation for the relief of Sheriff Gasherie.

The charge that Ormsby County had failed to make good its promise to provide quarters for the Legislature free of charge caused a commotion on the floor of the House which is described in section 31.

EDITORS ENTERPRISE: I have just returned from the Capital, where I have been a Legislative spectator for a while. The strongest conviction which the experience of my visit forced upon my mind was, that the Capital ought to be removed from Carson City.

I think you would be of my opinion if you could see with your own eyes, and hear with your own ears, the doings of the Legislature for a few days.

My first and best reason for thinking the Capital ought to be removed is, that while it remains in Carson, the Legislative Assembly is beyond the pale of newspaper criticism—beyond its restraining influence, and consequently beyond the jurisdiction of the people, in a manner, since the people are left in ignorance of what their servants are doing, and cannot protest against their acts until it is too late. Your reports of proceedings take up as much room in the city papers as can well be spared, I suppose, and they are ample enough for all intents and purposes—or rather, they would be, if the Virginia newspapers could stay in Carson and criticize these proceedings, and also the members, editorially, occasionally. A mere skeleton report carries but an indifferent conception of the transactions of a Legislative body to the minds of the people. For instance, in the style and after the manner of one of these synopses: Mr. Stewart gave notice of a bill entitled an Act to audit the claim of D. J. Gasherie. A day or so afterward, we learn that according to former notice, Mr. Stewart introduced his bill. You hear of it again in some committee report. And again, as having been reported "favorably" by a Committee of the Whole. Next, your report says Mr. Stewart's bill passed by so many ayes, and so many noes. The work is done; none of your readers have the slightest idea what Mr. Gasherie's claim was for, and neither does one of them imagine himself even remotely interested in knowing anything about it. Yet the chief portion of your readers, I take it, were very particularly interested in that bill—because they will have to contribute money from their own pockets to pay Mr. Gasherie's claim; and they were further interested, on general principles, because the passage of that bill inflicted a great wrong upon the Territory. Now, if the Legislature had been in session in Virginia, under the eyes of the press, instead of those of six or seven idle lobby members, I doubt if Mr. Stewart would have introduced the bill; I doubt if the Committee of the Whole would have presumed to consider it; I know the House and the Council would not have passed it. When Mr. Elliott rose in his place and objected that this was a bill to provide payment of a sum out of the Territorial Treasury, amounting to between $1,800 and $1,900, for the maintenance by Sheriff Gasherie, of several Ormsby county paupers, the newspapers would have promptly seconded him in the suggestion that Ormsby county maintain her own paupers, and pay the bill out of her own pocket. And when Mr. Stewart acknowledged the justness of the suggestion, but said Ormsby had bankrupted herself by purchasing a set of fine county buildings, and must therefore beg this favor at the hands of the people of the whole Territory, the newspapers would have known all about it, would have demurred, and the members, with a sense of responsibility thus forced upon them would have intentionally voted no upon the bill, instead of voting aye without really knowing, perhaps, what particular measure was before the House. Moreover, several other outrageous laws, already passed, could never have been passed in Virginia. Twenty-thousand dollars of the people's money have been asked for to build a seminary in Carson City and present it to two of her citizens—a private affair, and no more public in its character than Mr. Chauvel's fencing school here, and no more deserving of a Territorial appropriation of $20,000. Members were not wanting to vote for the measure, and to advocate it strongly. The bill would even have passed, probably, if Messrs. Clagett, and Elliott had withheld their earnest opposition to it. Yet a bill to provide for the establishment and maintenance of a public mining college—a polytechnic school—has excited small interest among the members. They forget that a mining education can be best acquired here in the Territory—they forget, also, that the Seminary could offer no inducements of a similar nature, since our citizens, for many years to come, will prefer to educate their daughters at the inexpensive and efficient seminaries of Benicia, San Jose, and Santa Clara. The Seminary bill was resurrected on Saturday, consolidated with the Polytechnic bill, $30,000 of public money added, and again brought before the Legislature. So—$20,000 for a building, and a tax of 1 per cent. on $30,000,000 of property, for "sundries." A crowd of young gentlemen and ladies in one building might affect the matter of public morals more than that of public education, I think. The school is not located, in the bill, but the Ormsby delegation propose to have it established in Carson. The Governor is to appoint the trustees, and they are to fix upon a location, I believe. A mining school in a town fifteen miles from a mine, would be a beneficial thing, in the abstract. Yet this $50,000 bill may pass, after all. So may the act to purchase Mr. Curry's prison for $80,000 more—$130,000 to Carson, by way of compensation for the stream of iniquitous private franchises which has been flowing from one or two members of her delegation during the entire session. Could these bills, unmodified, pass, if the people could be thoroughly posted as to their merits, by the press? I suppose not. Clagett, Brumfield, Elliott, and two or three other intelligent, industrious and upright members have saved the credit of the Lower House, and protected the interests of the people, in nearly every case where it has been done at all—but they have received no commendation for it; neither have idle members, and members of easy integrity, been censured. It is because the people have been left in the dark as to who they ought to praise and who they ought to blame.

It was urged, last session, that Storey county was disposed to stow away, in her ravenous maw, everything that came in her way. That argument lost her the Capital, by one vote—that argument, and one other, which was a written pledge, on the part of Ormsby county, that if the Capital were permitted to remain in Carson, halls should be furnished for the use of the Legislature, free of charge. Storey county offered to erect capital buildings at her own expense, and move the officers and other governmental appurtenances within her lines, also at her own expense. Let Storey county make that proposition to-day, and it will be accepted. It is Ormsby county, now that is striving with extraordinary energy, to swallow all public benefits—not Storey. And Ormsby has failed to redeem her pledge—for she has charged the Legislature $500 for the use of her Court-house, and after making the contract, is now dissatisfied because the granting of a greater sum is refused her.

Four members of one branch of the Legislature support the Specific Contract bill because it will result to their personal advantage, in sums varying from $1,000 to $4,000. More than that number have supported private franchises on personal pecuniary grounds. One member would vote $20,000 to the Seminary because he would reap an advantage, in dollars and cents, from the passage of the bill. Inasmuch as these statements come from the gentlemen referred to, themselves, they are entitled to full credence. If there could be a merit attached to a wrong motive, I think that merit might be considered to be the small amount of intelligence required to keep from telling about it. But all Legislators are not diplomats. Would it not be well to place the Assembly where the press, and through the press the people, could look after it?

Mr. Clagett gave notice, on Saturday, of an Act to remove the Capital, and the bill will probably be formally introduced to-day (Monday). If the people of Storey county want the seat of government in their midst, let them signify it promptly and cordially.

A LOOKER-ON

31.

Legislative Proceedings
Carson City, February 16–20, 1864

☞ The passages reprinted here bear upon the last days of the session of the Legislature. Along with a few sentences of jollification, they present the legislative history of an effort to move the territorial capital from Carson City to Virginia City. Sam P. Davis tells a story—without mentioning a specific date—which purports to reveal the backstage history of this affair. Davis says that one night in Virginia City, Joseph T. Goodman, Rollin Daggett, and Jonas Seeley ("a prominent attorney") were "out painting the town." They hired a hack and, having had a good deal to drink, decided on the spur of the moment to go to Carson, twenty miles away, for the purpose of moving the capital to Virginia City. "Arriving early in the morning," Davis continues, "they took a short rest and rising about nine o'clock, they invaded the halls of legislation and announced their mission. They had money to burn and soon champagne was flowing freely in every saloon in Carson." Under these benign influences—runs the story—the House quickly passed a bill ordering the removal. The vote was expected to be close in the Council, but Goodman persuaded Abraham Curry to favor the bill and its passage seemed likely. Curry, however, soon repented of his promise and asked with tears in his eyes to be released from it. "Next day the Virginia City delegates were still celebrating what they regarded as a sure victory, but when the vote was taken in the Senate it was one short and Carson won."[1]

This anecdote may have some basis in fact, but a comparison of it with the reports of the proceedings of the Legislature in the *Enterprise* reveals a good deal of distortion. The bill for removal of the capital did not pass the House on February 16, the day on which Goodman and his companions arrived in Carson, but was referred to a special committee. The committee reported favorably on the bill next day, and it was then passed by a vote of 13 to 11.[2] A motion to reconsider was defeated on February 18. The bill reached the floor of the Council on the nineteenth, but after debate it was postponed indefinitely by a vote of 6 to 4. On February 20, the last day of the session, an obscure parliamentary maneuver again brought up the question of removal in the House. The result was a tie vote, which had the effect of killing the measure.[3]

The joke of presenting a comb to William H. Clagett was suggested by the presentation of a gold-headed ebony cane to Speaker A. J. Simmons of the House.

HOUSE—THIRTY-SIXTH DAY

CARSON, *February 16*

MAYOR Arick, Joe Goodman, George Birdsall, Young Harris, and other solid citizens of Virginia arrived at 3 this morning, having left home at midnight. They came down to see how the Capital question was going. Send a lot more down—the more the merrier, and the greater degree of interest is exhibited. Virginia seldom does things by halves—she generally comes out strong when she takes hold of a question.—MARK.]

· · · · · ·

Mr. McDonald moved a recess.

Mr. Clagett hoped the motion would not prevail. He wished to go on with the regular business—introduction of bills etc. [Sensation among opponents to the removal of the Capital.]

The motion was lost.

Mr. Clagett moved a call of the House. [Numerous objections.] The motion was carried—ayes 7, noes 5.

After a moment's delay, Mr. Dixson moved that further proceedings under the call be dispensed with. Lost.

The absentees, Messrs. Ungar and Curler, were brought forward and excused, and further proceedings under the call were then dispensed with.

Mr. Phillips moved a recess. Lost—ayes 9, noes 11.

Mr. Clagett then, pursuant to previous notice, introduced an Act to locate permanently the Capital of the Territory. [At Virginia—that city to provide suitable buildings for 5 years at her own cost, before October 1, 1864—otherwise the Act to be null and void.]

The bill was read in answer to numerous calls.

Mr. Elliott moved that the rules be suspended and the bill engrossed for a third reading.

Mr. Dixson strenuously objected, and said he couldn't see the object of rushing this bill through with such indecent haste. [Behold the virtuous member from Lander—the heart of the same being in Carson.—Mark.]

Mr. Ungar moved to refer the bill to the Storey delegation, with instructions to report forthwith.

Mr. Phillips moved to amend by substituting the Gold Hill portion of the Storey delegation.

Mr. Clagett hoped the amendments would be rejected and Mr. Elliott's motion agreed to, and in his remarks called attention to the fact that Ormsby county made a written pledge last year that she would furnish free halls to the Legislature from and after that session—but had violated her pledge, inasmuch as those same County Commissioners have charged and received $500 for the halls now being used by the Assembly.

Mr. Dixson did not want things rushed so—he wanted things printed; he didn't know anything about things, and he wanted time to gain information. He couldn't see what members meant by springing things in this way. [Emotion, indicative of the distress which a Lander member with his heart in Ormsby must naturally feel when he sees an attempt made to ravish Carson against her will.]

Mr. Dixson sat down weeping, and snuffling, and wiping his nose on his coat sleeve. [That's a joke of mine—he had a handkerchief with him.—Mark.]

Mr. Tennant called for the reading of Ormsby's pledge, and Mr. Clagett got it from Mr. Calder, and read it.

Mr. Stewart made an eloquent appeal in behalf of Ormsby county, and moved as a substitute to the three or four motions already before the House, that the bill be referred to a special committee, to consist of one member from each county, with instructions to report to-morrow morning. Carried; on a division—ayes 13, noes 4.

The Speaker appointed the committee as follows: Messrs. Clagett, Stewart, Curler, Dean, Elliott, Gove, McDonald, Tennant and Partridge.

HOUSE—THIRTY-SEVENTH DAY

CARSON, *February 17*

[Dallam, of the Carson *Independent,* makes a full and unqualified apology to me this morning—an entire column of it. He says he was not in his right mind at the time, and hardly ever is. Now, when a man comes out like that, and owns up with such pleasant candor, I think I ought to accept his apology. Consequently, we will call it square. It is flattering to me to observe that Dallam's editorials display great ability this morning, and that the paper shows an extraordinary degree of improvement in every respect. A becoming modesty should characterize us all—it is not for me to say who the credit is due to for the improvements mentioned. I only say I am glad to see the *Independent* looking healthy and vigorous again.—MARK.]

PETITION

Mr. Stewart presented a petition, signed by most of the responsible citizens of Ormsby, he said, setting forth that it had just come to a knowledge of the fact that the Ormsby Commissioners had pledged free Legislative Halls, and violated that pledge. The petitioners promise that the rent money shall be at once refunded.

Mr. Stewart also presented a communication from the Secretary of the Territory acknowledging the receipt of the full amount of the rent money ($500) as paid over to him by the petitioners yesterday.

Mr. Stewart moved the reference of the two documents to the Special Committee on removal of the Capital.

Mr. McDonald objected that the Committee spoken of were ready now to report, according to instructions. He moved to lay the papers on the table, to be taken up at pleasure. Carried.

QUESTION OF PRIVILEGE

Mr. Stewart rose to a question of privilege, and spoke at considerable length upon two editorials in the ENTERPRISE in relation to the removal of the capital, and a communication upon the same subject in the same paper, written by one "Looker-On," but whom Mr. Stewart, with ghastly humor and with relentless and malignant irony, persisted in calling "Looker On or *Hanger-On*, I don't know which!" He said the Gasherie bill for supporting Ormsby county paupers, and which expense the Territory was asked to pay, only amounted to $877, instead of the large amount stated by the writer of the article!

[The amount being less, don't you see, the principle is not the same. Of course. Certainly. Wherefore? Why not? The gentleman's question of privilege was well taken. As long as the paupers did not cost, or propose to cost the Territory much, it was impertinent in a newspaper to mention it. That is the way Mr. Stewart and I look at it.—MARK.]

Mr. Stewart said the balance of the money was cash paid out of Mr. Gasherie's own pocket in the catching of Territorial criminals, and of course as anybody would willingly acknowledge, it was the Territory's place to pay it.

. . . . . .

Mr. Clagett, from the Special Committee on the removal of the capital, presented a majority report favoring the removal.

Mr. Stewart, from the same committee, presented a minority report recommending the indefinite postponement of the bill.

Mr. Dixson moved the reference of both reports to Committee of the Whole.

Mr. McDonald moved to amend by accepting the majority report.

On a division, Mr. Dixson's motion prevailed—13 to 11.

Mr. Clagett called for the reading of the amendments recommended by the majority report, which was done. [Stipulates that Virginia shall also furnish Supreme Court rooms and Clerk's offices for five years.—REP.]

Mr. Stewart moved that the Ormsby petition and the communication from the Secretary of the Territory be referred to Committee of the Whole. Carried.

Mr. Barclay moved a re-consideration of the vote by which the bill and the above documents were referred to Committee of the Whole. Lost by the following vote:

AYES—Messrs. Barclay, Clagett, Curler, Elliott, Gillespie, Heaton, McDonald, Nelson, Requa, Tennant, Ungar—11.

NOES—Messrs. Brumfield, Calder, Dean, Dixson, Fisher, Gove, Hess, Hunter, Jones, Phillips, Stewart, Trask, Mr. Speaker—13.

Mr. Elliott moved that the Capital Bill be made the special order for tomorrow morning at 11 A.M. Lost by the following vote (required a two-thirds vote to carry):

AYES—Messrs. Barclay, Calder, Clagett, Elliott, Fisher, Gillespie, Heaton, McDonald, Nelson, Phillips, Requa, Tennant, Ungar and Mr. Speaker—14.

NOES—Messrs. Brumfield, Curler, Dean, Dixson, Gove, Hess, Hunter, Jones, Stewart and Trask—10.

Mr. Brumfield moved to change the time to 12 o'clock Saturday night (the moment when the Legislature adjourns finally).

Mr. Clagett opposed the motion.

Lost, by the following vote:

AYES—Messrs. Brumfield, Dean, Dixson, Gove, Hess, Hunter, Jones, Stewart—9.

NOES—Messrs. Barclay, Calder, Clagett, Curler, Elliott, Fisher, Gillespie, Heaton, McDonald, Nelson, Phillips, Requa, Tennant, Trask, Ungar, Mr. Speaker—16.

Mr. Clagett said that in order to stop this frittering away of valuable time, and in order to get a test vote, he would move that the bill be considered engrossed and ordered to a third reading. Carried by the following vote:

AYES—Messrs. Barclay, Brumfield, Calder, Curler, Clagett, Elliott, Fisher, Gillespie, Gove, Heaton, Hunter, Jones, McDonald, Nelson, Phillips, Requa, Stewart, Tennant, Trask, Ungar—20.

NOES—Messrs. Dean, Dixson, Hess, Mr. Speaker—4.

Mr. McDonald moved that the bill be read by title only. Carried.

FINAL PASSAGE OF THE CAPITAL BILL

The bill was accordingly read a third time by title, and finally passed, by the following vote:

AYES—Messrs. Barclay, Calder, Clagett, Curler, Elliott, Gillespie,

Heaton, McDonald, Nelson, Requa, Tennant, Ungar and Mr. Speaker—13.

NOES—Messrs. Brumfield, Dean, Dixson, Fisher, Gove, Hess, Hunter, Jones, Phillips, Stewart and Trask—11.

HOUSE—THIRTY-EIGHTH DAY

Carson, *February 18*

THE CAPITAL QUESTION

Mr. Calder, according to previous notice, moved a reconsideration of the vote of yesterday, by which the Capital bill passed. He said his objections had been removed by the bond submitted by Mr. Stewart.

Mr. Clagett spoke at some length on the subject, in demonstration of the fact that a bond could not be drawn under such circumstances that would be valid and binding.

Mr. Brumfield replied rather warmly. In reply to the old argument about newspaper criticism which could be brought to bear on the Legislature if the Capital were in Virginia, he was especially bitter on the *Bulletin*—said he supposed it would be the favorite— that paper which was to have been teeming with mining taxation articles to-day, but was silent—had been purchased again, doubtless. As for the advantage a community might derive from the presence of the Capital, he couldn't appreciate the proposition; he didn't want the Capital at Virginia; he was going there to live, and he didn't want to be bothered with it. As to buying the Capital with the bond now before the House, neither Ormsby county nor the Legislature had a right to buy and sell the Capital.

After some further debate, Mr. Gillespie moved the previous question, which motion prevailed, and discussion was blockaded.

The motion to reconsider was then put and lost [!—REP.] by the following tie vote [clinching the thing as far as the House is concerned].

AYES—Messrs. Brumfield, Dean, Dixson, Fisher, Gove, Hess, Hunter, Jones, Phillips, Stewart and Trask—11.

NOES—Messrs. Calder, Clagett, Curler, Elliott, Gillespie, Heaton, McDonald, Nelson, Tennant, Ungar and Mr. Speaker—11.

ABSENT—Mr. Requa—don't know whether he dodged or not.

DODGED THE ISSUE—Mr. Barclay.

After the above bully proceedings, and on motion of Mr. Mc-
Donald, the House took a recess until 2:30 P.M.

Thursday Afternoon

. . . . . .

The Sergeant-at-Arms brought in Messrs. Dean, Phillips, Tennant, Jones, Gillespie and Ungar.

Mr. Dean had been talking over family matters. Mr. Phillips had
been engineering a lawsuit. Mr. Tennant had been on committee
business. Messrs. Jones and Gillespie were playing billiards, and
Mr. Ungar's child was sick and he had been playing marbles with
her.

Mr. Brumfield moved that Mr. Ungar be granted leave of absence to continue playing marbles with her. [Laughter.]

A motion to fine Mr. Gillespie a box of cigars for engaging in the
unholy practice of playing billiards, was lost by a tie vote—10 to
10 [notwithstanding that youth has a remittance at Wells, Fargo's
from his creditors in Virginia, and which he denied the same.—
MARK.]

The absentees were all excused.

Friday Afternoon

[CARSON, *February 19*]

. . . . . .

Mr. Gillespie moved to reduce the Sergeant-at-Arms' salary to
$9 per day, and strike out that portion which gives the reporters $7
per day.

Mr. Barclay said Mr. Gillespie was not so economical when he
presented his own bill.

Mr. Fisher said he ought to remember the verse,

> "The mercy I to others show,
> That mercy show to me."

Considering the mercy shown him by the House, his opposition
comes with a bad grace from him.

[I feel called upon to observe that Mr. Gillespie got huffy—I
would prefer to call it by a milder term, but I cannot conscientiously do so. Mr. Gillespie got huffy.—REP.]

After some further debate, Mr. Gillespie explained that there was no vindictiveness in him—all his motives were dictated from on high—from on high, sir!—[Tremendous applause.] He went on and made further and even more aggravatedly absurd remarks.

Mr. Barclay said it was customary to pay the reporters.

Mr. Gillespie's motion in relation to the reporters was lost, by the following vote:

AYES—Messrs. Clagett, Gillespie, Hess, Hunter, Nelson, Phillips, Tennant and Trask—8.

NOES—Messrs. Barclay, Brumfield, Calder, Curler, Dean, Dixson, Fisher, Gove, Heaton, Jones, McDonald, Stewart, Ungar and Mr. Speaker—15.

COUNCIL—AFTERNOON SESSION—THIRTY-NINTH DAY

Carson, *February 19*

REMOVAL OF THE CAPITAL

Mr. Daggett moved that the Capital bill be taken from the table.

Mr. Coddington moved that the bill be indefinitely postponed.

Upon the latter's motion a lengthy discussion ensued. Mr. Daggett opposing, and Messrs Curry, Coddington, Sturtevant, Negus and Hall supporting it.

Mr. Curry presented a communication from certain citizens of Carson City, binding themselves in the sum of $20,000, to furnish suitable halls and rooms for the Legislature and Territorial offices free of cost, provided that the Capital be allowed to remain at Carson City, while Nevada remained a Territory.

At the close of the debate, the motion to indefinitely postpone was carried by the following vote:

AYES—Messrs. Coddington, Curry, Negus, Sturtevant, Waldron, Mr. President.

NOES—Messrs. Daggett, Flagg, Sheldon, Thompson.

HOUSE—LAST DAY—FORTIETH

Carson, *February 20*

The Chaplain not being present, Mr. Fisher suggested that the Virginia reporter be requested to officiate in his place.

By courtesy of the House, the Virginia reporter was allowed to explain that he was not on it. [Excused.]

Mr. Phillips moved a call of the House. Carried.

Mr. Gillespie was produced before the bar of the House.

Mr. Brumfield moved, as the heaviest punishment that could be inflicted upon him, that he be denied the comfort of making a single motion for the space of an hour. [Laughter.]

Mr. Barclay moved that he be fined $5, and the same be paid to the Sergeant-at-Arms.

Mr. Phillips moved to amend by contributing the money to the Sanitary Fund.

The motions were lost.

Messrs. Dixson and Hunter were brought in and fined a box of cigars each.

The Sergeant-at-Arms said Mr. Clagett was sick in bed.

The Speaker said he must come anyhow.

Mr. Fisher wanted the editor of the *Independent* sent for. [Laughter.]

The Speaker said he did not think Mr. Clagett needed purging. [Laughter.]

Mr. Heaton came forward and was excused.

NOTICE

Mr. Stewart gave notice of an act to permanently locate the Capital on the South side of Capt. Pray's saw mill on Lake Tahoe, in Douglas county. [Sensation.]

[But nothing further appears in the record concerning this proposed bill.—H. N. S.]
. . . . . .

A Message was received from the Council asking the return of the bill for the removal of the Capital. [Another of those grave Council jokes—REP.]

In view of these portentous symptoms, a call of the House was ordered.

After calling the roll, Mr. Stewart moved that further proceedings under the call be dispensed with.

The Chair decided the motion carried.

A motion to indefinitely postpone the Council message was lost— ayes 9, noes 11.

The motion to comply with the Council's request, carried—ayes

11, noes 8. [Confusion and contention—so to speak. The vote was even taken over again, with the following result:]

AYES—Messrs. Barclay, Calder, Clagett, Elliott, Gillespie, Heaton, McDonald, Nelson, Tennant, Ungar and Mr. Speaker—11.

NOES—Messrs. Brumfield, Curler, Dean, Dixson, Fisher, Gove, Hunter, Jones, Phillips, Stewart and Trask—11.

Mr. Speaker *pro tem.*—Mr. Fisher—decided the motion lost.

Mr. Barclay wished to remind our worthy reporter that he didn't dodge the question this time. [His head is right. I cannot even swear that he dodged it before, with malice aforethought. Good authority says his absence before was unavoidable. I believe it. A man who votes as firmly as Mr. Barclay does for reporters against log-rolling members, would be apt to stick to his points upon all occasions when the same was possible. How's that?—REP.]

Saturday Afternoon

. . . . . .

Council bill to amend the Act to prohibit gambling. The bill was read. [The Clerk pronounces the names of all games glibly, and without any perceptible foreign accent.—REP.]

. . . . . .

Saturday Night

. . . . . .

[Mr. Stewart drew his everlasting toll-road on the House again. This has been the old regular result of every five minutes idleness to-day.—REP.] . . . . . .

THIRD HOUSE

The institution resolved itself into a respectable body, as expressed in the above heading.

Mr. Thos. Hannah was elected assistant Clerk, and came forward and took the oath.

Mr. Clagett introduced a voluminous bill for the relief of certain citizens of Ormsby county. [It appropriates Curry's Warm Springs —gives it to these parties as a franchise for a swimming school— and—never mind, I will cease reporting and listen to the fun.— REP.]

. . . . . .

[The *Independent* of this morning touched upon Mr. Clagett's seeming repugnance to the use of the comb. On this hint, Mr. Barclay and other members of the House, had procured a prodigious wooden comb and conferred upon your servant the honor of presenting it.—REP.]

Mr. Mark Twain inquired if testimonials were still in order, and received an affirmative reply from the Speaker. He arose in his place and addressed Mr. Clagett as follows: [Never mind publishing it again. I had no speech prepared, and therefore I was obliged to infringe upon etiquette to some extent—that is to say, I had to take Mr. Fisher's speech (apologizing to that gentleman, of course) and read it to Mr. Clagett, merely saying "comb" where the word "cane" occurred, and "legislator" in the place of "parliamentarian," and slinging in a few "as it weres," and "so to speaks," etc., to add grace and vigor to the composition. I think I must be a pretty good reader—the audience appeared to admire Fisher's speech more when I delivered it than they did when he delivered it himself.]

Mr. Clagett received the testimonial, and replied felicitously— as he is wont to do. He concluded by saying it was a college practice to give the ugliest student a penknife, with instructions to give it to a man uglier than himself, if he should ever find one. He liked the idea—he thought it his duty to confer the comb upon some person whose hair needed its offices more than his own. [He passed it over to Mr. Hunter, of Washoe. Applause and Laughter.]

Baskets of wine were now brought in, with the compliments of Theodore Winters, President of the Washoe Agricultural, Mining and Mechanical Society, and the House rested awhile to drink health and prosperity to that gentleman.

Shortly after, other baskets were produced, per order, and at the expense of the Speaker, and the operation of drinking was further continued.

HUNTER'S MEMORIAL

Mr. Hunter, by request, came forward and read a long, solemn, magnificent, hifalutin memorial about the mines, religion, chemistry, social etiquette, agriculture, and other matter proper to a document of this kind. The House applauded tempestuously—and laughed. They laughed immoderately. Why they did it, I cannot imagine, for I never heard an essay like this one before in my life. Now that is honest. Mr. Hunter finally got angry and refused to finish reading the discourse, but when it was explained to him that only lobby members had been laughing all the time he was satisfied of course. I would like to hear the memorial read in Virginia.

Mr. Stewart, from the special Committee, reported that the Governor had no further communications to make.

Mr. Elliott offered a resolution that the House adjourn *sine die* at 11:30 P.M.

Mr. McDonald, true to his old regular motion [to adjourn] moved to amend by making the hour 12 P.M. The motion prevailed.

And from this time until midnight, fun ran high.

At 12 P.M. Mr. Speaker declared the House adjourned *sine die*.

The members went up to the Governor's and had a good time for an hour. The old man is as competent as any that walks, to make an evening pass pleasantly. Wine, music, anecdotes and sentiments composed the programme.

At 2 A.M. the exhilarated members closed the frolic by serenading the Speaker, at the White House.

32.

Letter from Mark Twain
Carson City, [April 25, 1864]

☞ This letter is dated only "Monday"; but since it was published in the *Territorial Enterprise* on Thursday, April 28, 1864, the date of composition must be April 25.

William C. Jaynes, a barkeeper in Daley's Exchange Bar, Virginia City, had shot and killed P. H. Dowd in the Gem Saloon, Gold Hill, on March 7, 1864, as the result of a quarrel about settlement of their former partnership in operating the saloon.[1] Jaynes was sentenced to life imprisonment.[2]

Horace Smith, a lawyer, was shot by Captain F. W. H. Johnson, agent for Wells, Fargo and Company, in Virginia City on October 28, 1863, and died from the effects of the wound the following December. Johnson was eventually acquitted.[3]

The case of Alderman J. Earl of Virginia City turned upon the question whether residence for six months in the city was necessary to make him eligible for office.[4]

The committee of Carson ladies arranging the fancy-dress ball for the benefit of the Sanitary Fund had been organized on April 18. Because of the importance this organization later assumed in Mark Twain's life, it is worth recording that Orion Clemens had been appointed president of the Sanitary Commission of Ormsby County on April 14.[5] Mollie Clemens served as secretary pro tem. at the organizing meeting of the committee for the ball. The officers elected were: Mrs. W. K. Cutler, president; Mrs. H. F. Rice, vice-president; Mrs. H. H. Ross, secretary; and Mrs. S. D. King, treasurer.[6]

EDS. ENTERPRISE: The road from Virginia to Carson—as traveled by Wilson's coaches—is in excellent condition, the same being neither muddy nor very dusty. The stages do not even stop to rest on the chalk hill.

We came by the penitentiary, but I did not consider it worth while to stop at the institution more than a few minutes, inasmuch as I had been in it before. Bob Howland, the Warden, was at his post, and I had sufficient confidence in him to leave him there. He is probably there yet. N.B.—When you journey in this direction, stop at the penitentiary and examine the native silver fish on exhibition there in the aquarium. They are caught in the Warm Springs. They are very like gold-fish, only they are longer, and not so wide, and are white instead of yellow, and also differ from gold-fish to some extent in the respect that they do not resemble them. This description may sound a little incoherent, but then I have set it down just as I got it from Bob Howland, in whom I have every confidence. Mr. Curry is erecting a handsome stone edifice at the Warm Springs, to be used as a hotel.

I heard in the stage, and also since I arrived here, that an organized effort will shortly be made to rescue Jaynes, the murderer, from the Storey county jail. Whether it be true or not, it will not be amiss to put the officers on their guard with a hint.

The Supreme Court began its session here to-day, and adjourned over until to-morrow, after hearing arguments for a new trial of Johnson for killing Horace Smith. The ground upon which a new trial is sought, is that some testimony was admitted upon the first trial in the District Court which should have been ruled out. I have spoken with District Attorney Corson on the subject, and he thinks the movement for a rehearing will not succeed. From present appearances, I think Alderman Earl will hold his seat for some time yet (if the sacred ambition to sit in a high place in spite of law and gospel to the contrary shall continue to animate him), as it has already been decided to submit his case, through the District and City Attorneys, to the District Court, and the long session now anticipated for the Supreme Court, will doubtless delay his trial for some time. It would have been better, wouldn't it, for the Council to have declared his seat vacant, and allowed him to take legal steps for its restitution himself?

Governor Nye has not yet returned. It is said he will start back to Carson to-morrow.

Acting-Governor Clemens made a requisition upon H. F. Rice, Esq., a day or two since, for offices for the Secretary of the Territory, rent-free, in accordance with the contract entered into by certain citizens during the late session of the Legislature when the subject of removing the Capital to Virginia was agitated. The requisition was duly honored, and in the course of the week, handsome offices will be fitted up in the second story of the north end of the county buildings for the use of the Secretary and his clerks.

Mr. Colburn, or Coleman, or whatever his name is—the young man with a penchant for trying unique experiments, and who was accused of committing a rape on an infant here three years ago—is in trouble again. A young girl who alleges that he seduced her in California some time ago, is over here suing him for damages in the Probate Court.

Your carrier here neglects some of his subscribers as often as two or three times a week, sometimes, or else his papers are stolen after he leaves them. Let the matter be attended to—the people hunger after Dan's intellectual rubbish.

The ladies gave a festival here last Friday for the benefit of my chronic brick church. The net proceeds amounted to upwards of $500, and will be applied to furnishing the edifice, which is still in a high state of preservation, and is gradually but surely becoming really ornamental. That is the church for the benefit of which I delivered a Governor's message once, and consequently I still take a religious interest in its welfare. I could sling a strong prayer for its prosperity, occasionally, if I thought it would do any good. However, perhaps it wouldn't—it would certainly be taking chances anyhow.

The ladies are making extraordinary preparations for a grand fancy-dress ball, to come off in the county buildings here on the 5th of May, for the benefit of the great St. Louis Sanitary Fair. The most pecuniary results are anticipated from it, and I imagine, from the interest that is being taken in the matter, the ladies of Gold Hill had better be looking to their laurels, lest the fame of their recent brilliant effort in the Sanitary line be dimmed somewhat by the financial achievements of this forthcoming ball.

The infernal telegraph monopoly saddled upon this Territory by the last Legislature, in the passage of that infamous special Humboldt telegraph bill, and afterwards clinched by a still more rascally enactment on the same occasion, is bearing its fruits, and the people here, as well as at Virginia, are beginning to wince under illegal and exorbitant telegraphic charges. They double the tariff allowed by law, and a man has to submit to the imposition, because he cannot afford the time and trouble of going to law for a trifle of five or ten dollars, notwithstanding the comfort and satisfaction he would derive from worrying the monopolists. The moment that law received the Governor's signature last winter, you will recollect the Telegraph Company doubled their prices for dispatches to and from San Francisco. And that is not the worst they have done, if common report be true. This common report says the telegraph is used by its owners to aid them in stock-gambling schemes. I recollect that on the night the jury went out in the Savage and North Potosi case and failed to agree, our San Francisco dispatch failed to come to hand, and the reason assigned was that a dispatch of 3,000 words was being sent from Virginia to San Francisco and the line could not be used for other messages. Now that Telegraph Company may have made money by trading in North Potosi on that occasion, but who is young enough to believe they ever got two dollars and a half for that voluminous imaginary dispatch? That telegraph is a humbug. The Company are allowed to charge $3.50 for the first ten words across the continent, and must submit to a considerable deduction on longer dispatches—but they take the liberty of increasing that rate some thirty-five per cent, and people have to put up with it. Colonel Cradlebaugh tells me that last year, when he was a delegate at Washington from this Territory, they always charged him more for dispatches sent here than if they went through to California. The Government pays the Overland Telegraph Company $40,000 a year, with the understanding that Government messages are to pass over the lines free of charge—but I know of several dispatches of this character that were not permitted to leave the telegraph offices until they were paid for. It is properly the District Attorney's business to look after these telegraphic speculators, and that officer ought to be reminded of the fact. The next Grand Jury here will endeavor to make it interesting to the Telegraph Company.

Gillespie's monument—the ratty old Agricultural Fair shanty—still rears its ghastly form in the plaza, and serves to remind me of that statesman's extraordinary career in the House of Representatives. It consisted in saving to his country the usual, but extravagant sum of eight or ten dollars a day extra pay to Legislative reporters, and in making a speech in favor of the Sierra Seminary bill which had the effect of killing that really worthy measure. All through the session Gillespie was mighty handy about smashing the life out of any little incipient law that he chose to befriend, with one of his calamitous speeches. His vote was patent, too; his "nay" invariably passed a bill, and his "aye" was the deadest thing! [My language may be unrefined, but it has the virtue of being uncommonly strong.] But that monument in the plaza looks as hungry as Gillespie does himself, and much more unsightly, and I look for one of them to eat the other some day, if they ever get close enough together.

I depart for Silver Mountain in the Esmeralda stage at 7 o'clock to-morrow morning. It is the early bird that catches the worm, but I would not get up at that time in the morning for a thousand worms, if I were not obliged to.

MARK TWAIN

PART THREE

"THE AFFAIR WAS A SILLY JOKE"

33.

History of the Gold and Silver Bars—
How They Do Things in Washoe
Virginia City, May 16, 1864

☞ This letter, preserved as an unidentified clipping in a scrapbook in
the MTP, was published in a St. Louis newspaper, presumably in late
May or June 1864, but has never been reprinted.[1] Although it takes the
form of a personal letter to Jane Clemens and Pamela Clemens Moffett,
it has the air of having been written for publication (as were the letters
to members of the Clemens family published in the Keokuk *Gate City*
in 1861–1862). The dispatch Mark Twain says he will try to find time to
write for the *Republican* was probably never written; at any rate, it did

185

not appear in either the daily or the weekly edition of the paper during May or June, 1864.

The dates supplied in brackets are based upon an article in the Gold Hill *Evening News* for Tuesday, May 17, 1864 (p. 2), under the heading "The Austin Flour Sack."

A LADY of this city put the ball in motion which rolled on and raised for our Sanitary Fair the gold bricks and silver bars from Nevada. The following interesting letter gives the *modus operandi* of "raising the wind" in Washoe. It is very readable both for its style and its facts:

VIRGINIA CITY, Nevada Territory, midnight [Monday, May 16, 1864].—I don't know the day of the month or of the week; consult the postmark.

My Dear Mother and Sister: I had rather die in Washoe than *live* in some countries. The old California motto is applicable here: "We have lived like paupers that we might give like princes." Virginia is only a small town, about three times as large as Hannibal, and Gold Hill is about the same size as Hannibal. Silver City and Dayton are mere villages—but you ought to see them roll out the twenty dollar pieces when their blood is up. It makes no difference what the object is, if you just get them stirred up once they are bound to respond.

I think they like that Sanitary Fund because it affords them such a bully opportunity of giving away their money. They are slow until you move them, though. When Pamela wrote us to try and do something for the St. Louis Fair, I went after the President of the Storey County Sanitary Commission [A. B. Paul], who is an old St. Louisian—I had never taken much interest in sanitary matters before. He went to work sending calls to the several counties to contribute, and I, being chief of our editorial corps, then, went to scribbling editorials. But we couldn't make the riffle.

Paul got the ladies of Gold Hill to give a ball, and a silver brick worth $3,000 was the result, but that wouldn't go far, you know.— Then we got up a meeting in Virginia, and only got $1,500 or $1,800, and that made us sick. We tried it again, and almost concluded to disband the audience without trying to do anything—but we went on, kept it up all the afternoon and raised $3,500, and had about concluded it was no use to try to get up a sanitary excitement. We began to think we were going to make a mighty poor show at the St. Louis Fair, when along came RUEL GRIDLEY (you remember him), whom I hadn't seen for 15 years, and he brought help. He is a Copperhead, or as he calls himself, "Union to the backbone, but a Copperhead in sympathies."—He lives in Austin, Reese river—a town half as big as Hannibal. He made an eccentric wager with a Republican named Hereford that if a Republican Mayor were elected there, he would give Hereford a 50-pound sack of flour, and carry it to him on his shoulder, a mile and a quarter, with a brass band at his heels playing "John Brown," and if a Democrat were elected, Hereford was to carry the flour to the tune of "Dixie." Ruel lost the bet, and carried the flour, with the band and the whole town at his heels. Hereford gave the flour back to Ruel, and about that time one of Paul's letters arrived, and Ruel put the flour up at auction and sold it for the benefit of the St. Louis Fair for five thousand three hundred dollars. The news came here, but it didn't work on the people much. However, when Ruel got here yesterday [Sunday, May 15], with his sack, on his way to the States, Paul thought we might make some use of it. We put it up at auction and it only brought five or six hundred dollars. He lives in Gold Hill, and he said he was so disgusted with Virginia that he would try his own town, and if she failed he would leave the country. This morning [Monday, May 16] at eleven o'clock he had two open carriages—one for reporters and the other for the speakers—got a brass band and we started for Gold Hill. When we got there Ruel gave the history of the flour sack, and said that from what he could see people outside of Austin didn't care much for flour. But they soon made him sing small. Gold Hill raised Austin out of her boots, and paid nearly seven thousand dollars in gold for the sack of flour. Ruel threw up the sponge!

Then we went down to little Silver City and sold it for $1,500 or $1,700. From there we went to the village of Dayton and sold it for somewhere in the neighborhood of $2,000. Carson is considerably larger than either of these three towns, but it has a lousy, lazy, worthless, poverty-stricken population, and the universal opinion was that we couldn't raise $500 . . . there. So we started home again about $10,000 better off than when we left in the morning.

We got to Gold Hill at 4 in the afternoon, and found the streets crowded, and they hailed us from all sides with "Virginia's boomin'!" "Virginia's mad!" "Virginia's got her back up!" "You better go 'long to Virginia; they say they'll be d——d if the whole Territory combined shall beat them!" and a hundred other such exclamations. Wherefore we journeyed into Virginia with a long procession at our heels, coming up to see the fun. We got to the meeting place after dark, and found the neighboring buildings illuminated and the adjacent streets completely blocked up with people. Then the fun commenced, and I wished Pamela could have been there to see her own private project bringing forth its fruit and culminating in such a sweeping excitement away out here among barren mountains, while she herself, unconscious of what her hands had done, and unaware of the row she was kicking up, was probably sitting quietly at home and thinking it a dreary sort of a world, full of disappointments, and labors unrequited, and hopes unblessed with fruition. I speak of the row as hers, for if she had not written us, the St. Louis Fair would probably have never heard from Washoe. She has certainly secured $30,000 or $40,000 worth of greenbacks from us by her own efforts.

Well, the fun commenced, and the very first dash made Austin take a back seat, and strode half way up to Gold Hill. It was a bid for the sack of flour by the men employed in the Gould & Curry mine and mill, of three thousand five hundred dollars! They went ahead of Austin two hundred dollars. Then followed half a dozen bids of five hundred dollars each, and the thing was fairly under way. In two hours and a half Virginia cleaned out the Territory and paid nearly $13,000 for the sack of flour! How's that? Nearly a dollar a head for every man, woman and child in the camp, in two hours and a half; and on four hours' notice. New York couldn't come up to that ratio in the same length of time. And then the offices of all our big mines are located in San Francisco, and when that city makes a big dash for the Sanitary fund, the heaviest end of it comes always from those very offices.

The other day the *Daily Union* gave $200, and I gave $300, under instructions from the proprietors always to "go them a hundred better." To-night the *Union* bid $100, and I bid $150 for the *Enterprise.* I had to go to the office to make up my report, and the *Union* fellows came back and bid another $100. It was provoking, because I had orders to run our bid up to $1,000, if necessary, and I only struck the *Union* lightly to draw them on. But I guess we'll make them hunt their holes yet, before we are done with them.

If I have time to-morrow, I will send a dispatch, by request, to the St. Louis *Republican.*

I stated in the paper once that Virginia could raise half a ton of pure silver in six hours for the St. Louis Fair, if they could get her mad—she went over that weight to-night in two hours and a half. If all our bars for the St. Louis Fair had no gold in them, their weight would not fall far short of a ton.

Yours affectionately   SAM

34.

Letter from Samuel L. Clemens to Mrs. Orion Clemens
Virginia City, May 20, 1864

☞ This letter from Mark Twain to his sister-in-law, Mary Eleanor ("Mollie") Stotts Clemens, has not been published before. The original is in MTP; the text is published here by permission of the Trustees of the Mark Twain Estate (copyright, 1957, The Mark Twain Co., Inc.).

It will be recalled (§32, above) that Mollie Clemens was a member of the group of ladies of Carson who had arranged the fancy-dress ball on May 5 for the benefit of the Sanitary Fund. "This letter" is the open letter to the editors of the *Territorial Enterprise* dated May 18, 1864, which is reproduced as section 38, below. "Dan" is of course Mark Twain's colleague Dan De Quille (William Wright).

There is no evidence that Mark Twain took any action against Dr. H. H. Ross.

Although the texts of articles which appeared in newspapers of the 1860's have been normalized in spelling and, to a degree, in punctuation, this previously unpublished letter by Mark Twain and the three others included below in sections 39, 40, and 41 are transcribed exactly from the original manuscripts in Mark Twain's hand. Canceled passages in these letters are enclosed in brackets.

Virginia, *May 20*

My Dear Mollie:

I have had nothing but trouble & vexation since the Sanitary trip, & now this letter comes to aggravate me a thousand times worse. If it were from a man, I would answer it with a challenge, as the easiest way of getting out of a bad scrape, although I know I am in the wrong & would not be justified in doing such a thing. I wrote the squib the ladies letter refers to, & although I could give the names of the parties who made the offensive remarks I shall not do it, because they were said in drunken jest and no harm was meant by them. But for a misfortune of my own, they never would have seen the light. That misfortune was, that that item about the sack of flour slipped into the paper without either my consent or Dan's. We kept that Sanitary spree up for several days, & I wrote & laid that item before Dan when I was not sober (I shall not get drunk again, Mollie,)—and said he, "Is this a joke?" I told him "Yes." He said he would not like such a joke as that to be perpetrated upon him, & that it would wound the feelings of the ladies of Carson. He asked me if I wanted to do that, & I said "No, of course not." [& I threw it on the table] While we were talking, the manuscript lay on the table, & we forgot it & left it there when we went to the theatre, & [nev] I never thought of it again until I received this letter tonight, for I have not read a copy of the Enterprise for a week. I suppose the foreman, prospecting for copy, found it, & seeing that it was in my handwriting, thought it was to be published, & carried it off.

Now Mollie, whatever blame there is, rests with me alone, for if I had not [been just] had just sense enough to submit the article to Dan's better judgment, it would have been published all the same, & not by any mistake, either. Since it has made the ladies angry, I am sorry the thing occurred, & that is all I can do, for you will see yourself that their communication is altogether unanswerable. I cannot publish that, & explain it by saying the affair was a silly joke, & that I & all concerned were drunk. No—I'll die first.

Therefore, do one of two things: Either satisfy those ladies that I dealt honorably by them when I consented to let Dan suppress that article upon his assertion that its [would] publication would wound their feelings—or else make them appoint a man to avenge the wrong done them, with weapons in fair & open field.

They will understand at a glance that I cannot submit to the humiliation of publishing myself as a liar (according to the terms of their letter,) [& they will also understand] so long as I have the other alternative of either challenging or being challenged.

Mollie, the Sanitary expedition has been very disastrous to me. Aside from this trouble, (which I feel [worst] deepest,) I have two other quarrels on my hands, engendered on that day, & as yet I cannot tell how either of them is to end.

Mollie, I shall say nothing about this business until I hear from you. If they insist upon the publication of that letter, I shall still refuse, but Dr Ross shall hear from me, for I suspect that he is at the bottom of the whole business.

Your affectionate
Brother,
SAM

35.

Personal Correspondence

☞ This correspondence was published in the *Territorial Enterprise* on Tuesday, May 24, 1864. It has been reprinted, except for letters I and VI, by Ivan Benson (*Mark Twain's Western Years,* pp. 183–186, from the Sacramento *Union,* May 26, 1864), and less fully by Effie Mona Mack (*Mark Twain in Nevada,* pp. 317–321). Miss Mack (pp. 315–316) reprints the editorial and the "communication" from the *Union* (May 21, 1864) referred to in Mark Twain's letters to Laird.

[I]

ENTERPRISE OFFICE,
Saturday, May 21, 1864

JAMES LAIRD, ESQ.—*Sir:* In your paper of the present date appeared two anonymous articles, in which a series of insults were leveled at the writer of an editorial in Thursday's ENTERPRISE, headed "How is it?—How it is." I wrote that editorial.

Some time since it was stated in the Virginia *Union* that its proprietors were alone responsible for all articles published in its columns. You being the proper person, by seniority, to apply to in cases of this kind, I demand of you a public retraction of the insulting articles I have mentioned, or satisfaction. I require an immediate answer to this note. The bearer of this—Mr. Stephen Gillis—will receive any communication you may see fit to make.

Sam. L. Clemens

[II]

Office of the Virginia Daily Union ⎱
Virginia, May 21, 1864 ⎰

Samuel Clemens, Esq.—Mr. James Laird has just handed me your note of this date. Permit me to say that I am the *author* of the article appearing in this morning's *Union*. I am responsible for it. I have nothing to retract. Respectfully,

J. W. Wilmington

[III]

Enterprise Office, ⎱
Saturday Evening, May 21, 1864 ⎰

James Laird, Esq.—*Sir:*—I wrote you a note this afternoon demanding a published retraction of insults that appeared in two articles in the *Union* of this morning—or satisfaction. I have since received what purports to be a reply, written by a person who signs himself "J. W. Wilmington," in which he assumes the authorship and responsibility of one of said infamous articles. Mr. Wilmington is a person entirely unknown to me in the matter, and has nothing to do with it. In the columns of your paper you have declared *your own* responsibility for *all* articles appearing in it, and any farther attempt to make a catspaw of any other individual and thus shirk a responsibility that you had previously assumed will show that *you* are a cowardly sneak. I now *peremptorily* demand of you the satisfaction due to a gentleman—without alternative.

Sam. L. Clemens

[IV]

Office of the Virginia Daily Union, ⎱
Virginia, Saturday evening, May 21st, 1864 ⎰

Sam'l. Clemens, Esq.:—Your note of this evening is received. To the first portion of it I will briefly reply, that Mr. J. W. Wilmington, the avowed author of the article to which you object, is a gentleman now in the employ of the *Union* office. He formerly was one of the proprietors of the Cincinnati *Enquirer*. He was Captain of a Company in the Sixth Ohio Regiment, and fought at Shiloh. His responsibility and character can be vouched for to your abundant satisfaction.

For all editorials appearing in the *Union*, the proprietors are personally responsible; for communications, they hold themselves ready, when properly called upon, either to give the name and address of the author, or failing that, to be themselves responsible.

The editorial in the ENTERPRISE headed "How is it?" out of which this controversy grew, was an attack made upon the printers of the *Union*. It was replied to by a *Union* printer, and a representative of the printers, who in a communication denounced the writer of that article as a liar, a poltroon and a puppy. You announce yourself as the writer of the article which provoked this communication, and demand "satisfaction"—which satisfaction the writer informs you, over his own signature, he is quite ready to afford. I have no right, under the rulings of the code you have invoked, to step in and assume Mr. Wilmington's position, nor would he allow me to do so. You demand of me, in your last letter, the satisfaction due to a gentleman, and couple the demand with offensive remarks. When you have earned the right to the title by complying with the usual custom, I shall be most happy to afford you any satisfaction you desire at any time and in any place. In short, Mr. Wilmington has a prior claim upon your attention. When he is through with you, I shall be at your service. If you decline to meet him after challenging him, you will prove yourself to be what he has charged you with being: "a liar, a poltroon and a puppy," and as such, cannot of course be entitled to the consideration of a gentleman.

Respectfully,

JAMES L. LAIRD

[V]

ENTERPRISE OFFICE, VIRGINIA CITY ⎱
May 21, 1864—9 o'clock, P.M. ⎰

JAMES L. LAIRD, ESQ.—*Sir:* Your reply to my last note—in which I *peremptorily demanded satisfaction of you, without alternative*—is just received, and to my utter astonishment you still endeavor to shield your craven carcass behind the person of an individual who in spite of *your* introduction is entirely unknown to me, and upon whose shoulders you *cannot* throw the whole responsibility. You acknowledge and reaffirm in this note that "For all *editorials* appearing in the *Union*, the *proprietors are personally responsible*." Now, sir, had there appeared no *editorial* on the subject endorsing and reiterating the slanderous and disgraceful insults heaped upon me in the "communication," I would have simply called upon you and demanded the name of its author, and upon your answer would have depended my farther action. But the "Editorial" alluded to was equally vile and slanderous as the "communication," and being an "Editorial" would naturally have more weight in the minds of readers. It was the following undignified and abominably insulting slander appearing in your "Editorial" headed "The 'How is it' issue," that occasioned my sending you first an *alternative* and then a *peremptory challenge*:

"Never before in a long period of newspaper intercourse—never before in any contact with a cotemporary, however unprincipled he might have been, have we found an opponent in statement or in discussion, who had no gentlemanly sense of professional propriety, who conveyed in every word, and in every purpose of all his words, such a groveling disregard for truth, decency and courtesy as to seem to court the distinction, only, of being understood as a vulgar liar. Meeting one who prefers falsehood; whose instincts are all toward falsehood; whose thought is falsification; whose aim is vilification through insincere professions of honesty; one whose only merit is thus described, and who evidently desires to be thus known, the obstacles presented are entirely insurmountable, and whoever would touch them fully, should expect to be abominably defiled."—*Union, May 21*

You assume in your last note, that I "have challenged Mr. Wilmington," and that he has informed me "over his own signature," that he is quite ready to afford me "satisfaction." Both assumptions are utterly false. I have twice challenged *you*, and you have twice attempted to shirk the responsibility. *Mr. W's* note could not possibly be an answer to my demand of satisfaction from *you*; and besides, his note simply avowed authorship of a certain "communication" that appeared simultaneously with your libelous "editorial," and states that its author had "nothing to retract." For your gratification, however, I will remark that Mr. Wilmington's case *will be attended to in due time* by a distant acquaintance of his who is not willing to see him suffer in obscurity. In the meantime, if you do not wish yourself posted as a coward, you will *at once accept my peremptory challenge, which I now reiterate.*

SAM. L. CLEMENS

[VI]

OFFICE TERRITORIAL ENTERPRISE ⎱
VIRGINIA, *May 21, 1864* ⎰

J. W. WILMINGTON—*Sir:* You are, perhaps, far from those who are wont to advise and care for you, else you would see the policy of minding your own business and letting that of other people alone. Under these circumstances, therefore, I take the liberty of suggesting that you are getting out of your sphere. *A contemptible ass and coward* like yourself should only meddle in the affairs of *gentlemen* when called upon to do so. I approve and endorse the course of my principal in this matter, and if your sensitive disposition is aroused by any proceeding of his, I have only to say that I can be found at the ENTERPRISE office, and always at your service.

S. E. GILLIS

[To the above, Mr. Wilmington gave a verbal reply to Mr. Millard—the gentleman through whom the note was conveyed to him—stating that he had no quarrel with Mr. Gillis; that he had written his communication only in defense of the craft, and did not desire a quarrel with a member of that craft; he showed Mr. G's note to Mr. Millard, who read it, but made no comments upon it.]

[VII]

OFFICE OF THE VIRGINIA DAILY UNION, ⎱
Monday Morning, *May 23, 1864* ⎰

SAMUEL CLEMENS, ESQ.:—In reply to your lengthy communication, I have only to say that in your note opening this correspondence, you demanded satisfaction for a communication in the *Union* which branded the writer of an article in the ENTERPRISE as a *liar*, a *poltroon* and a puppy. You declare yourself to be the writer of the ENTERPRISE article, and the avowed author of the *Union* communication stands ready to afford satisfaction. Any attempt to evade a meeting with him and force one upon me will utterly fail, as I have no right under the rulings of the code, to meet or hold any communication with you in this connection. The *threat* of being posted as a coward cannot have the slightest effect upon the position I have assumed in the matter. If you think this correspondence reflects credit upon *you*, I advise you by all means to publish it; in the meantime you must excuse me from receiving any more long epistles from you.

James L. Laird

I denounce Mr. Laird as an unmitigated liar, because he says I published an editorial in which I attacked the printers employed on the *Union*, whereas there is nothing in that editorial which can be so construed. Moreover, he is a liar on general principles, and from natural instinct. I denounce him as an abject coward, because it has been stated in his paper that its proprietors are responsible for all articles appearing in its columns, yet he backs down from that position; because he acknowledges the "code," but will not live up to it; because he says himself that he is responsible for all "editorials," and then backs down from that also; and because he insults me in his note marked "IV," and yet refuses to fight me. Finally, he is a fool, because he cannot understand that a publisher is bound to stand responsible for any and all articles printed by him, whether he wants to do it or not.

Sam. L. Clemens

36.

"Miscegenation"

☞ The authorship of this unsigned editorial, published May 24, 1864, in the *Territorial Enterprise*, is clear from the writer's acknowledgment of the authorship of the "How Is It?" editorial in the same paper.

The word "miscegenation" was one of the most widely publicized and most controversial slogans of the presidential campaign of 1864. It had been coined for political purposes by David Goodman Croly, city editor of the violently Democratic New York *World*, and had been introduced to the public as the title of an anonymous pamphlet by Croly and George Wakeman, a younger colleague on the staff of the *World*.[1] *Miscegenation: The Theory of the Blending of the Races, Applied to the American White Man and Negro,* a pamphlet of seventy-two pages, was published in New York just before Christmas of 1863. The work was a hoax. The authors hoped to arouse the hostility of voters toward the Republican party by circulating an enthusiastic advocacy of intermarriage between whites and Negroes as a statement of Republican opinion. An especially ingenious political maneuver was a passage declaring the Irish to be inferior to Negroes and urging them to accept intermarriage with the Negro as a solution to their problem. The pamphlet attracted much attention. It figured in debates in the House of Representatives, and was even discussed at length in the London press. Although the nature of the hoax was not fully recognized during the campaign— some observers seem to have considered it to be the work of an obtuse but sincere abolitionist fanatic—Republican politicians recognized the potential danger to their cause from the dissemination of the notion that Republicans advocated social equality for the Negro. The Chicago *Tribune,* for example, said editorially on March 18, 1864, that the supposed Republican advocacy of miscegenation was "the 'phantom bouquet' of the copperhead fancy." The comment was quoted in the Virginia City *Daily Union* on April 23 (p. 1). The fact that Mark Twain had the impulse, however fleeting, to use "miscegenation" as a term of reproach suggests that he had not entirely lost his unexamined Southern tendency to sympathize with the Democrats' hostility to the Negro, even though he did not share their opposition to Lincoln's administration. His reference to a miscegenation society in the East was apparently directed at the National Freedman's Relief Association, then recently organized as a private philanthropy. On May 24, 1864, the *Daily Union* (p. 2) announced that the Association was "about to solicit contributions from the good people of Virginia" and urged support for it.

Wᴇ published a rumor, the other day, that the moneys collected at the Carson Fancy Dress Ball were to be diverted from the Sanitary Fund and sent forward to aid a "miscegenation" or some other sort of Society in the East. We also stated that the rumor was a hoax. And it was—we were perfectly right. However, four ladies are offended. We cannot quarrel with ladies—the very thought of such a thing is repulsive; neither can we consent to offend them—even unwittingly—without being sorry for the misfortune, and seeking their forgiveness, which is a kindness we hope they will not refuse. We intended no harm, as they would understand easily enough if they knew the history of this offense of ours, but we must suppress that history, since it would rather be amusing than otherwise, and the amusement would be at our expense. We have no love for that kind of amusement—and the same trait belongs to human nature generally. One lady complained that we should at least have answered the note they sent us. It is true. There is small excuse for our neglect of a common politeness like that, yet we venture to apologize for it, and will still hope for pardon, just the same. We have noticed one thing in this whole business—and also in many an instance which has gone before it—and that is, that we resemble the majority of our species in the respect that we are very apt to get entirely in the wrong, even when there is no seeming necessity for it; but to offset this vice, we claim one of the virtues of our species, which is that we are ready to repair such wrongs when we discover them.

37.

Two Editorials in the Gold Hill *Evening News*
May 24, 1864

HOITY! TOITY!!

THE cross-firing that has been going on for a week past between the *Union* and the *Enterprise,* concerning a donation made by the employees of the former paper to the Sanitary Fund, has at last culminated in a serious row, and the bloody and barbarous code has been appealed to. Nearly a column of this morning's *Enterprise* is devoted to the publication of the correspondence between Sam Clemens (Mark Twain) and James L. Laird, and Mr. Wilmington, who comes in as an intervenor, and assumes the responsibility of the article for the publication of which Clemens holds Laird to an account. Laird declines to accede to the proposition of Clemens, and the latter proceeds to "post" him, with all those epithets in such case by the code made and provided. This is emphatically a bad egg. In the first place, the cause of the quarrel was not one calculated to enlist public sympathy; neither did the discussion of the question demand the use of the language which was resorted to. If the matter results in bloodshed, the victim will not be mourned as a martyr in a holy cause, nor the victor crowned with laurel as the champion of right. The sentiment of a civilized community revolts at the appeal to the bloody code on every trifling cause of offense. There is another reason, and that a very serious one, why we object to the code being called into requisition on slight occasions among the editorial fraternity. We have noticed that there is a proneness to fire at the legs, and that "there is a divinity that *un*-shapes our *ends*" to the extent that one of the parties is ever afterwards remarkable for the gait vulgarly styled the "step and go fetch it." We have, albeit living in a duelling community; lo! these many years, managed thus far to keep step with the balance of our fellow citizens; and have no fancy, now that we are passing into the "sere and yaller," to have every impudent scallawag on the street accosting us with, "How are you, old limpy?" This thing must be put stop [*sic*].

A FALSTAFFIAN DUEL

As we go to press, a rumor is rife in town that Pete Hopkins, of Carson, having heard that his friend Mark Twain was about to enter into a contract to be killed, has come to the rescue and assumed the dying part. Pete has had no rest since that terrible massacre at Dutch Nick's, and is desirous of dying a savage death; besides, he thinks he would make a better target than Mark, in which opinion we coincide. Blood, or *something else,* is likely to grow out of the difficulty, unless the parties can be made to believe, in the language of Bulwer, that "the pen is mightier than the sword." The duel will perhaps come off in the pine forest at Empire City. Horrible! most horrible!

38.

The *Enterprise* Libel of the Ladies of Carson

☞ A letter published in the Virginia City *Daily Union,* May 26–27, 1864.

CARSON CITY, *May 21st, 1864*

VIRGINIA DAILY UNION: The following communication, in reply to a libelous article which appeared in the Enterprise of the 18th inst., was sent to that journal for publication, but thus far no notice has been taken of it. By inserting it in your columns, you will confer a favor upon the ladies whose names are appended, and, *perhaps*, draw a reply from "Mark Twain," the author of the scurrilous item.

CITIZEN

CARSON CITY, *May 18th, 1864*

EDITORS OF ENTERPRISE: In your issue of yesterday, you state "that the reason the Flour Sack was not taken from Dayton to Carson, was because it was stated that the money raised at the Sanitary Fancy Dress Ball, recently held in Carson for the St. Louis Fair, had been diverted from its legitimate course, and was to be sent to aid a Miscegenation Society somewhere in the East; and it was feared the proceeds of the sack might be similarly disposed of." You apparently mollify the statement by saying "that it was a hoax, but not all a hoax, for an effort is being made to divert those funds from their proper course."

In behalf of the ladies who originated and assisted in carrying out the programme, let us say that the whole statement is a *tissue of falsehoods,* made for *malicious* purposes, and we demand the name of the author. The ball was gotten up in aid of the Sanitary Commission, and *not* for the St. Louis Fair. At a meeting of the ladies, held in this city last week, no decision was arrived at as to whether the proceeds of the ball should be sent to St. Louis or New York, but one thing *was decided,* that they should go to the aid of the sick and wounded soldiers, who are fighting the battles of our country, *and for no other purpose.* The only discussion had upon the subject was whether the funds should be forwarded to St. Louis or New York, and this grew out of a circular received from St. Louis, by one of the members, stating "that a portion of the proceeds of the St. Louis Fair, were to be applied to the aid of the Freedmen's Society." In order to have no mistake in the matter, and that the funds should all be applied to the Sanitary Commission, it was proposed by some of the ladies that the money be sent to New York, but no final decision was arrived at. In conclusion, let us say that the ladies having the matter in charge, consider themselves capable of deciding as to what shall be done with the money, without the aid of outsiders, who are probably desirous of acquiring some *glory* by appropriating the efforts of the ladies to themselves.

Mrs. W. K. Cutler, *President*
Mrs. H. F. Rice, *Vice President*
Mrs. S. D. King, *Treasurer*
Mrs. H. H. Ross, *Sec'y San. Ball*

The ladies signing the above card, sent it to the editors of the "Enterprise," and not to any individual. The assumption in "Enterprise" of May 24th, that they were expecting an answer from "Mark Twain," except through the "Enterprise," is his, not theirs.

Citizen

39.

Letter from Samuel L. Clemens to Orion Clemens
Virginia City, May 25, 1864

☞ The original of this previously unpublished letter is in MTP. Published here by permission of the Mark Twain Estate (copyright, 1957, The Mark Twain Co., Inc.).

For information about William H. Clagett, see the Biographical Directory.

It is not entirely clear just who were the three persons from whom Mark Twain thought he might receive a challenge, or what was the nature of the additional quarrels he had on hand, or how he considered he had triumphed over the ladies of Carson. The man to whom he says he has sent a challenge is presumably Laird.

The biographer of Mark Twain should note that on this particular day he was carrying a revolver.

Va, *Wednesday* A.M.

My Dear Bro.

Don't stump for the Sanitary Fund—Billy Clagett says he certainly will not. If I have been so unlucky as to rob you of some of your popularity by that unfortunate item, I claim at your hands that you neither increase nor diminish it by so fruitless a proceeding as making speeches for the Fund. I am mighty sick of that fund—it has caused me all my d——d troubles—& I shall leave the

Territory when your first speech is announced, & leave it for good.

I see by the Union of this morning, that those ladies have seduced from me what I consider was a sufficient apology, [under] coming from a man open to a challenge from three persons, & already awaiting the issue of such a message to another—they got out of me what no *man* would ever have got, & then—well, they are ladies, & I shall not speak harshly of them. Now although the Union folks have kept quiet this morning, (much against my expectations,) I still have a quarrel or two on hand—so that this flour sack business may rest, as far as Carson is concerned. I shall take no notice of it at all, except to mash Mr Laird over the head with my revolver for publishing it if I meet him to-day—otherwise, I do nothing. I consider that I have triumphed over those ladies at last, & I am quits with them. But when I forgive the injury—or forget it— [may] or fail to set up a score against it, as opportunity offers—may I be able to console myself for it with the consciousness that I have become a marvellously better man. [At] I have no intention of *hunting* for the puppy, Laird, Mollie, but he had better let me have 24 hours unmolested, to get cool in.

[We await the result of]

But for Heaven's sake give me at least the peace & quiet it will afford me to know that no stumping is to be done for the unlucky Sanitary Fund.   Yro Bro

SAM

40.

Letter from Samuel L. Clemens to Orion Clemens
Virginia City, May 26, 1864

☞ The original of this previously unpublished letter is in MTP. Published here by permission of the Trustees of the Mark Twain Estate (copyright, 1957, the Mark Twain Co., Inc.).

It should be noted that at this point Mark Twain and Steve Gillis intended to remain in San Francisco a month and then go East. They may have had in mind the plan for trying to sell the silver mine in New York mentioned in "Sources of Controversy," in Part One.

Mark Twain's courage and belligerence are substantiated by the fact that the fire-eating Gillis had vetoed one of his proposed courses of action on the score that it would not be safe.

The Hale & Norcross was one of the important mines on the Comstock Lode, in Virginia City. Until 1864 it had not been nearly so productive as its neighbors, the Savage, Chollar, and Potosi. But in 1866–1867, and especially after John W. Mackay, James G. Fair, James C. Flood, and William S. O'Brien got control of it in 1869, it was to prove highly profitable.[1] Mark Twain presumably refers to Hale & Norcross stock held by him and Orion. There is no evidence that either of the brothers realized any substantial return from their mining speculations.

VA, *May 26, 1864.*

MY DEAR BRO—

Send me two hundred dollars *if you can spare it comfortably.*— However, never mind—you can send it to San Francisco if you prefer. Steve & I are going to the States. We leave Sunday morning per Henness Pass. Say nothing about it, of course. We are not afraid of the grand jury, but Washoe has long since grown irksome to us, & we want to leave it anyhow.

We have thoroughly canvassed the Carson business, & concluded we dare not do anything, either to Laird or Carson men without spoiling our chances of getting away. However, if there is any chance of the husbands of those women challenging *me*, I don't want a straw put in the way of it. I'll wait for them a month, if necessary, & fight them with *any* weapon they choose. I thought of challenging one of them & then crossing the line to await the result, but Steve says it would not be safe, situated as we are.

When I get to the Bay—where we shall remain a month—I will fix the Hale & Norcross in a safe shape.

My best love to Mollie,

SAM

41.

Draft of a Letter from Samuel L. Clemens
to W. K. Cutler

Virginia City, May 28, 1864

☞ The original of this document, in Mark Twain's handwriting, is in the Dan De Quille Papers, Bancroft Library, University of California, Berkeley. Published here by permission of the Bancroft Library and of the Trustees of the Mark Twain Estate (copyright 1957, The Mark

Twain Co., Inc.). The editor wishes to acknowledge the kindness of Mr. Cecil G. Tilton in bringing the note to his attention.

The letter was never sent. It is endorsed on the back in another handwriting, as follows: "Mark Twain to Cutler, First draft of document left on my desk when a second was written and sent. Nothing came of the matter. Dan De Quille."

Virginia, *May 28, 1864.*

W. K. Cutler—

Sir—To-day, I have received a letter from you, in which you assume that you have been offended and insulted by certain acts of mine. Having apologized once for that offensive conduct, I shall not do it again. Your recourse is in a challenge. I am ready to accept it.

Having made my arrangements—before I received your note— to leave for California, & having no time to fool away on a common bummer like you, I want an immediate reply to this.

42.

An Editorial in the Gold Hill *Evening News*
May 30, 1864

☞ Dutch Nick's and the Hopkins family figure in Mark Twain's "Empire City massacre" hoax. See headnotes to sections 12 and 29.

AN EXILE

Among the few immortal names of the departed—that is, those who departed yesterday morning per California stage—we notice that of Mark Twain. We don't wonder. Mark Twain's beard is full of dirt, and his face is black before the people of Washoe. Giving way to the idiosyncratic eccentricities of an erratic mind, Mark has indulged in the game infernal—in short, "played hell." Shifting the *locale* of his tales of fiction from the Forest of Dutch Nick's to Carson City; the *dramatis personae* thereof from the Hopkins family to the fair Ladies of the Ladies' Fair; and the plot thereof from murder to miscegenation—he slopped. The indignation aroused by his enormities has been too crushing to be borne by living man, though sheathed with the brass and triple cheek of Mark Twain.

Thrice the brinded cat hath mewed,
Thrice, and once the hedge-pig whined.

Thrice the card of the indignant ladies has appeared in the columns of the *Union,* and once the Carson *Independent* contains the following:

LADIES' SANITARY SOCIETY.—The ladies interested in the Sanitary Commission met in the parlor of the Ormsby House on Thursday evening last, for the purpose of ascertaining the amount of funds derived from all sources in aid of the Sanitary Fund. After deducting all expenses, it was found they had just $2,000, which was forwarded to Dr. Bellows, President of the National Sanitary Commission, yesterday. A vote of thanks was tendered to His Excellency Governor Nye, for his able lecture delivered in aid of the Fund, and to the *Independent* office for many favors in the way of printing; also to the officers of the society, and ladies who have assisted in the undertaking. The ladies all seemed highly pleased with their efforts, and we are informed that before adjourning they gave three cheers for the *immortal four,* and three groans for the *Territorial Enterprise.*

Those groans were not for the *Enterprise* in the abstract, but for the *Enterprise* as the vehicle of Mark Twain's abominations. He has *vamosed,* cut stick, absquatulated; and among the pine forests of the Sierras, or amid the purlieus of the city of earthquakes, he will tarry awhile, and the office of the *Enterprise* will become purified, and by the united efforts of Goodman and Dan De Quille once more merit the sweet smiles of the ladies of Carson.

Sources of the Items Included in This Volume

(The scrapbooks are in MTP)

20. Doings in Nevada, January 4, 1864 — New York *Sunday Mercury*, Feb. 7, 1864, p. 3

21. Letter from Mark Twain, January 10, 1864 — Scrapbook 4, p. 4

22. Legislative Proceedings, January 12, 1864 — Scrapbook 3, p. 83

23. Legislative Proceedings, January 13, 1864 — Scrapbook 4, p. 3

24. Letter from Mark Twain, January 14, 1864 — Scrapbook 4, p. 4

25. Legislative Proceedings, January 14–27, 1864 — Scrapbook 4, pp. 3, 86, 94, 141

26. Legislative Proceedings, January 28, 1864 — Scrapbook 3, p. 140

27. Letter from Mark Twain, February 5, 1864 — Scrapbook 3, p. 106

28. Legislative Proceedings, February 8–15, 1864 — Scrapbook 3, pp. 102–104, 106, 108, 109–110

29. Letter from Mark Twain, February 13, 1864 — Scrapbook 3, p. 111

30. The Removal of the Capital, February 15, 1864 — Scrapbook 3, p. 111

31. Legislative Proceedings, February 16–20, 1864 — Scrapbook 3, pp. 112–114, 116–118

32. Letter from Mark Twain, April 25, 1864 — Scrapbook 3, p. 144

33. History of the Gold and Silver Bars—How They Do Things in Washoe, May 16, 1864 — Scrapbook 1, p. 59

34. Letter from Samuel L. Clemens to Mrs. Orion Clemens, Virginia City, May 20, 1864 — Original in MTP

35. Personal Correspondence, published May 24, 1864 — Scrapbook 3, p. 146

36. Miscegenation, published May 24, 1864 — Scrapbook 3, p. 146

37. (*a*) Hoity! Toity! (*b*) A Falstaffian Duel — Gold Hill *Evening News*, May 24, 1864, pp. 2, 3

38. The "Enterprise" Libel of the Ladies of Carson — Virginia City *Daily Union*, May 26–27, 1864, p. 2

39. Letter from Samuel L. Clemens to Orion Clemens, Virginia City, May 25, 1864 — Original in MTP

40. Letter from Samuel L. Clemens to Orion Clemens, Virginia City, May 26, 1864 — Original in MTP

41. Draft (Unsent) of a Letter from Samuel L. Clemens to W. K. Cutler, Virginia City, May 28, 1864

Original in Dan De Quille Papers, Bancroft Library

42. An Exile

Gold Hill *Evening News,* May 20, 1864, p. 2

NOTES TO PART ONE
"Those Were the Days!"
(Pages 3–30)

[1] *Mark Twain's Letters,* ed. A. B. Paine (hereafter *Letters*), II, 773.

[2] *Letters,* I, 187.

[3] *Roughing It,* II, 12. The yield of the Comstock mines increased from $6,000,000 in 1862 to $12,400,000 in 1863 and $16,000,000 in 1864; but depression hit toward the end of that year, and production did not recover fully until the mid-1870's (Grant H. Smith, *History of the Comstock Lode,* pp. 32, 58, 164–165). In midsummer of 1863 the population of Virginia City reached 15,000 (*ibid.,* p. 28).

[4] *Letters,* I, 82.

[5] *Ibid.,* p. 85.

[6] *Ibid.,* p. 82.

[7] *Ibid.,* p. 83.

[8] Samuel L. Clemens (hereafter SLC) to William H. Clagett, Esmeralda, Nevada Territory, Sept. 9, 1862, typescript (hereafter TS) in Mark Twain Papers, University of California Library, Berkeley (hereafter MTP).

[9] Ivan Benson, *Mark Twain's Western Years,* p. 175.

[10] Virginia City *Evening Bulletin,* Aug. 24, 1863, p. 3; Oct. 8, 1863, p. 3.

[11] E. M. Branch, "Chronological Bibliography," *passim.*

¹² The Grant H. Smith Papers in the Bancroft Library, University of California, Berkeley, contain two additional articles by Mark Twain belonging to this period which have not been printed in any book. They are: (1) an article reprinted in the *Alta California,* date unspecified, from the *Territorial Enterprise* of Aug. 29, 1862, describing the duel on Aug. 28 in which Joe Goodman shot Tom Fitch in the knee; (2) an article from an unidentified source, date unspecified, entitled "The Spanish" and describing a trip through one of the mines on the Comstock Lode. In a MS note Smith asserts that the article appeared in the *Enterprise* on Feb. 2, 1863; but this date seems improbable because that Feb. 2 was a Monday and the paper was not published on Mondays.

¹³ A. B. Paine, *Mark Twain, A Biography* (hereafter *Biography*), Appendix C, I, in Vol. III, pp. 1597–1599; Benson, *op. cit.,* pp. 176–177.

¹⁴ SLC to Jane Clemens and Pamela Clemens Moffett, original in MTP. Paine (*Letters,* I, 101–102) publishes part of this letter.

¹⁵ Grant H. Smith says in his unpublished study "Mark Twain in Nevada" (Grant H. Smith Papers, Carton 3, p. 74 n.) that Albert B. Paine gave this scrapbook to Willard S. Morse of Pasadena on the occasion of Paine's visit to Nevada and California in 1907—three years before Mark Twain's death.

¹⁶ *Biography,* I, 222.

¹⁷ *Mark Twain in Eruption,* ed. Bernard De Voto, p. 392. The remark seems to refer to the second Territorial Legislature, in 1862, but the pseudonym was not in use at that time. Mark Twain had telescoped his recollections of this session and the next, in 1864.

¹⁸ Letter to the *Territorial Enterprise,* Dec. 31, 1863, § 18.

¹⁹ A. J. Marsh, *Marsh's New Manual of Reformed Phonetic Short-Hand* (first published in 1868), San Francisco, 1892. The alphabet is based on that of Isaac Pitman. Marsh is listed as "general reporter, Sacramento Daily and Weekly Union" in Leonard Mears, *Sacramento Directory for the Years 1863–4,* p. 90. When he reported the Nevada Constitutional Convention of 1864, his residence was still listed as Sacramento (Myron Angel, ed., *History of Nevada,* p. 86). Extensive shorthand reporting of political speeches for newspapers was apparently a novelty in the West. The Virginia City *Daily Union* remarked editorially on Jan. 6, 1864 (p. 1): "The fine art of phonographic reporting and the persistency with which it is being employed by the press, is subjecting the public men of the country to an unaccustomed and dreadful ordeal."

²⁰ In 1909, more than forty-five years later, Mark Twain wrote an article entitled "A Simplified Alphabet" advocating the general use of Burnz's "Alphabet of Phonic Shorthand," which was, like the Marsh alphabet, based on that of Pitman (*What is Man? and Other Essays,* pp. 256–264). Paine's date of 1899, on p. 256, is probably erroneous, for the MS itself (Paine No. 103, MTP) bears the date "1908–9" in Paine's

hand. Mark Twain proposes to use the Burnz alphabet but to *"spell every word out."* With characteristic enthusiasm he declares: "That admirable alphabet, that brilliant alphabet, that inspired alphabet, can be learned in an hour or two. In a week the student can learn to write it with some little facility, and to read it with considerable ease. I . . . saw it tried in a public school in Nevada forty-five years ago, and was so impressed by the incident that it has remained in my memory ever since." (In § 24 Mark Twain describes this visit to Lawlor's school. He says the boys used Graham's system of shorthand, but the difference among various modifications of Pitman was slight.) In the course of the 1909 essay he remarks (p. 261), "I am not pretending to write that character well. I have never had a lesson, and I am copying the letters from the book." This statement carries conviction, and other evidence supports it. Among the Mark Twain Papers are 38 notebooks in his own handwriting, the earliest dating from his days on the Mississippi River as a cub pilot, the latest from 1905. One of these (given the number 4 by Paine) belongs to the years 1864–1865. The first entry in it reads, "About 1st June left Va, N.T., 1864, & went to San F, Cal." On p. [7] there are two entries written partly in a phonetic alphabet. Since Mark Twain was using a pencil, he could not follow exactly the system of light and heavy strokes on which Marsh's alphabet relied, but the intention is evidently to use Marsh's symbols for consonants in rather awkward conjunction with ordinary nonphonetic vowel signs. The shorthand symbols are clumsily made—the writer was obviously a novice. There is one later instance of shorthand symbols in this notebook (indecipherable but apparently a single word) and six lines of symbols, again indecipherable, in a notebook of 1882 (No. 16, MTP). I am aware of no other instances of Mark Twain's use of shorthand except a dozen pages of exercises apparently written at the time he was composing the essay of 1909, and of course the manuscript of the essay itself, which is illustrated with cuts of shorthand words and phrases written by the author.

[21] "Reporters in the Convention," *Territorial Enterprise*, Nov. 23, 1863, in Scrapbook 2, p. 145, MTP. The letter is unsigned, but Marsh's authorship is indicated by internal evidence.

[22] *Territorial Enterprise*, undated clipping, Scrapbook 2, p. 153, MTP.

[23] Virginia City *Daily Union*, Feb. 2, 1864, p. 2. Rice used the pseudonym "Carl" in writing letters to the *Union*.

[24] "Legislative Proceedings," *Territorial Enterprise*, Feb. 21, 1864, in Scrapbook 3, p. 116 (House), p. 117 (Council). A motion to pay the *Enterprise* $300.00 for publishing the Constitution was defeated (p. 116). The rates of pay for reporters seem to reflect currency inflation. Rice and one A. W. Oliver had been given a bonus of $3.00 a day for the first session of the Legislature in 1861 (*Laws of the Territory of Nevada, Passed at the First Regular Session of the Legislative Assembly*, p. 284). During

the second session, in 1862, the bonus paid to Clemens and Rice had been $6.00 a day ("Letter from Nevada Territory," Sacramento *Union*, Dec. 22, 1862, p. 8).

²⁵ *Territorial Enterprise*, Jan. 16, 1864, in Scrapbook 3, p. 86.

²⁶ *Ibid.*, Feb. 14, 1864, in Scrapbook 3, p. 109.

²⁷ *Ibid.*, Feb. 12, 1864, in Scrapbook 3, p. 107. "Barry" was probably a nickname for "Baruch." In the next passage quoted the name is rendered "Barrac."

²⁸ *Ibid.*, Feb. 23, 1864, in Scrapbook 3, p. 118.

²⁹ *Ibid.* The *Union* omitted the account of this incident from the dispatch covering the proceedings of the legislature, but "Carl" described it in his "Letter from Carson" (Virginia City *Daily Union*, Feb. 23, 1864, p. 2). "Carl" was a little dry concerning the antics of the legislators: "There was a vast deal of native wit of a high order wasted during the remainder of the session, which closed about midnight, to the joy of every man, woman and child in this burg."

³⁰ SLC to Jane Clemens and Pamela Clemens Moffett, Steamboat Springs, Nevada Territory, Aug. 19, 1863, typescript in MTP. Paine publishes this letter in part (*Letters*, I, 91–93) but omits the passage quoted here. I have not been able to identify the bill Mark Twain says he killed.

³¹ *Territorial Enterprise*, Jan. 5, 1864, in Scrapbook 3, p. 79.

³² *Mark Twain's Autobiography*, ed. A. B. Paine, II, 307–308.

³³ *Laws of the Territory of Nevada, Passed at the Second Regular Session of the Legislative Assembly*, pp. 162–163 (hereafter *Laws, Second Session*). Orion Clemens wrote to his wife on January 2, 1862, from Carson City: "The Legislature passed a fee bill in my favor, allowing me to charge fees on copying, &c.; but it doesn't amount to much" (original in MTP).

³⁴ *Laws of the Territory of Nevada, Passed at the Third Regular Session of the Legislative Assembly*, p. 49 (hereafter *Laws, Third Session*).

³⁵ "Letter from Carson," Virginia City *Daily Union*, Feb. 12, 1864, p. 3.

³⁶ *Laws, Second Session*, p. 91. This legislation supplemented a vaguer statute passed by the first legislature directing the Secretary to take custody of all records of Carson County, and allowing him fifteen cents a folio for copying (*Laws of the Territory of Nevada, Passed at the First Regular Session of the Legislative Assembly*, p. 286; hereafter *Laws, First Session*).

³⁷ Virginia City *Daily Union*, Jan. 30, 1864, p. 1. Perhaps "Carl" overstates the amount of money: the published report of the Territorial Auditor shows that for the period Nov. 1, 1862—Dec. 31, 1863, Orion drew $5,713.30 for "copying county Records." His salary for this period was $1,416.67 (*Annual Reports of the Secretary of the Territory, Territorial Auditor, Treasurer, Superintendent of Public Instruction, and Adjutant-General, January 13, 1864*, p. 7 of Auditor's report).

³⁸ SLC to Jane Clemens and Pamela Clemens Moffett, San Francisco,

[May ? 1863], original in MTP. He had written to the same correspondents a few months earlier: "I pick up a foot or two occasionally for lying about somebody's mine" (SLC to Jane Clemens and Pamela Clemens Moffett, Virginia City, Feb. 16, 1863, in Webster, ed., *Mark Twain, Business Man*, p. 77). But in interpreting this statement one should remember that the frontier humorist habitually referred to his art as "lying." In this same letter (p. 78), Mark Twain says: "What do you show my letters for? Can't you let me tell a lie occasionally to keep my hand in for the public, without exposing me?"

[30] SLC to Jane Clemens and Pamela Clemens Moffett, July 18, [1863], original in MTP. He was probably referring to a story written for the *Enterprise* of that day, the general tenor of which can be inferred from a passage in his weekly letter to the San Francisco *Call*, dated July 19: "The 'North Ophir' is coming into favor again. As nuggets of pure silver as large as pieces of chalk were found in liberal quantities in the ledge, the mine was pronounced 'salted,' and the stock fell from $60 to $13 a foot. However, during the last day or two a hundred experienced miners have examined the claim, and laughed at the idea of its having been salted. . . . Their testimony has removed the stain from the North Ophir's character, and the stock has already begun to recover" (reprinted in "Mark's Letters to San Francisco *Call*," ed. A. E. Hutcheson, *Twainian*, Jan.–Feb., 1952, p. 4).

[40] SLC to Orion Clemens, Esmeralda, July 30, 1862, in *Letters*, I, 83; *Roughing It*, II, 4, 16. On Feb. 16, 1863, he wrote that his salary from the paper was six dollars a day (Webster, ed., *Mark Twain, Business Man*, p. 77).

[41] SLC to Jane Clemens and Pamela Clemens Moffett, Virginia City, Aug. 5, [1863], original in MTP. It is significant that this convincing statement about the meagerness of his financial resources was made only a few weeks after a visit to San Francisco during which he had tried hard to make money speculating in mining stocks (SLC to Orion Clemens, San Francisco, June 20, 1863, original in MTP).

[42] Mark Twain's salary on the *Call* was apparently $140.00 a month— less than his salary on the *Enterprise* (SLC to Jane Clemens and Pamela Clemens Moffett, San Francisco, Oct. 19, 1864, typescript in MTP). In Virginia City, where prices were possibly higher than in San Francisco, he and his roommate had paid $70.00 a month for a room which they shared, and $50.00 a month each for board. With laundry, Mark Twain found that "it costs me $100 a month to live" (SLC to Jane Clemens and Pamela Clemens Moffett, Virginia City, July 18, 1863, typescript in MTP). This was not a self-indulgent budget: on July 7, 1863 (p. 3), the Virginia City *Evening Bulletin* named $100.00 a month as the cost of living "respectably" for a single man.

[43] *Roughing It*, II, 136–137.

[44] The term was current in Nevada during the 1860's. In announc-

ing Mark Twain's lecture on the Sandwich Islands to be delivered in Virginia City, the *Daily Union* called him a "wandering Bohemian" (Oct. 29, 1866, p. 3) and an "old Bohemian" (Oct. 31, p. 3), and remarked: "We have heard of Bohemians falling so low as to become candidates for Governor, Congress or U. S. Senator, but when one condescends to turn lecturer we—well, Mark we are glad to see you at your old home after so long an absence" (Oct. 29, p. 3).

⁴⁵ SLC to Jane Clemens and Pamela Clemens Moffett, Virginia City, Aug. 5, [1863], original in MTP.

⁴⁶ William Wright, "Reporting with Mark Twain," *Californian Illustrated Magazine*, IV (1893), 170, 171.

⁴⁷ *Territorial Enterprise*, Nov. 8, 1863, in Scrapbook 2, p. 109, MTP.

⁴⁸ "Nevada and the Civil War," in S. P. Davis, ed., *History of Nevada*, I, 270–271; and see the headnote to § 8, below.

⁴⁹ Letter from Nevada Territory," Sacramento *Union*, Dec. 18, 1862, p. 1.

⁵⁰ *Ibid.*, Dec. 23, 1862, p. 1.

⁵¹ Below, § 25; G. H. Smith, "Mark Twain in Nevada," p. 57.

⁵² For example, a long speech by James Stark, reported in *Territorial Enterprise*, Nov. 13, 1863, in Scrapbook 2, pp. 121–122, MTP.

⁵³ For example, Virginia City *Daily Union*, Jan. 6, 1864, p. 2.

⁵⁴ Gold Hill *Evening News*, Jan. 12, 1864, p. 2, asserting that the *Union*, in Carson City, before it was moved to Virginia City, had been known as a Copperhead sheet; Virginia *Evening Bulletin*, quoted in Gold Hill *Evening News*, Jan. 15, 1864, p. 2, charging that John Church of the *Union* had openly cheered for Jeff Davis; *Territorial Enterprise*, Jan. 15, 1864, Scrapbook 3, p. 84, MTP, claiming that both Church and his partner Samuel A. Gessner had pro-Confederate sympathies; Virginia City *Daily Union*, Jan. 12, 1864, p. 2, hotly disclaiming Copperhead sentiments and counterattacking with the assertion that the *Enterprise* had "drifted several times" during 1863 "into the Copperhead ranks." The *Union* declared that William M. Stewart was closely associated with the *Enterprise* and that both were of "doubtful loyalty."

⁵⁵ *Roughing It*, II, 123.

⁵⁶ Fred W. Lorch, "Mark Twain and the 'Campaign That Failed,'" *American Literature*, XII (January, 1941), 454–470; John Gerber, "Mark Twain's 'Private Campaign,'" *Civil War History*, I (March, 1955), 37–60.

⁵⁷ SLC to William H. Clagett, Carson City, March 8, 1862, TS in MTP. Despite the rather bantering tone of Mark Twain's description of his experiences in the Confederate militia unit in "The Private History of a Campaign That Failed" (first published in 1885; reprinted in *Merry Tales*, 1892; included subsequently in *The American Claimant and Other Stories and Sketches*, 1899, etc.), and the mordant criticism of Southern society (especially of slavery) in *Adventures of Huckleberry Finn* and elsewhere, Mark Twain was capable in later years of falling

into the rhetorical clichés of neo-Confederate sentimentality. Introducing Col. Henry Watterson at a commemoration of Lincoln's birthday in Carnegie Hall, New York, in 1901, he said: "I was born and reared in a slave state; my father was a slave owner; and in the Civil War I was a second lieutenant in the Confederate service. For a while. . . . We of the South were not ashamed; for, like the men of the North, we were fighting for flags we loved; and when men fight for these things, and under these convictions, with nothing sordid to tarnish their cause, that cause is holy, the blood spilled for it is sacred, the life that is laid down for it is consecrated. . . . we are not ashamed that we did our endeavor; we did our bravest best against despairing odds, for the cause which was precious to us and which our conscience approved." (*Mark Twain's Speeches,* ed. A. B. Paine, [1923], pp. 229, 230.)

⁵⁸ Smith, "Mark Twain in Nevada," p. 57. Frank Fuller, who had known Mark Twain in Nevada in the 1860's, told Albert B. Paine that twenty years later James W. Nye had said Mark Twain was "a damned Secessionist" ("Letters from Frank Fuller," *Twainian,* July–August, 1956, p. 1).

⁵⁹ "Letter from Nevada Territory," Sacramento *Union,* Dec. 23, 1862, p. 1.

⁶⁰ Note 5 to headnote of § 16, and headnote of § 26, below; SLC to Robert Fulton, [Dublin, N.H.], May 24, 1905, in *Letters,* II, 773. Clayton's arrest in the summer of 1863 did not lead to his being ostracized; he presided over the burlesque Third House of the Legislature the following December.

⁶¹ Smith, *op. cit.,* p. 107.

⁶² SLC to William Clagett, Carson City, Feb. 28, 1862, TS in MTP.

⁶³ SLC to William Clagett, Esmeralda, Sept 9, 1862, TS in MTP.

⁶⁴ SLC to Pamela Clemens Moffett, Virginia City, March 18, 1864, original in MTP.

⁶⁵ *Territorial Enterprise,* dispatch dated Dec. 5, 1863, in Scrapbook 3, p. 24.

⁶⁶ *Ibid.,* dispatch dated Dec. 7, 1863, in Scrapbook 3, p. 28.

⁶⁷ *Ibid.,* dispatch dated Dec. 10, 1863, in Scrapbook 3, p. 36.

⁶⁸ Benson, *Mark Twain's Western Years,* p. 73, quoted from the San Francisco *Golden Era,* Dec. 6, 1863.

⁶⁹ See § 5, below.

⁷⁰ *Mark Twain's Travels with Mr. Brown,* eds. Franklin Walker and G. E. Dane.

⁷¹ The germ from which this chapter developed is in a letter by Mark Twain to the San Francisco *Call,* dated Aug. 20, 1863, which is reprinted in "Mark's Letters to San Francisco *Call,*" A. E. Hutcheson, ed., *Twainian,* March–April, 1952, p. 4, and May–June, 1952, p. 1.

⁷² *Letters,* I, 92.

⁷³ Grant H. Smith, who spent his boyhood in Virginia City, exemplifies

a personal hostility to Mark Twain that seems to have been preserved in oral tradition. According to Smith, "old-time Comstockers" in the 1870's said that he was "a 'smart Alec,' always showing-off and trying to make others appear ridiculous; that he was without manners, lazy, selfish and a liar" (Smith, *op. cit.*, p. 76). Charges of this sort are so vague that they have little significance beyond their function as projections of unconscious emotions. But the hostility is a historical fact which should be recorded.

[74] Quoted by E. M. Branch, *The Literary Apprenticeship of Mark Twain*, p. 290, note 113.

[75] R. G. Lillard, "Contemporary Reaction to 'The Empire City Massacre,'" *American Literature*, XVI (November, 1944), 198–203.

[76] "'The Third House' and Other Burlesques," Virginia City *Daily Union*, Jan. 30, 1864, p. 2.

[77] G. H. Smith, *The History of the Comstock Lode*, p. 48.

[78] *Roughing It*, II, 113.

[79] *Ibid.*, II, 115, 117–118.

[80] *Autobiography*, I, 354–360.

[81] Benson, *Mark Twain's Western Years*, p. 112; DeLancey Ferguson, "Mark Twain's Comstock Duel: The Birth of a Legend," *American Literature*, XIV (March, 1942), 66–70. Cyril Clemens' effort to reinstate the legendary account ("'The Birth of a Legend' Again," *American Literature*, XV [March, 1943], 64–65), is not convincing.

[82] *Biography*, I, 250–252.

[83] Gold Hill *Evening News*, May 17, 1864, p. 2.

[84] *Letters*, I, 97–98.

[85] In his *Autobiography* (I, 360), which clothes this affair in an aura of fiction, Mark Twain says: "Mr. Cutler had come up from Carson City, and sent a man over with a challenge from the hotel. Steve [Gillis] went over to pacify him ... Steve gave him fifteen minutes to get out of the hotel, and half an hour to get out of town, or there would be results ... Mr. Cutler went off toward Carson, a convinced and reformed man."

[86] For example, "Carl" reported to the *Daily Union* from Carson City on Feb. 20, 1864 (p. 3), that Abraham Curry had struck one L. D. Strong, a commissioner of Ormsby County, in the face with enough force to draw blood. A jury released Curry although he had admitted giving the blow. There is no mention of a challenge from the victim of this affront.

[87] Letter of Mark Twain to the San Francisco *Call* dated Aug. 2, 1863, reprinted in "Mark's Letters to San Francisco *Call*," A. E. Hutcheson, ed., *Twainian*, March–April, 1952, p. 1.

[88] Quoted in Angel, *History of Nevada*, p. 292. The role of spoilsport seems ill-suited to Jack Perry the fire laddie and mighty warrior.

[89] News story in *Territorial Enterprise* of Sept. 29, 1863, reprinted in San Francisco *Alta California*, Oct. 1, 1863, p. 1. S. P. Davis has a detailed account of the duel (*History of Nevada*, I, 451–452), varying in

some respects from Mark Twain's contemporary report; and Mark Twain mentions it in his *Autobiography* (I, 351–354), although without a date.

[90] *Autobiography*, I, 359.

[91] *Biography*, I, 252.

[92] John W. North was prominent in Nevada politics; in 1864 he was a justice of the Supreme Court (H. H. Bancroft, *History of Nevada, Colorado, and Wyoming*, pp. 157–158, 173; here, by inadvertence, Bancroft has the name "James W. North").

[93] *Laws, First Session*, chap. xxviii, sec. 36, p. 61. The same legislature made gambling a felony (p. 53), but open gambling was taken for granted in Virginia City throughout the territorial period. Goodman and Fitch crossed into California for their second duel; but the challenge was sent and accepted in Nevada.

[94] *Biography*, I, 252.

[95] Branch, "Chronological Bibliography," p. 134. The article (which is not extant in its original form) was reprinted in the San Francisco *Golden Era* on June 26, 1864, under the title " 'Mark Twain' in the Metropolis" and is included in *The Washoe Giant in San Francisco*, ed. Franklin Walker, pp. 74–76.

[96] SLC to Orion and Mollie Clemens, San Francisco, Oct. 19, 1865; SLC to Jane Clemens and Pamela Clemens Moffett, San Francisco, Jan. 20, 1866; originals in MTP.

[97] *Biography*, I, 294–297; W. F. Frear, *Mark Twain and Hawaii*, pp. 207–209, 422. In Scrapbook 1, p. 71 (MTP), there is a clipping from an unidentified newspaper which contains an open letter to Mark Twain dated Oct. 30, 1866, asking him to lecture in Carson City. Although this was a familiar device of publicity, the phrasing of the letter seems to have a more than perfunctory warmth. It is signed by two business firms and 112 individuals (including A. W. Tjader, C. M. Brosnan, A. Curry, Henry R. Mighels, C. N. Noteware, and H. F. Rice—but *not* W. K. Cutler). It states that the people of Carson "remember you in times gone by as one of its citizens, and . . . have none other than the most kindly remembrances of you." Of course, the fact that such a reassurance was given may suggest some uncertainty about current opinion of Mark Twain in Carson City.

[98] The characterization is that of Arthur McEwen, San Francisco *Examiner*, Jan. 22, 1893, p. 15.

NOTES TO PART TWO
"The Office of Reporter"
(Pages 33–182)

SECTION 1

[1] *Mark Twain in Eruption,* ed. Bernard De Voto, pp. 390–391.

[2] Wright left in December and was gone nine months (Dan De Quille, "Reporting with Mark Twain," *Californian Illustrated Magazine,* IV [1893], 170).

[3] *Roughing It,* II, 6–7.

[4] SLC to Jane Clemens and Pamela Clemens Moffett, Steamboat Springs, Nevada Territory, Aug. 19, 1863, typescript in MTP; see also *Mark Twain's Autobiography,* II, 307.

[5] *Mark Twain in Eruption,* p. 392; *Autobiography,* II, 307–308. At the end of the session, the Council adopted a resolution thanking Clemens and Clement T. Rice (reporter for the Virginia *Union*) for "their full and accurate reports of the proceedings" ("Letter from Nevada Territory," Sacramento *Union,* Dec. 23, 1862, p. 1).

[6] Unsigned editorial in Scrapbook 1, p. 58. Although the clipping is undated, it can be assigned to the 1862 session because it refers to "Sam Clemens" instead of to "Mark Twain."

[7] Myron Angel, ed., *History of Nevada,* p. 80.

[8] *Roughing It,* I, 182.

[9] *Laws, Second Session,* p. 213; *Laws, Third Session,* p. 178.

[10] See Angel, *op. cit.,* pp. 555, 606; R. G. Lillard, "Studies in Washoe Journalism and Humor," pp. 73–74.

[11] Wells Drury, *An Editor on the Comstock Lode,* p. 21.

[12] SLC to Robert Fulton, [Dublin, N.H.], May 24, 1905, in *Letters,* II, 773.

SECTION 2

[1] Unpublished letter of Dr. Charles L. Anderson to his wife, Carson City, Sept. 17, 1862, photostat in Bancroft Library, University of California, Berkeley.

[2] Oct. 28, 1863; reprinted in Appendix C of Paine, *Biography,* III, 1597–1599.

SECTION 4

[1] A clipping in Scrapbook 2, p. 18, MTP, which contains a letter dated Feb. 18, 1863, also includes a masthead with the statement, "*The Enterprise* is published daily, Mondays excepted." At other periods the days of publication of the paper were changed.

[2] *Letters,* I, 87.

[3] Reprinted in "Goodman's Assistance on the Biography," *Twainian*, May–June, 1956, p. 3. "The Sugar Loaf" is not extant.

[4] Reprinted again in E. M. Mack, *Mark Twain in Nevada*, pp. 224–227.

[5] *Biography*, I, 295–296. Dan De Quille quoted a slightly different version of the song as Mark Twain's contribution to the entertainment of the company at the dinner given for him, De Quille, and Ada Clare by Adah Isaacs Menken in Virginia City in 1864 ("Salad Days of Mark Twain," San Francisco *Examiner*, March 19, 1893, p. 14).

SECTION 5

[1] "Letter from Nevada Territory," Sacramento *Union*, Nov. 26, 1862, p. 3.

SECTION 6

[1] Unpublished letter of Dr. Charles L. Anderson to his wife, Carson City, Feb. 6, 1863, photostat in Bancroft Library.

[2] G. C. Odell, *Annals of the New York Stage*, VII, 281–282, 431–432.

SECTION 7

[1] He had left Virginia City by May 3 ("Mark Twain," *Territorial Enterprise*, May 3, 1863, in Scrapbook 2, p. 43, MTP). He describes his return in a letter to the San Francisco *Call* dated July 5, 1863, reprinted in "Mark's Letters to San Francisco *Call*," ed. A. E. Hutcheson, *Twainian*, Jan.–Feb., 1952, p. 1.

SECTION 8

[1] R. M. Dorson, "Mose the Far-famed and World-renowned," *American Literature*, XV (November, 1943), 288–300.

[2] *Roughing It*, Vol. II, chap. vi.

[3] S. P. Davis, *History of Nevada*, I, 269–271.

[4] Mark Twain in San Francisco *Call*, Aug. 6, 1863, reprinted in *Twainian*, May, 1944, p. 5.

[5] Angel, *History of Nevada*, p. 292.

[6] *Biography*, I, 234–235.

[7] SLC to Jane Clemens and Pamela Clemens Moffett, Steamboat Springs, Aug. 19, 1863, in *Letters*, I, 91–93.

[8] E. M. Branch, "Chronological Bibliography," p. 129.

SECTION 10

[1] Ivan Benson, *Mark Twain's Western Years*, p. 95.

[2] *Biography*, I, 248.

[3] Virginia City *Daily Union*, Feb. 28, 1864, p. 3.

[4] Reprinted in *The Washoe Giant in San Francisco*, ed. Franklin Walker, pp. 33–38.

SECTION 11

[1] San Francisco *Call*, Aug. 2, 1863, reprinted in *Twainian*, March–April, 1952, p. 1.
[2] Scrapbook 2, p. 89, MTP.
[3] *Roughing It*, II, 113.

SECTION 12

[1] A convention had met at Genoa in 1859 to draw up a territorial constitution (Angel, *History of Nevada*, pp. 63–64).
[2] *Ibid.*, pp. 84–85.
[3] See §20, below.
[4] Angel, *op. cit.*, p. 86.
[5] The *Enterprise* for that date is not extant. In *Mark Twain's Western Years* (pp. 176–177) Benson reprints the text as carried by the San Francisco *Bulletin* on Oct. 31, 1863.
[6] R. G. Lillard, "Contemporary Reaction to 'The Empire City Massacre,'" *American Literature*, XVI (November, 1944), 198–203.

SECTION 13

[1] Reproduced in Angel, *History of Nevada*, p. 81.

SECTION 14

[1] Angel, *History of Nevada*, p. 215.

SECTION 15

[1] Text of the speech, from *Territorial Enterprise*, in Scrapbook 3, pp. 63–65, MTP; news story in the *Enterprise*, Dec. 20, 1863, in Scrapbook 3, p. 50.
[2] Virginia City *Union*, Jan. 8, 1864, p. 2.
[3] *Ibid.*, Jan. 12, 1864, p. 1.
[4] "Why He Favors a State Government," *ibid.*, Jan. 17, 1864, p. 2; "Bribery and Corruption," *ibid.*, Jan. 19, 1864, p. 2; "Some of the Untruths and Some of the Truths of the Election," *ibid.*, Jan. 21, 1864, p. 2.
[5] Angel, *History of Nevada*, p. 85; Bancroft, *History of Nevada, Colorado, and Wyoming*, pp. 178–179.
[6] Angel, *op. cit.*, pp. 84–85; editorial, "Under the Circumstances," *Daily Union*, Jan. 3, 1864, p. 2; editorial, "Our Cause and Our Candidates," *Territorial Enterprise*, Jan. 5, 1864, in Scrapbook 3, p. 79, MTP.
[7] *Roughing It*, I, 137–143.

SECTION 16

[1] The editor wishes to acknowledge the courtesy of the authorities of the Yale University Library in allowing him to consult the Scrapbook in the Morse-Frear Collection.
[2] R. G. Lillard, "Studies in Washoe Journalism and Humor," p. 11.

[3] "Letter from Nevada Territory," Sacramento *Union,* Nov. 18, 1862, p. 2.

[4] A copy of the broadside is in the Houghton Library at Harvard, and there is a photostat in MTP. Claude M. Simpson, Jr., reprints the text of the broadside with explanatory notes in "Captain Jim and the 'Third House,'" *Western Folklore,* IX (April, 1950), 101–110.

[5] Clayton was arrested in the summer of 1863 by the military authorities "for persisting in the utterance of disloyal sentiments" (letter by Mark Twain to San Francisco *Call,* dated Aug. 2, 1863, reprinted in *Twainian,* March–April, 1952, p. 2). He does not seem to have been imprisoned very long: he presided over the meeting of the Third House which Mark Twain addressed on Jan. 27, 1864 (headnote to §26, below). He is mentioned again as presiding officer in 1867 and 1869 (Lillard, *op. cit.,* pp. 17, 18, quoting Gold Hill *News,* Jan. 7, 1867, and Carson *Daily Appeal,* Jan. 29 and Feb. 5, 1869). Professor Simpson suggests that the address may have been written by J. Ross Brown, Dan De Quille, or Clement T. Rice (Simpson, *op. cit.,* p. 102), but Clayton seems a more likely candidate.

[6] "Letter from Nevada Territory," Sacramento *Union,* Dec. 18, 1862, p. 1.

[7] Letter from Charles L. Anderson to his wife, Nov. 16, 1863, photostat in Bancroft Library.

[8] Article XVI, text in *Territorial Enterprise,* Dec. 18, 1863, in Scrapbook 3, p. 47, MTP.

SECTION 17

[1] Branch, "Chronological Bibliography," p. 131; *Letters,* I, 93–94.

[2] Angel, *History of Nevada,* p. 220. H. H. Bancroft (*History of Nevada, Colorado, and Wyoming,* p. 171 n.) also has the name as Mrs. E. G. Cutler.

SECTION 18

[1] Virginia City *Daily Union,* Jan. 1, 1864, p. 3.

[2] Bancroft, *History of Nevada, Colorado, and Wyoming,* pp. 178–179; see also the headnote to §15.

[3] Bancroft, *op. cit.,* pp. 179, 187.

SECTION 20

[1] I am grateful to Mr. Philip Foner for checking the files of the *Mercury* in the New York Public Library to ascertain the date of publication of Mark Twain's letter.

[2] Branch, "Chronological Bibliography," p. 131.

[3] Branch, *Literary Apprenticeship of Mark Twain,* p. 291, note 126.

[4] Text of the letter in S. C. Webster, ed., *Mark Twain, Business Man,* pp. 79–80.

SECTION 21

[1] Virginia City *Daily Union,* Jan. 13, 1864, p. 3.
[2] V. L. Parrington, *The Romantic Revolution in America,* pp. 227–228, 306–308.
[3] See headnote to §17, above.
[4] Artemus Ward to SLC, Austin, Nevada Territory, Jan. 1, 1864, in *Letters,* I, 93–94.
[5] Paine, *Biography,* I, 239–242; *Letters,* I, 94; Lillard, "Studies in Washoe Journalism and Humor," pp. 80–83.
[6] Paine's version in the *Letters* (I, 93–94) is incomplete.

SECTION 23

[1] Work Projects Administration, San Francisco Theatre Research Series, Vol. XIV: *A History of Burlesque,* by Ettore Rella (mimeographed), p. 52.
[2] G. C. Odell, *Annals of the New York Stage,* V, 436–437.
[3] T. A. Brown, *A History of the New York Stage,* II, 126.
[4] Odell, *op. cit.,* VII, 28, 141, 154, 224, 256, 427, etc.

SECTION 24

[1] J. W. Kelly, *Second Directory of Nevada,* p. 97.
[2] "Carl," "Letter from Carson," Virginia City *Union,* Jan. 17, 1864, p. 2.

SECTION 25

[1] "Concerning Notaries," in *The Washoe Giant in San Francisco,* pp. 67–70; original version in Scrapbook 3, p. 103, MTP.
[2] Letter of Orion Clemens to Sacramento *Union,* reprinted in *Territorial Enterprise,* [Jan. 24, 1864], Scrapbook 3, p. 96, MTP.

SECTION 26

[1] See §16, above.
[2] The invitation and Mark Twain's reply, both dated Jan. 23, 1864, were published in the Carson *Daily Independent* (Scrapbook 4, p. 3, MTP).
[3] Mack, *Mark Twain in Nevada,* pp. 276–277.
[4] SLC to Pamela Clemens Moffett, Virginia City, original in MTP. The photograph is reproduced in Benson, *Mark Twain's Western Years* (facing p. 32).
[5] Virginia City *Daily Union,* Jan. 30, 1864, p. 1. It will be noted that "Carl's" dispatch places the meeting of the Third House on Jan. 28; Mark Twain's dispatch places it on Jan. 27. Miss Mack (*Mark Twain in Nevada,* p. 277) places the meeting on a Wednesday, which would make the date the twenty-seventh.
[6] Headnote to §6, above. The shortage of women on the frontier brought girls into circulation early.

[7] Mrs. Carrie L. Headrick to Albert B. Paine, Gardenville, Nevada, n.d. [probably 1907], in "Mining Days Sweetheart of Mark Twain," *Twainian*, May–June, 1956, p. 2. Parts of Mrs. Headrick's letter are paraphrased in Paine, *Biography*, I, 246–247. Mrs. Headrick was slightly confused about the incident: she spoke of a box and of a curtain's going up, as if the speech had been delivered in a theater rather than in a courtroom. But she was, after all, not present at the speech itself, and there is no reason to question her recollection of the main outlines of her disappointment.

SECTION 27

[1] Scrapbook 2, p. 93, MTP.

[2] Virginia City *Daily Union*, Jan. 30, 1864, p. 2. The district (or prosecuting) attorney for Storey County from Sept. 2, 1863, to Nov. 6, 1866, was Dighton Corson (Angel, *History of Nevada*, p. 607), but no evidence connects him with Mark Twain or with the pseudonym "Meriden." In April, 1864, Mark Twain seems to be on good terms with District Attorney Corson (see § 32, below).

[3] MS note, Scrapbook 3, p. 121, MTP.

SECTION 29

[1] Angel, *History of Nevada*, p. 313.

SECTION 31

[1] Davis, *History of Nevada*, II, 976–977.

[2] "Legislative Proceedings," *Territorial Enterprise*, Feb. 18, 1864, in Scrapbook 3, p. 113, MTP.

[3] *Ibid.*, Feb. 21, 1864, in Scrapbook 3, p. 117.

SECTION 32

[1] Virginia City *Daily Union*, March 8, 1864, p. 3.

[2] Angel, *History of Nevada*, p. 345.

[3] *Ibid.*

[4] *Daily Union*, April 22, 1864, p. 3.

[5] *Ibid.*, April 16, 1864, in Scrapbook 3, p. 139, MTP.

[6] *Ibid.*, April 21, 1864, p. 2, quoting the Carson *Independent*.

NOTES TO PART THREE

"The Affair Was a Silly Joke"
(Pages 185–205)

SECTION 33

[1] The type face of the clipping in the MTP does not resemble the type faces used in 1864 by the *Missouri Republican*, the *Democrat*, or the *Daily Union*, of St. Louis. Checks of broken files of the *Republican* and *Democrat* for May and June, 1864, in the Missouri State Historical

Society, Columbia, by Mr. Harvey McCaleb, and of a complete file of the daily and weekly *Republican* by Mrs. Frances Biese in the Missouri Historical Society, St. Louis, have failed to reveal precisely when or where Mark Twain's letter was published.

Section 36

[1] The account of this pamphlet which follows is based upon the pamphlet itself and upon the admirably thorough article by Sidney Kaplan, "The Miscegenation Issue in the Election of 1864," *Journal of Negro History*, XXXIV (July, 1949), 274–343.

Section 40

[1] Smith, *History of the Comstock Lode*, pp. 116–120.

Biographical Directory

☞ Like the good reporter he was, Mark Twain mentioned many people in his dispatches to the *Territorial Enterprise*—more than 250, in fact, in the pieces collected in this volume. It is not easy to find authentic information about most of these residents of early Nevada. This directory embodies such biographical data as are available—and relevant—concerning forty of the men and women who figure most vividly in Mark Twain's dispatches.

ARICK, RUFUS E.

Mayor of Virginia City, 1863–1864; unsuccessful Democratic candidate for lieutenant governor in 1864.

BALDWIN, ALEXANDER W. ("SANDY")

One of the leading attorneys of the Territory, associated with William M. Stewart as counsel for the Ophir and Yellow Jacket companies. Elected to the Council from Storey County in 1863 and 1864.

BROSNAN, CORNELIUS M.

A Virginia City lawyer of Irish birth who was brought to the United States at the age of 14 by his parents. He came to California in 1850 and to Nevada in 1863. He was a delegate to the constitutional conventions of 1863 and 1864 and was elected a justice of the first Supreme Court of Nevada in 1864.

BROWN, K. B. ("KETTLE-BELLY")

A celebrated gambler, sportsman, and boon companion, of Virginia City; chief engineer of the volunteer fire department.

BRUMFIELD, W. H.

An attorney of Carson City; representative from Ormsby County in the second and third Territorial Legislatures.

CHAPIN, SAMUEL A.

A native of Massachusetts who had lived for ten years in Michigan. He came to California in 1850 and to Virginia City in 1860. He had mining interests, dealt in lumber, and was a delegate to the constitutional conventions of 1863 and 1864.

CLAGETT, WILLIAM H. ("BILLY")

An attorney whom Mark Twain had known as a law student in Keokuk, Iowa, and as a companion on the excursion to the Humboldt district in the winter of 1861–1862. He was elected to the Assembly from Humboldt County in 1862 and 1863, and to the state House of Representatives in 1864. A photograph of Clagett, A. J. Simmons (Speaker of the House in the second Territorial Legislature, 1862), and Mark Twain is reproduced in Benson, *Mark Twain's Western Years* (facing p. 32). In 1866 Clagett moved to Montana Territory and was elected delegate to the U. S. Congress from there in 1871.

CLAPP, MISS HANNAH K.

A schoolteacher who came to Nevada from Michigan, one of the first women residents of Carson City. In 1861 she established a private school for boys and girls called the Sierra Seminary. The first Territorial Legislature chartered this school, but a proposed subsidy for it was never voted.

CLAYTON, HAL

Prosecuting attorney in the court at Carson City under the government of Utah Territory, 1860; presiding officer of the "Third House" during the first and second Territorial Legislatures, 1861–1862, and again during the sessions of 1864, 1867, and 1869. In July, 1863, he was arrested by the military authorities for "persisting in the utterance of disloyal sentiments."

CLEMENS, ORION

Elder brother of Mark Twain, a newspaper man in Missouri and Iowa, who had been appointed territorial secretary in 1861. In the frequent and prolonged absences of Governor James W. Nye he served as acting governor, holding this office, for example, from December 27, 1862, to July 24, 1863. He was Union nominee for secretary of state in the slate of candidates put up in the election of January 19, 1864, when the first state constitution was rejected by the voters.

CURRY, ABRAHAM V. Z.

A pioneer merchant who came to Nevada in 1858; the principal founder of Carson City. Curry filed one of the two claims subsequently consolidated in the famous Gould & Curry mine, but he sold out his interest early for a small sum. Mark Twain praised his many services to the community in *Roughing It* (Vol. I, chap. xxv). He served as a representative in the second Territorial Legislature and as a councilman in the third.

CUTLER, MRS. W. K.

A noted singer and elocutionist, associated with Miss H. K. Clapp in conducting the Sierra Seminary. She was president of the women's organization of Carson City that arranged a ball for the benefit of the Sanitary Fund, and was one of the signers of the letter protesting Mark Twain's insinuation that the proceeds were to be sent to a "miscegenation society."

DAGGETT, ROLLIN M.

A native of New York who spent his childhood in Ohio and came to the Pacific Coast overland in 1849. After a period of prospecting and working as a journeyman printer he established the *Golden Era* in San Francisco in 1852. In 1860 he established the *Daily Evening Mirror* in the same city. Coming to Nevada in 1862, he became a broker, and in 1863 was elected to the Territorial Council. In 1864 he joined the staff of the Virginia City *Territorial Enterprise*. Member of Congress, 1879–1881; minister to Hawaii, 1882–1885; subsequently a journalist in San Francisco.

DE QUILLE, DAN
See Wright, William.

DIXSON, E. C.

Probate judge of Ormsby County, 1861–1863, and representative from Lander County in the third Territorial Legislature.

FITCH, THOMAS

A journalist, lawyer, and politician, noted for his oratory. He was born in New York but migrated to Wisconsin and then to California, where he worked on newspapers in San Francisco and Placerville. Having been admitted to the bar, he was elected to the California legislature in 1862.

He came to Nevada in 1863 and was for a time editor of the Virginia City *Daily Union*. In 1863 he founded the *Occidental*, a short-lived weekly literary magazine described in *Roughing It* (Vol. II, chap. x). He was a delegate from Storey County to the Constitutional Convention of 1863; served as district attorney of Washoe City, 1865–1866; and in 1868 was elected to Congress.

GILLESPIE, WILLIAM M.

A native of New York who came to Virginia City in 1861. He was clerk of the first Territorial Legislature; representative from Storey County in the third Territorial Legislature; and delegate from Storey County and secretary of the constitutional conventions of 1863 and 1864.

GILLIS, STEPHEN E.

A compositor on the *Territorial Enterprise*, one of Mark Twain's closest friends. Gillis, who was born in Mississippi, was a noted fighter and an incurable practical joker. He moved on to San Francisco with Mark in 1864, and the two men continued to be companions until Mark Twain left California for the East in 1866.

GOODMAN, JOSEPH T.

A native of New York who came to California while he was still a boy. He worked as compositor and writer on the San Francisco *Golden Era*, and in 1861, at the age of 23, joined with Denis McCarthy in buying the *Territorial Enterprise*. He was a proprietor and editor of the paper during Mark Twain's period on the staff. In the boom of the 1870's he made a fortune speculating in mining stocks, but went broke soon afterward, and John M. Mackay lent him the money to buy a grape ranch in Fresno County, California. In the 1880's he sold out and entered journalism again in the Bay Region. He was interested in Central American archaeology and succeeded in making an important contribution to the deciphering of the Maya calendar and numerical system. His monograph *The Archaic Maya Inscriptions* was published under the auspices of A. P. Maudslay in London in 1897.

HOPKINS, PETER

Proprietor of the Magnolia Saloon in Carson City.

JOHNSON, J. NEELY

A native of Indiana who came to California in 1849 and was elected governor in 1855. Moving to Nevada in 1860, he entered the practice of law in Carson City. He was a delegate to the constitutional conventions of 1863 and 1864 and was appointed a justice of the State Supreme Court in 1867.

LAIRD, JAMES L.

One of three proprietors of the Carson City *Silver Age*, 1860–1862. In November, 1862, the paper was moved to Virginia City and renamed the *Daily Union*.

LARROWE, MARCUS D.

A native of New York who settled in Austin, Lander County, in 1861. He was district attorney for the second district, 1861–1863; a delegate to the Constitutional Convention of 1863; and Union nominee for justice of the Supreme Court of Nevada in the election of January 19, 1864.

LOVEJOY, JOHN K.

An unusually flamboyant and opinionated journalist. In 1863 he took over the Washoe City *Times* and changed its name to *The Old Pah-Utah*, but he sold his interest in 1864 and moved to Virginia City, where he founded the short-lived *Daily Old Piute*. He served as a representative in the second Territorial Legislature.

MITCHELL, MILES N.

A native of New York who came to California in 1851 and to Virginia City in 1860. He was speaker of the Assembly in the first Territorial Legislature, delegate to the Constitutional Convention of 1863, and Union nominee for governor in the election of January 19, 1864.

MOTT, GORDON N.

Appointed judge of the first district of Nevada Territory, 1861, and elected Territorial Delegate to Congress, 1862. In September, 1863, he resigned from the bench at the height of tension over the Chollar-Potosi litigation. It was charged that he was bribed to resign by the Potosi Company managers.

MUSSER, JOHN J.

A lawyer who had come to Washoe in 1858 with Abraham Curry and had been one of the founders of Carson City. In 1859 he was sent to Washington by the settlers in western Utah Territory to urge Congress to establish the Territory of Nevada. He was appointed prosecuting attorney for the second district in 1863.

NORTH, JOHN W.

A native of New York who had emigrated to Minnesota before coming to Nevada as first surveyor general of the Territory in 1861. When Gordon N. Mott was compelled to resign as judge of the first district in 1863, during the celebrated Chollar-Potosi litigation, North was appointed to replace him. North rendered a decision in favor of the Potosi, was in turn attacked, especially by William M. Stewart, attorney for the Chollar company, and resigned from the bench in 1864. He served as president of the Constitutional Convention of 1863.

NYE, JAMES W.

A native of New York; district attorney and judge, Madison County, New York, 1839–1848; president of the Metropolitan Board of Police, New York City, 1857–1860; Governor of Nevada Territory, 1861–1864; United States Senator from Nevada, 1864–1873.

PERRY, JOHN VAN BUREN ("JACK")

City marshal of Virginia City; foreman, Hook and Ladder Co. No. 1. An ardent Unionist, and apparently a type not unlike Buck Fanshaw in *Roughing It.*

RICE, CLEMENT T.

A reporter for the Virginia City *Daily Union* whom Mark Twain called "the Unreliable." He wrote under the pseudonym "Carl."

SMALL, JAMES W.

A native of Ohio who came to Nevada in 1863 and ran a hotel in Lake Valley. He was a delegate from Douglas County to the Constitutional Convention of 1863.

STARK, JAMES

An actor, born in Nova Scotia, who had appeared in Shakespearian roles in New York in the 1840's. In the early 1860's he operated a mining and milling business in Aurora. He was a member of the Esmeralda delegation to the Constitutional Convention of 1863. In 1866 he returned, without great success, to the New York stage.

STERNS, L. O.

An attorney, a resident of Aurora, who served as a delegate to the Constitutional Convention of 1863.

STEWART, WILLIAM M.

The most prominent lawyer in Nevada during Mark Twain's residence there, counsel for the principal mining companies and a skilled courtroom strategist who commanded enormous fees. He had been born in New York, but grew up in Ohio; and he had attended Yale for a year before coming to California in 1850. After prospecting for a time, he studied law and was admitted to the bar in 1852. He held the office of attorney general of California in 1854, and migrated to Nevada in 1860, where he served as a member of the Territorial Council in 1861 and of the Constitutional Convention of 1863. He was United States Senator from Nevada 1864–1875, and returned to the Senate 1887–1905.

STURTEVANT, JAMES H.

A native of New York who came to California in 1850 and to the Truckee Valley in 1857, where he engaged in farming. He was a member of the Assembly in all the Territorial Legislatures and a delegate to the Constitutional Convention of 1864. In 1863 he married Emma Curry, daughter of Abraham Curry.

TRUMBO, JOHN K.

A real-estate dealer of Carson City. In 1859 he had served as clerk of the first meeting held for the purpose of taking steps to organize a territorial government in Nevada.

WASSON, WARREN

An authentic "Pi-Ute" who had come to Nevada in 1857. He was at various times a rancher, an Indian agent, a United States marshal, and an assessor of Internal Revenue.

WINTERS, THEODORE

A native of Illinois who came to California overland in 1849 and to Washoe City in 1857. He was one of the most successful farmers and stock raisers in the territory. His race horses were especially celebrated, and he maintained a race track on his ranch. He had substantial holdings in the Ophir Silver Mining Company.

WRIGHT, WILLIAM ("DAN DE QUILLE")

Mark Twain's closest friend in Virginia City. He was born in Ohio in 1829 but removed with his family to Iowa in 1847 and came to California in 1857. After a period of prospecting in California and Nevada, he began contributing to the San Francisco *Golden Era*. In 1862 Joseph T. Goodman hired him as a reporter on the *Territorial Enterprise*. He stayed with the paper until it suspended publication in the 1890's, gaining a wide reputation as a writer and contributing to many other western journals. He was author of *The Big Bonanza* (published by the American Publishing Company of Hartford in 1877). After the *Territorial Enterprise* went under, John Mackay gave Wright a pension, but he died within a year or two (in 1898).

YOUNGS, SAMUEL

A native of New York who came to Nevada in 1860 and settled as a merchant in Aurora. He was an assemblyman in the first Territorial Legislature and a delegate to the Constitutional Convention of 1863.

Works Cited

ANDERSON, CHARLES LEWIS. Letters to his wife, written from Carson City, September 6, 1862—June 20, 1863. Photographic copies of the manuscript letters, Bancroft Library, University of California, Berkeley.

ANGEL, MYRON, ed. *History of Nevada*. Oakland: Thompson & West, 1881.

Annual Reports of the Secretary of the Territory, Territorial Auditor, Treasurer, Superintendent of Public Instruction, and Adjutant-General, January 13, 1864. Carson City, 1864.

BANCROFT, HUBERT H., *History of Nevada, Colorado, and Wyoming* (*Works*, Vol. XXV). San Francisco, 1890.

BENSON, IVAN. *Mark Twain's Western Years*. Stanford, California: Stanford University Press, c. 1938.

BRANCH, EDGAR M. "A Chronological Bibliography of the Writings of Samuel Clemens to June 8, 1867," *American Literature*, XVIII (May, 1946), 109–159.

———. *The Literary Apprenticeship of Mark Twain*. Urbana, Illinois: University of Illinois Press, 1950.

BROWN, T. ALLSTON. *A History of the New York Stage*. 3 vols. New York: Dodd, Mead & Co., 1903.

CLEMENS, SAMUEL L. *Mark Twain in Eruption*, ed. Bernard De Voto. New York: Harper & Brothers, c. 1940.

———. *Mark Twain's Autobiography*, ed. Albert B. Paine. 2 vols. New York: Harper & Brothers, c. 1924.

———. *Mark Twain's Letters*, ed. Albert B. Paine. 2 vols. New York: Harper & Brothers, c. 1917.

———. *Mark Twain's Speeches,* ed. Albert B. Paine. New York: Harper & Brothers, c. 1923.

———. *Mark Twain's Travels with Mr. Brown,* ed. Franklin Walker and G. Ezra Dane. New York: Alfred A. Knopf, 1940.

———. "Mark's Letters to San Francisco *Call* from Virginia City, Nevada Territory, July 9th to November 19th, 1863," ed. A. E. Hutcheson, *Twainian,* January–February, 1952—May–June, 1952.

———. *Roughing It,* 2 vols. New York: Harper & Brothers, n.d.

———. *The Washoe Giant in San Francisco,* ed. Franklin Walker. San Francisco: George Fields, 1938.

———. *What Is Man? and Other Essays.* New York: Harper & Brothers, 1917.

CLEMENS, SAMUEL L., and BRET HARTE. *Sketches of the Sixties,* ed. John Howell. San Francisco: John Howell, 1927.

DAVIS, SAM P., ed. *The History of Nevada.* 2 vols. Reno, Nevada: Elms Publishing Co., 1913.

DRURY, WELLS. *An Editor on the Comstock Lode.* New York: Farrar & Rinehart, 1936.

FREAR, WALTER F. *Mark Twain and Hawaii.* Chicago: Lakeside Press, 1947.

Gold Hill Evening News, Gold Hill, Nevada, October, 1863—May, 1864.

[Gould & Curry Silver Mining Co.], *Views of the Works of the Gould & Curry Silver Mining Co., Virginia, N. T.,* San Francisco, [1864].

KELLY, J. WELLS. *Second Directory of Nevada Territory,* Virginia City, 1863.

Laws of the Territory of Nevada, Passed at the First Regular Session of the Legislative Assembly. San Francisco, 1862.

Laws of the Territory of Nevada, Passed at the Second Regular Session of the Legislative Assembly. Virginia City, Nevada, 1863.

Laws of the Territory of Nevada, Passed at the Third Regular Session of the Legislative Assembly. Virginia City, Nevada, 1864.

LILLARD, RICHARD G. "Studies in Washoe Journalism and Humor." Unpublished Ph.D. dissertation, State University of Iowa, 1943.

MACK, EFFIE MONA. *Mark Twain in Nevada.* New York: Charles Scribner's Sons, 1947.

MARSH, ANDREW J. *Marsh's New Manual of Reformed Phonetic Short-Hand.* 3d ed. San Francisco, 1892.

MEARS, LEONARD. *Sacramento Directory for the Years 1863–4.* Sacramento, 1863.

ODELL, GEORGE C. *Annals of the New York Stage.* 15 vols. New York: Columbia University Press, 1927–1949.

PAINE, ALBERT B. *Mark Twain, A Biography.* 3 vols. New York: Harper & Brothers, c. 1912.

PARRINGTON, VERNON L. *Main Currents in American Thought.* 3 vols. in 1. New York: Harcourt, Brace & Co., c. 1927, 1930. Vol. II (*The Romantic Revolution in America*).

RABB, KATE M., ed. *Wit and Humor of America.* Vol. V. Indianapolis: The Bobbs-Merrill Company, 1907.

SMITH, GRANT H. Papers (Bancroft Library, University of California, Berkeley; Carton 3, containing unpublished typescript "Mark Twain in Nevada," and miscellaneous notes, photostats, photographs, etc., bearing on Mark Twain).

————. *The History of the Comstock Lode 1850–1920.* (University of Nevada *Bulletin,* Vol. XXXVII, No. 3, July 1, 1943; Geology and Mining Series, No. 37.)

THOMPSON & WEST. *History of Nevada. See* Angel, Myron.

Virginia *Daily Union,* Virginia City, Nevada, January–June, 1864.

WEBSTER, SAMUEL C., ed. *Mark Twain, Business Man.* Boston: Little, Brown & Co., 1946.

WORK PROJECTS ADMINISTRATION, NORTHERN CALIFORNIA. San Francisco Theatre Research Series, ed. Lawrence Estavan, Vol. XIV: *A History of Burlesque,* by Ettore Rella (mimeographed), San Francisco, 1940.

Index

(Note.—Italicized page numbers refer to the Biographical Directory. Periodicals are listed under place of publication. The lists of page references are selective rather than inclusive, especially in such entries as "Clemens, Samuel L.," "Carson City (Nevada)," "Virginia City (Nevada)," and "Virginia City *Daily Territorial Enterprise*." The following categories of names are omitted: (1) names which appear only in records of votes or of attendance in the Territorial Legislature; (2) names which appear only once, without significant information in the text; (3) names of persons not resident in Nevada Territory who have no direct relation to events described in the text; (4) names which are introduced as parts of citations.)

235

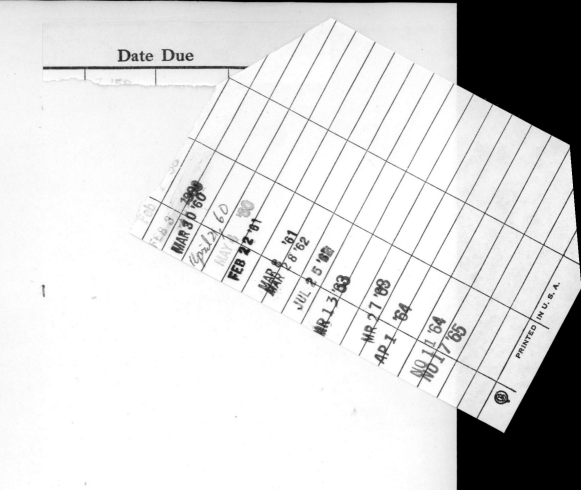